The Dynamics of Growth

Scientific Principles at Work in the
Worldwide Advancement of the Bahá'í Faith

I knew not what amazement was
Until I made Thy love my cause.
O how amazing would it be
If I were not amazed by Thee!

Bahá'u'lláh, in *Gems of Divine Mysteries*,
Quoted from the *Díván* of Ibn-i-Fáriḍ

The Dynamics of Growth

Scientific Principles at Work in the
Worldwide Advancement of the Bahá'í Faith

Jena Khadem Khodadad

GEORGE RONALD
OXFORD

George Ronald, Publisher
Oxford
www.grbooks.com

© Jena Khadem Khodadad 2016
All Rights Reserved

Reprinted 2017

A catalogue record for this book is available from the British Library
ISBN 978-0-85398-602-7

Cover design: Steiner Graphics

CONTENTS

Preface — ix
Acknowledgements — xix

Introduction: Focus on Growth: Essential to the Mission
   of the Bahá'í Faith — 1

PART 1

1. The Nature of Growth — 15
2. Enhancing Growth from Within — 40
3. The Flow of Plans and Growth — 67
4. Crystallization and Growth — 103
5. The Science of Chaos and Thousandfold Growth — 114

PART 2

6. The Twofold Process and Growth — 131
7. The Flow of History and Growth — 153
8. The Paradigm of Oneness of Religion and Growth — 178
9. Progressive Revelation and Growth — 197

PART 3

10. The Worldwide Bahá'í Community and the Unification
    of World Society — 213

Glossary — 229
Bibliography — 257
Notes and References — 267

*This book is dedicated
to*

my husband, Manucher

and

to the memory of my parents

*my father
Zikrullah Khadem*

and

*my mother
Javidukht Khadem*

PREFACE

The moment I started to compose this book I knew that writing its preface would be a task at once challenging and yet fulfilling.

It would be challenging, for herein I must convey to the reader – succinctly yet convincingly – the intent, the why, the what, and the how of this writing. I must ask myself: What prompted me to write on the dynamics of growth of the Bahá'í Faith in a manner which may be perceived uncommon, unconventional? Will a book centred on the application of scientific concepts and principles to the growth and advancement of the worldwide Bahá'í community – a process which is fundamentally spiritual – be well received? Can the use of metaphors, analogies, similes, and principles from science shed valuable insights on the dynamics of growth in the Bahá'í Faith?

Reflection on these questions firmed my resolve to proceed. In line with the Bahá'í principle of the harmony of science and religion, perspectives from science can add a valuable dimension to understanding the question of growth. Bahá'u'lláh and 'Abdu'l-Bahá make extensive use of analogies, metaphors and similes. 'Abdu'l-Bahá encourages their use in numerous passages, among them his talk on 'intelligible realities and their expression through sensible forms'.[1]

Once I decided to pursue this line of writing, my challenge became twofold: how to overcome the conventional barriers to this mode of discussion and how to convey my arguments to readers – from diverse backgrounds – in a manner that is cogent, clear and meaningful.

How it happened

The genesis of this book

The Dynamics of Growth owes its genesis to years of reflection and contemplation on a number of metaphors, analogies, similes, examples and principles from several fields, mostly from the natural sciences.

A significant source of this writing stems from my academic pursuits: study, instruction, and research, specifically in the disciplines of cell biology and neuroscience. Scientific concepts and principles as signposts disclose new vistas of expanded meaning on spiritual matters. Reflection on certain fundamental scientific principles operative in dynamic systems has enhanced my understanding of the process of growth of the Bahá'í Faith.

In particular, my chosen field of study – cell and molecular biology – brings together and integrates principles from biology, chemistry and physics in understanding the functions of living cells and tissues. Cell biology, a field replete with fascinating insights on living systems continues to enrich my appreciation of the growth process. It demands and encourages rigorous inquiry into mechanisms that lie at the very foundation of life. Neuroscience provides valuable insights; it addresses systems that are central to human consciousness, sensation and action.

Other areas of special interest are the philosophy of history and philosophy of science; these offer metaphors, analogies and perspectives rich with depths of insights, which have expanded my appreciation of the scientific and spiritual principles entailed in the process of growth of the Bahá'í Faith. They make special contributions to discussions in Chapters 7 and 8. The flow of the course of history, its direction, progression and culmination in a unified history of humankind, holds rich insights on those essential factors which are bound to influence the advancement of the Bahá'í Faith. The stages entailed in the progressive advancement of scientific truth have fascinating counterparts in the stages entailed in the Bahá'í premise of the oneness of religion and 'progressive revelation'.

The Bahá'í worldview provides guidance and inspiration for this book. It presents an expanded paradigm for our times. It is a dynamic spiritual system whose author is Bahá'u'lláh, whose expounders are 'Abdu'l-Bahá, the appointed successor to Bahá'u'lláh, and Shoghi Effendi, the appointed successor to 'Abdu'l-Bahá and the Guardian of the Bahá'í Faith.

There are three Central Figures of the Bahá'í Faith. The Báb (1819-1850), Forerunner to Bahá'u'lláh, and Bahá'u'lláh (1817-1892), the Inaugurator of the Bahá'í Dispensation, are Manifestations of God (for an explanation of this term see the Glossary). 'Abdu'l-Bahá

(1844–1921), appointed by Bahá'u'lláh as His Successor and the Centre of His Covenant, is the third Central Figure of the Bahá'í Faith. Shoghi Effendi (1897–1957) was appointed by 'Abdu'l-Bahá as the Guardian of the Bahá'í Faith and the Interpreter of its sacred texts. The twin successors to 'Abdu'l-Bahá were Shoghi Effendi[2] and the Universal House of Justice, the supreme governing body of the Bahá'í Faith, elected for the first time in 1963.

The writings of Bahá'u'lláh, 'Abdu'l-Bahá, Shoghi Effendi and the Universal House of Justice will be quoted in this book.

My interest in the question of growth

Over the years, the question of growth has continued to intrigue me; my interest was moderate at first but became more pressing with time. The earlier years of my life were spent in a country dominated by Shi'ah Islam and in a school dominated by Christian missionary zeal. At a young age, it became apparent to me that the solutions to alienation and discord among religions require a paradigm that can bring together all religions in harmony and fellowship. More specifically, there is a need for the long-sought-after *unified theory of religion*. It then became evident that such a theory – to be termed more precisely, *a unified premise* of religion – is already in existence through the Bahá'í principle of the oneness of religion known as 'progressive revelation'. It became increasingly clear that the solutions to the dilemmas facing humanity are to be found through the worldview presented by the Bahá'í Faith. Faced with a nagging question, I asked myself: When will this Bahá'í worldview, this *unified premise of religion*, the oneness of religion, become known and recognized by the masses? The next obvious question followed: When will this Faith grow in a measure that is commensurate with its mission of embracing all of humankind? How long will it take?

On one hand, much progress was being made in the Bahá'í world as exciting news was coming from all corners of the world about victories won; the light of Bahá'u'lláh had penetrated into yet another country, yet another territory, yet another distant island. Nonetheless, amidst such jubilations, I felt an overwhelming sense of urgency; the exigencies of the times – the pressing needs of humanity – required solutions which only the Bahá'í Faith could provide. As a child, my appreciation of time and process was lacking.

As I grew older, I knew that the impatience of my childhood and youth must be tempered with patience. Integration and assimilation into the collective consciousness of such a *seemingly revolutionary* and ground-breaking worldview require time and fortitude. The ingrained habits of the mind are not readily overcome.

In my later years, I had the opportunity and privilege of serving over a span of years on agencies and institutions of the Bahá'í Faith in the United States of America at national, regional and local levels. The centrepiece of the mandate of the Bahá'í National Teaching Committee[3] and the Regional Bahá'í Council of the Central States[4] was significant enhancement in the growth of the Bahá'í community. Once again, the question of growth resurfaced at the forefront of my consciousness. Once again, the importance of accelerated growth of this Faith, whose offerings provide solutions to the pressing needs of humankind, dominated my thinking. At this point, I bring to mind a passage from one of the messages of the Universal House of Justice: 'The Order brought by Bahá'u'lláh is intended to guide the progress and resolve the problems of society' and that there is the need for a 'vast expansion in our membership'.[5]

Over the years, a number of factors came together, germane to the overarching worldview of the Bahá'í Faith and the mandate for its growth and advancement. These included: scientific concepts and principles, the process of advancement of scientific knowledge, a fundamental perspective on the course of history, insights gleaned from service on Bahá'í institutions, and personal experience in sharing the Bahá'í Faith with others. The convergence of these and their relevance to the question of growth were gratifying; with the passage of time they continued to enlighten and expand my understanding. Consequently, I welcomed opportunities to share these insights with audiences through presentations at various conferences in plenary sessions, classes, and workshops, in the United States as well as in other countries.

These presentations were especially meaningful, as audiences were composed of a wide diversity of backgrounds, beliefs and disciplines. At Landegg Academy in Switzerland, the audience was composed of youth and college age, in the Czech and Slovak Republics of scientists and non-scientists, and in Auckland, New Zealand of Bahá'ís and their guests. The interest, comments and suggestions as well as critiques from those in attendance were invaluable to the development and refinement of my thinking. This was the beginning of the idea – though nebulous at first – to consider cultivating some of these themes into written form.

The seed of this book was planted when I shared the podium at a plenary session at the Green Lake Bahá'í Conference[6] with Dr John Hatcher. My presentation was on the theme of the crystallization of the Bahá'í worldwide community. Soon after, John urged me to develop the thoughts from that talk into written form. That seed began to germinate. Then, a few years later, after reading a brief coverage in the *New Zealand Bahá'í Newsletter*[7] on a presentation I had given in Auckland, New Zealand, on 'The Science of Growth', Dr Peter Khan wrote to me to emphasize the importance of the development of this theme. Additionally, I received encouragement for this writing from Mr Glenford Mitchell and Dr Bahieh Mitchell. These led me to the decision to compose *The Dynamics of Growth: Scientific Principles at Work in the Worldwide Advancement of the Bahá'í Faith*.

Such an undertaking at first seemed simple, as to some extent I had already developed these thoughts, together with respective diagrams illustrating them. Little did I realize, however, that major challenges would lie ahead.

Challenges to this writing

The *first* challenge was how to communicate these themes in writing to a readership from diverse disciplines and backgrounds. The *second* was how to effectively relate concepts from natural sciences to spiritual principles. The *third* was how to relate convincingly scientific metaphors and analogies to the question of growth of the Bahá'í Faith. The *fourth* was a fundamental question – the intrinsic value of this mode of approach to 'understanding' the growth of the Bahá'í Faith, as assurance has been given by Bahá'u'lláh through these words: 'Soon will all that dwell on earth be enlisted under these banners.'[8] Thus His Faith is destined to grow and become worldwide.

Response to these challenges. Regarding the first challenge: How to effectively communicate these themes to a varied readership? A written communication, unlike a spoken one, does not provide the opportunity to gauge its effectiveness by observing and interacting with the audience; therefore, I know that I must communicate my arguments with utmost clarity.

Regarding the second challenge: How to relate convincingly concepts from the natural sciences to spiritual principles? On numerous occasions, 'Abdu'l-Bahá encouraged the use of principles from the natural sciences to the understanding of spiritual precepts. Contrary to prevailing notions, there need not be a separation between the heart and the mind – between sentiment and intellect. Some arrive at their beliefs first through the intellect, others through the heart. Greater understanding and certitude are attained when each of these paths is complemented by the other. Many set out on the path of belief through the heart; however, when later the dimension of the mind, the intellect, is added, they are bound to be taken to a yet higher level of conviction.

Regarding the third challenge: How to effectively relate metaphors and analogies from science to the question of the growth of the Bahá'í Faith? All the chapters in *The Dynamics of Growth* use metaphors and analogies, mostly from the natural sciences with a few from the social sciences, to elucidate and clarify fundamental concepts. The sacred scriptures of the Bahá'í Faith are replete with such metaphors, analogies and similes. 'Abdu'l-Bahá specifically encourages their use.[9] In line with a fundamental principle of the Bahá'í Faith, there is no dichotomy between science and religion; they go hand in hand.

Regarding the fourth challenge: Is there value in this mode of approach to the growth of Bahá'í Faith, as assurance has been given by Bahá'u'lláh that His Faith will grow and become worldwide? I know, however, how these insights have increased my appreciation of growth as a process.

The discussions presented in this book are in line and in accordance with what we have learnt from the Universal House of Justice about the current progress of the Bahá'í community. The Universal House of Justice in a recent message expresses confidence about growth: 'Indeed, in an increasing number of settings the movement of a population towards Bahá'u'lláh's vision for a new society appears no longer merely as an enthralling prospect but as an emerging reality,' while at the same time recognizing that in some 'surroundings marked progress is yet to occur'[10] and that 'In places, the flow is a steady stream, in some, already a river. Now is not the moment for any soul to linger upon the bank – let all lend themselves to the onward surge.'[11]

At this time, as the Bahá'í world community is positioned for its accelerated large-scale growth, it is of special value to reflect on those factors which may empower the surge in growth.

Reflection on the discussions presented in various chapters of this book can enhance appreciation of the process of growth addressed through the systematic plans guided by the Universal House of Justice. These discussions focus attention on those growth-enhancing elements which are implemented through the plans of the Bahá'í world. Furthermore, they can increase one's understanding that growth is a dynamic process and that unforeseen and unanticipated factors can suddenly propel its significant acceleration. Additionally, these arguments point to the impact of the course of history on the growth of the Bahá'í Faith. Recognition and adoption of the Bahá'í premise of the oneness of religion can bring about a significant surge in growth. These questions and many more warrant reflection.

In sum, there are a number of reasons for writing this book. The application of scientific principles to the growth of the Bahá'í Faith extends beyond traditional approaches and barriers thus offering an important dimension to the discussion on growth.

As I came to appreciate the importance of sharing this understanding, I started a process which became the labour of many years. Throughout, I continued to reflect on whether such a discussion could in some measure help appreciation of the growth of a Faith destined to permeate the consciousness of world society. The solutions it offers to the dilemmas facing humankind must surely assure its ultimate victory. This Faith has a vast treasury of authenticated sacred writings and world-redeeming principles. It has its saints, its heroes and heroines dedicated to the plans of the Bahá'í world. There is a *Hand that directs its destiny.*

I pondered, however, on how the insights conveyed by this book have enhanced my own understanding of the process of growth. In this process there are phases wherein growth is occurring through the building up of resources. Such periods, as gleaned from the phases in the growth cycle of a biological cell, discussed in Chapter 1, are significant for gauging and ensuring vitality and sustainability of growth. Insights imparted through reflection on several themes in this book confirm that sustainable growth requires balance between expansion and consolidation and that individual and collective action are fundamental to the fulfilment of Bahá'u'lláh's vision for humanity.

Perchance others, who share my eagerness and impatience for growth, can reflect on: those factors which are entailed in growth in dynamic systems (Chapter 1); those factors which can enhance growth from within (Chapter 2); those factors from outside the Baháʼí community that can accelerate growth (Chapter 5); and that the growth of the Baháʼí Faith may be viewed as a crystallization process with two distinctive and sequential stages: slow growth during the nucleation phase followed by rapid growth during the crystal formation phase, as discussed in Chapter 4.

To the reader

In writing this book I knew what I wanted to impart. I recognize, nevertheless, that conveying thoughts and scientific theories – such as the generation of the laser beam, or the science of chaos and its butterfly effect in a manner which is succinct and at the same time meaningful would require significant effort. I have tried to address these through repeated revisions of my explanations of certain concepts which are essentially scientific, but clearly with spiritual implications. My hope is that I have succeeded in communicating to readers from backgrounds other than science these scientific principles with clarity and without compromise of accuracy. This has been a venture into unchartered territory.

I ask the reader's indulgence. I have attempted to discuss the scientific arguments in familiar terms, and have provided a glossary of the names, concepts and terminologies used throughout this book. The ultimate judgement – whether I have succeeded in this challenging task – must rest with each reader.

The afterglow

This writing has been *fulfilling*. I have experienced moments of elation in suddenly making a direct connection between these scientific principles and the growth of the Baháʼí Faith.

Writing *The Dynamics of Growth* required reflection, in greater depth, on the writings of Shoghi Effendi. As an admirer of Shoghi Effendi, whose physical presence I had undeservedly attained, I became exhilarated by his personage, his writings – the profundity and ever timeliness of the insights therein. I am continually reminded of ʻAbduʼl-Baháʼs statement about Shoghi Effendi: 'ages and centuries will bear traces of him'.[12]

My sense of elation springs from the vast treasury of this Faith – emanating from the Twin Manifestations, the Báb and Bahá'u'lláh, and from 'Abdu'l-Bahá and Shoghi Effendi. This writing has increased the depth of my dedication to the Universal House of Justice – now guiding the worldwide growth of the Bahá'í world. Each of the themes in this book leads one to that guidance.

In conclusion, upon the completion of the last chapter of this book I realized that a few additional chapters could further enrich it. Then, by chance, I came upon a statement of Tai' Tung, the 13th-century Chinese scholar: 'Were I to await perfection, my book would never be finished.'[13] Such serendipity I took to heart. I knew that I must remain content, at this point in time, with the current ten chapters.

In closing, I would like to express that the journey of many years was well worth it – due to the impact it has had on my innermost being. In reality, this book wrote me.

I stand in awe before the grandeur of the Bahá'í Faith. The following verses from Rumi are a reminder to my soul of that 'beauty that cannot be spoken' and the enormity of fully grasping the challenge of growth and the task that lies ahead. Though I have ventured into this field, I am nevertheless acutely aware that I am 'like an ant that's gotten into the granary . . . trying to lug out a grain that is way too big':

> *Friend, we're travelling together.*
> *Throw off your tiredness. Let me show you*
> *one tiny spot of the beauty that cannot be spoken.*
> *I'm like an ant that's gotten into the granary,*
> *ludicrously happy, and trying to lug out*
> *a grain that is way too big.*[14]

ACKNOWLEDGEMENTS

At the outset, I want to express my immense gratitude to my father, Zikrullah Khadem, whose scholarly interests in the sacred texts of the great religions of the world – Zoroastrian, Hindu, Buddhist, Jewish, Christian, Muslim, the Bábi and Bahá'í Faiths – were intense and fervent. His passion for these studies was due to the unshakeable conviction he had in their sacredness. At a young age he became consecrated to the Revelation of Bahá'u'lláh, the Faith destined to bring together within its embrace all religions. Throughout his life he immersed himself in the ocean of its writings. Impassioned, he often exclaimed in wonderment, 'O God increase my astonishment in Thee.'[1] A lifetime spent in quest of knowledge and service is an example which his children can only hope to emulate.

Composing *The Dynamics of Growth: Scientific Principles at Work in the Worldwide Advancement of the Bahá'í Faith* has been an adventure uplifting and cathartic – drawing me ever closer to him whose life, from youth to old age, was centred on the growth and worldwide expansion of the Bahá'í Faith.

I want to express my abundant gratitude to my mother, Javidukht Khadem, who shared my father's passion for the Bahá'í Faith and remained throughout her life his loving partner, collaborator and supporter. I am indebted to her in more ways than words can express. Her service, over fifty years, dedicated to the growth of the Bahá'í Faith in the United States, was indefatigable and passionate. Her encouragement that I should write this book, followed by persistent reminders over the years, lent impetus to this writing. I am greatly indebted to my husband, Dr Manucher Khodadad. Throughout the years of our lives together he has been a source of constant encouragement and support in all my undertakings. Once I set out to write this book he patiently accepted the interruptions which would be introduced into his life. His continuing belief in the value of this work has inspired me to stay the course.

I want to thank Dr John Hatcher, one of the first to suggest that I should develop, into written form, some of the thoughts which I had shared in one of my presentations at the Green Lake Bahá'í Conference. I feel indebted to Dr Peter Khan for his personal communication some years ago – wherein he encouraged me to develop the theme from a talk I had given on 'The Science of Growth' in Auckland, New Zealand. My appreciation goes to Mr Glenford Mitchell and Dr Bahieh Mitchell; after a conversation we had, some years in the past, on the application of scientific concepts to growth, they both urged its development into written form. Though I feel indebted to these individuals for their encouragement over the years, nevertheless I am at a loss to explain why a project they deemed of special value took so long to complete.

I want to express my appreciation to my brothers Mozhan, Riaz, Ramin and sister May for their dedication to the cause of growth and advancement of the Bahá'í Faith. I extend my special thanks to Mozhan, whose scholarly acumen I highly value, for his insightful suggestions after the critical reading of the entire manuscript at the earliest stage of its development.

I express my admiration for my granddaughters, Taylor, Isabel and Natalie Thurston whose level of interest and curiosity surpasses their young age. They draw attention to the importance of the role of upcoming generations of junior youth and youth in the advancement of Bahá'í beliefs. I thank my daughter, Camille, for nurturing in them an appreciation of their spiritual reality. I am proud of her strength and her advocacy of the advancement of women, essential to the oneness of humankind.

I also want to express my deepest sentiments to my sons, Nabil and Jian, for their dedication to the principles and ideals of the Bahá'í Faith. Each in his unique way is contributing to its growth and advancement. I thank Nabil for our valuable conversation on some of the themes of this book. To Jian, I owe special gratitude for his advice, suggestions and unrelenting encouragement. His insightful contributions during the latter phase of the development of this manuscript will do much toward its success. Work on this manuscript, has imparted a special quality to our mother–son bond which surpasses the mundane.

My special appreciation goes to Dr Feridun Khodadadeh – a physical chemist – for his interest and corroboration of certain scientific arguments presented in this book; his encouragement in the use of diagrams for elucidating certain scientific concepts was confirming.

ACKNOWLEDGEMENTS

I extend my appreciation to Marianne Smith Geula for her interest in this work and to Mary Bukowski with whom I have enjoyed meaningful and insightful conversations over the years, on certain themes introduced in this book.

I thank Thomas Murphy for his valuable contributions and extend my deepest appreciation to Dr Iraj Ayman, the founder of the Irfán Colloquium, for his unrelenting dedication to the cause of Bahá'í scholarship and his encouragement of certain themes covered in this book. The Irfán Colloquium has been an important forum for discourse, where I have presented, over the past several years, a few of the themes covered in this book.

I am grateful to several others for their encouragement and valuable suggestions: Dr Janet Khan, Dr Craig Loehle and Dr Anisa Nwachuku; Bijan Bayzaee for authentication of several sources; Isabel Jena Thurston for refining a few of the illustrations; Aaron Kreader for his artistic contributions to the diagrams in Chapter 6, and to Erica Leith, at George Ronald Publisher, for refinement of diagrams in preparation for publication.

I am deeply thankful, more than words can express, to May Hofman, my editor, for her knowledge, advice, wisdom and ever enthusiastic support. Her interest and encouragement never waned. I well remember that during the period of intense editing, each morning I would wake up early to be greeted by another email message bearing another round of edits from May, accompanied as always with encouraging words – what authors need to hear. Our literary interactions also had their poetic interludes by recalling selections from Handel's *Messiah*, as its passion related poignantly to certain concepts and chapters of this book.

INTRODUCTION

Focus on Growth: Essential to the Mission of the Bahá'í Faith

Attainment of the mission of Bahá'u'lláh for this age – the coming together of all races, tribes, nations, classes and religions in one world civilization – requires that its world-redeeming principles be made known to vast numbers of the inhabitants of this planet. Its precepts have the power to spark collective transformation in the character of the human race, tantamount to a *spiritual renaissance*. Such magnitude in societal change is the precondition for the establishment of a vital and sustainable global civilization. It is for this reason that the advancement of the Bahá'í community is fundamental to the actualization of the vision of Bahá'u'lláh for humanity.

Growth and advancement of the Bahá'í community is at the heart of this book. Although there is a rich repository of authoritative writings on this subject, application of scientific principles to the advancement of the Bahá'í Faith is a novel approach. It is anticipated that this study, developed from the perspective of a scientist, can offer a fresh point of view and make valuable contributions to the theme of growth. This work explores principles and insights using a number of scientific metaphors from the author's fields of study and interest. Reflection on these may impart an enhanced appreciation of the dynamics of growth of the Bahá'í community under the plans directed by its world governing body, the Universal House of Justice.

Importantly, the approach offered through this writing can bring into synergy perspectives from science and religion in affirmation of a fundamental assertion of the Bahá'í Faith: the principle of harmony between science and religion.

Several salient questions on the theme of growth warrant a brief preview in this introduction, leaving a more meaningful coverage to the ensuing chapters.

Certain fundamental considerations on growth

Reflection on expansion over time

From the inception of Bahá'u'lláh's Prophetic mission in the Síyáh-Chál[1] in 1853, the pattern of expansion of the Bahá'í community has displayed varying rates of growth from country to country, region to region and time to time, with periods of rapid growth as well as phases of slower growth. By 1893, in the span of forty years the Bahá'í Faith had already spread from the land of its birth and repression, Iran, to a few countries in Asia and Africa, North America,[2] and Europe. By 1920 the Bahá'í Faith had reached as far as Australia and in 1933 Shoghi Effendi announced that it had 'encircled the globe'.[3] The worldwide spread of the Bahá'í Faith will be discussed in Chapter 3, *The Flow of Plans and Growth*. By 1963, under the guidance of the plans of Shoghi Effendi, the Guardian of the Bahá'í Faith and the appointed successor to 'Abdu'l-Bahá, the Bahá'í community had achieved a phenomenal worldwide expansion[4] and continues to advance in its growth under the plans directed by the Universal House of Justice. As noted by that supreme body, each approach, over time, to the growth of the Bahá'í community was suited to its specific historical circumstance.[5]

At the time of this writing, the available statistics on its worldwide growth are remarkable. The Faith has spread to over 120,000 localities. Its community includes within its embrace over 2,112 indigenous tribes, races and ethnic groups. Its sacred writings have been translated into over 800 different languages.[6] The global spread of the Bahá'í Faith to all islands and corners of the world suggests that it is among the most geographically widespread religions.

The growth and advancement of the Bahá'í Faith is centred on its vision – the creation of 'the nucleus of a glorious global civilization'.[7] Toward the attainment of this lofty objective, the Bahá'í community invites the engagement of others – whether they are registered Bahá'ís or not – in the process of societal change and civilization building.

At this particular point in time, when the world population has exceeded seven billion and the Bahá'í population is still only a small fraction of that,[8] it is imperative that significant numbers of the inhabitants of the planet become imbued with the healing and regenerating message which the Bahá'í Faith offers to humanity. Thus its principles can become widespread and the transforming message of Bahá'u'lláh can *penetrate* and *suffuse* collective consciousness.

A vast ten-part majestic process

Regarding the growth and spread of the Bahá'í Faith, Shoghi Effendi in one of his messages to the Bahá'í world described a 'vast ten-part majestic process' which was set in motion at the dawn of the Adamic cycle.[9] The **eighth part** of that process he described as the *diffusion* of that light to over ninety-four sovereign states, dependencies and islands of the planet as a result of the prosecution of a series of national plans.[10] The **ninth part** of that process he described as the *further diffusion* of that same light to over one hundred and thirty-one additional territories and islands in both the Eastern and Western hemispheres through the operation of a decade-long world spiritual crusade.[11] He foreshadowed the **tenth part** of this mighty process, the *penetration* of that light, in the course of numerous crusades and successive epochs of both the Formative[12] and Golden Ages[13] of the Faith, into all the remaining territories of the globe. Shoghi Effendi signified this as 'the stage at which the light of God's triumphant Faith shining in all its power and glory will have *suffused* and enveloped the entire planet'.[14]

The stages of penetration and suffusion

The Universal House of Justice, in its 1964 Riḍván Message to the Bahá'ís of the world,[15] and again more recently in 2011,[16] called attention to this divinely propelled process described by Shoghi Effendi, who characterized the final stage as the '*penetration* of that light into all the remaining territories of the globe', envisioning its *suffusion*.

The stage of *diffusion*, characterized by the worldwide spread of the Bahá'í Faith undertaken by valiant heroes and heroines under the guidance of the Ten Year Global Spiritual Crusade, has already taken place. At this point in time, the *penetration* of that light and its *suffusion* are at the heart of the plans of the Bahá'í world. The efforts of Bahá'ís worldwide are now directed at the *penetration* and *suffusion* of the divine Word, toward the construction of the nucleus of that glorious global civilization. The question of the advancement of the Bahá'í Faith will continue to remain fundamental to the realization of the mission of Bahá'u'lláh for humanity.

Growth under the plans of the Bahá'í world

The growth of the Bahá'í community is addressed through plans guided by the Faith's successive world heads. The Universal House of Justice calls attention to the importance of planning – its role as well as its unique nature. The plans of the Bahá'í Faith are systematic; they identify objectives to be achieved and approaches for achieving them. Importantly, they strive to align the work of the Cause with the processes that are steadily unfolding in the world.[17]

Implementation of these plans requires: identification of specific tasks, alignment of the individual and communities with the institutions of the Bahá'í Faith, focus on the task, and individual as well as collective action. These requirements are discussed in Chapter 2, *Enhancing Growth from Within*, using scientific insights drawn from the metaphor of the laser beam. The evolution of the plans of the Bahá'í community – the unfolding stages of the Tablets of the Divine Plan[18] – is discussed in Chapter 3, *The Flow of Plans and Growth*.

Essential characteristics of growth

Quantitative and qualitative growth

Growth must include two essential and inseparable dimensions: quantitative and qualitative. For the Bahá'í community, quantitative growth is increase in the number of avowed believers as well as those populations imbued with the vision of Bahá'u'lláh for humanity. Qualitative growth is transformation: the outcome of assimilation of the spirit and principles of the Bahá'í Faith into one's consciousness, character and actions. This concept of growth remains fundamental to the creation of that vital and sustainable global civilization envisioned by Bahá'u'lláh, expounded by 'Abdu'l-Bahá and Shoghi Effendi, and addressed through the systematic plans of the Universal House of Justice. The importance of both quantitative and qualitative growth is emphasized in Chapter 1, *The Nature of Growth* and throughout this book.

INTRODUCTION: FOCUS ON GROWTH

Organic growth

The process of growth is fundamentally organic in nature.[19] This evokes principles from the science of biology; it means that the Baháʼí Faith – as a living organism or as an organ – develops and grows through a systematic process, in phases, in a timely fashion and in a highly coordinated sequence. It implies that there is a structure, an entity inherent within the system itself toward which the organ gradually develops until ultimately its destiny becomes manifest and its purpose is fulfilled. Therefore, that ultimate pattern and structure of the organ is *latent,* enfolded in those early cells at the very beginning.

The analogy of an organ, applied to the understanding of the organic growth of the Baháʼí Faith, as well as certain other related concepts, are discussed in Chapter 1, *The Nature of Growth*.

Current strategies of the plans

In order to advance the process of 'entry by troops',[20] the current plans of the Baháʼí world include two intimately linked approaches: *community building* and *capacity building*. Community building efforts centre their focus at the grassroots level in neighbourhoods and villages, wherever individuals are found to walk this path of service with the Baháʼís. Capacity is built through systematic training known as the 'institute process'[21] fostering knowledge, spiritual insight and practical skills for community building, and through ongoing learning acquired, over time, through a pattern of study, consultation, action and reflection with others. These processes are centred on participation in the core activities which include, at this time: study circles, devotional meetings, children's classes, and spiritual empowerment programmes for junior youth. Together they constitute a *framework for action*; they thus hold the potential for significant growth. The core activities, as well as community building and capacity building, are mentioned in Chapter 2 and discussed in Chapter 3, *The Flow of Plans and Growth*.

Issues of growth

Essential to the penetration and suffusion of the transforming message of Baháʼu'lláh is that the Baháʼí community should grow and its principles become widespread. As growth is integral to the plans of the Bahá'í world, certain fundamental questions warrant reflection. Among these are: What is the purpose of growth? What signifies growth? How can growth be measured?

The purpose of growth

The ultimate purpose of the growth of the Bahá'í community is transformation of both the individual and the collective. The achievement of this objective is through dissemination of the ideals, principles, and vision of Bahá'u'lláh for humanity, implemented under the systematic plans of the Bahá'í world; these are to be in tandem with learning how to put these teachings into practice through action.

What signifies the growth of the Bahá'í community?

Recent guidance from the Universal House of Justice conveys that the growth of the Bahá'í community must extend beyond the traditional measure of increase in the numbers of registered Bahá'ís. Its scope widens to also include those populations imbued with the vision of Bahá'u'lláh, even though not registered as Bahá'ís. Importantly, measures of growth include the involvement of those participating in the capacity building and community building endeavours of Bahá'ís.

The spread of Bahá'í ideals and principles is addressed through programmes of growth.[22] These are described by the Universal House of Justice in terms of the 'movement of a population, inspired by the purpose and principles of the Cause'.[23] Such populations can bring about societal change – a prelude to transformation of the masses.

Measures of growth

In assessing growth, certain numerical measures such as the number of those participating in programmes of growth; the number of learning sites; the number of those who have completed institute courses; or those serving as tutors of study circles, teachers of children's classes, and facilitators of junior youth empowerment programmes, can serve as effective indicators of growth. Increase is shown in all these parameters.[24] Furthermore, there is enhancement in the devotional and spiritual character of the Bahá'í community life.²⁵ All of these together signify that the Bahá'í community by expanding its capabilities is showing the way to accelerated growth.

Recently, an important measure of growth was a numerical goal in the Five Year Plan (2011–2016).²⁶ This charge – the establishment of programmes of growth in large numbers of clusters²⁷ worldwide – has generated momentum. The Universal House of Justice, heartened over the progress made, wrote in 2015 that 'efforts to set in motion the necessary pattern of activity have already begun in almost every one of the clusters' and noted that 'those defining features that must come to mark the further unfoldment of the growth process in a cluster are becoming gradually discernible'.²⁸

In this context, the Universal House of Justice anticipates an increase in the numbers of participants from tens serving hundreds to 'one or two hundred facilitating the participation of one or two thousand'²⁹ in a distinct geographic area. One can readily envision that increases in the numbers of such participants will set in motion a dynamic process, continuous and autocatalytic.³⁰ The potential for such an autocatalytic process is highlighted in Chapter 4, *Crystallization and Growth*. It must be emphasized that essential to meaningful growth is qualitative change or *transformation* – the purpose of Bahá'u'lláh's revelation.

The Bahá'í community and the oneness of humankind

Millions of Bahá'ís across the face of this planet endeavour toward the creation of the nucleus of the glorious world culture and civilization anticipated in the teachings of Bahá'u'lláh, mindful that the building of such a civilization is 'an enterprise of infinite complexity and scale'. A task of such magnitude requires a profound change, both at the level of the individual and in the structure of society. Bahá'u'lláh asserts that the object of every Revelation is transformation in the whole character of mankind.³¹ Bahá'ís worldwide strive toward advancing this lofty objective – a quest that has for long inspired the vision of visionaries, the verses of poets, and the prophecy of the prophets.

The Bahá'í community is geographically and culturally widespread. It represents a wide diversity of backgrounds – ethnic, racial, cultural, social and religious. Thus it represents a viable model, a microcosm of humanity dedicated to the cause of peace and oneness of the human race. Its adherents view themselves as members of a single human family. It is such a community that is engaged in a spiritual enterprise toward the advancement of present-day society into a world culture and civilization. Chapter 10, *The Worldwide Bahá'í Community and Unification of World Society*, presents the Bahá'í world community as a viable diaspora (see the Glossary) for bringing about the unification of the world.

The Bahá'í community, with its beginning in the mid-nineteenth century, is consecrated to the ideals and principles of the Bahá'í Cause. Bábí and Bahá'í history signifies a poignant, tender and moving saga of persecution, sacrifice, devotion and fervour of multitudes impassioned by the Báb and Bahá'u'lláh. Numerous were those heroes and heroines who served sacrificially to spread the message of Bahá'u'lláh to the masses, to all corners of the globe.

Organization of this book

This book is organized in three parts. The chapters employ metaphors, mostly from the natural sciences – the author's background – to illustrate certain scientific principles which may be at work in the process of the growth and expansion of the Bahá'í community. These are offered for the reader's reflection. Metaphors, analogies and similes are used throughout this writing. Similar devices have been used in all religions. Bahá'u'lláh and 'Abdu'l-Bahá make extensive use of such means in order to explain and elucidate certain matters and to expand and enhance perception and understanding. 'Abdu'l-Bahá explains and encourages their use and often asks the listener to reflect further on a specific example he provides – implying that this will lead to uncovering their hidden layers and dimensions. 'Abdu'l-Bahá was once asked why the teachings of all religions are expressed largely in parables and metaphors and not in the plain language of the people. He replied:

> Divine things are too deep to be expressed by common words. The heavenly teachings are expressed in parable in order to be understood and preserved for ages to come. When the spiritually minded dive deeply into the ocean of their meaning they bring to the surface the pearls of their inner significance. There is no greater pleasure than to study God's Word with a spiritual mind.[32]

INTRODUCTION: FOCUS ON GROWTH

It must be pointed out, nonetheless, that though such devices – as employed in this book – are offered in the interest of elucidating and expanding perceptions on certain essential points, they nevertheless, as all metaphors, analogies and similes, have their own limitations.

Part 1

Consisting of five chapters (Chapters 1 to 5), Part 1 is centred on the process of growth and advancement of the Bahá'í community.

Chapter 1, *The Nature of Growth.* This chapter addresses some of the essential conditions and factors that characterize growth in any dynamic system. These conditions are indispensable to vitality, vibrancy and sustainability of growth. Qualitative growth (or transformation) and quantitative growth are discussed as two inseparable dimensions of growth. Several metaphors and analogies from biological systems – such as growth of population of cells and the process of division (mitosis) of one cell into two – are explored; the insights therein are applied to the growth of the Bahá'í community.

Chapter 2, *Enhancing Growth from Within,* addresses those factors that are internal to the Bahá'í community and hold the potential to enhance its rate of growth. There are a number of factors that are indispensable to growth; these include vision, passion, ecstasy, action, and the building of strong indissoluble bonds, among others. This chapter also provides insights from a number of metaphors and analogies from science, such as the reflex arc of the nervous system, bonds connecting atoms in a compound, transition in phase of water from aqueous to steam, and the phenomenon of co-evolution. The metaphor of the laser beam – its generation, function, and action – holds rich insights. Its properties of coherence, alignment and focus are discussed in relation to individual and collective action.

Chapter 3, *The Flow of Plans and Growth,* discusses the progression of the plans of the Bahá'í world, from the Tablets of the Divine Plan of 'Abdu'l-Bahá to the plans of Shoghi Effendi and continuing on with the plans of the Universal House of Justice. These plans, to be understood as the unfolding stages of the Divine Plan of 'Abdu'l-Bahá, have guided the Bahá'í community systematically toward its remarkable worldwide spread. The recent plans of the Universal House of Justice place special focus on capacity building and community building – essential to growth.

Chapter 4, *Crystallization and Growth*, discusses the crystallization of the Bahá'í community; the insights gleaned from its analogue – crystallization of a substance in a solution – are discussed and offered for the reader's reflection. The process of crystal formation and the essential properties of a crystal serve as insightful metaphors for the growth of the Bahá'í community and the resultant properties of transformation, structure, beauty and purity of character.

Chapter 5, *The Science of Chaos and Thousandfold Growth*. This chapter is centred on certain 'growth-enhancing factors' that are external to the Bahá'í community and beyond its control and influence. When operational, however, these factors can bring about significant acceleration in the rate of growth of the Bahá'í Faith. This chapter offers fascinating insights gleaned from certain concepts and metaphors that can serve as analogues for a process which once in operation can wield immense power. Among these growth-enhancing factors are the phenomenon of Chaos including its 'butterfly effect' and its implications for the emergence of the World Order of Bahá'u'lláh.

Part 2

Part 2 (Chapters 6 to 9) includes certain selected concepts and precepts of the Bahá'í Faith that have direct relevance to the urgent needs of humanity in this era of globalization; these are bound to exert a strong impact on the worldwide acceptance and expansion of the Bahá'í Faith. It is for these reasons that once the Bahá'í Faith becomes widely known, once its light *penetrates* and *suffuses*[33] human consciousness (see above, 'A vast ten-part majestic process'), it can spark a conflagration of unimaginable magnitude and brilliancy.

The authoritative texts of the Bahá'í Faith on God, the nature of man, the immortality of the soul, and numerous other fundamental beliefs, provide answers to man's perennial questions and satisfy humankind's quest for spirituality. In considering the growth and expansion of the worldwide Bahá'í community, the following areas are selected for inclusion in this book: the twofold process of integration and disintegration (Chapter 6); Bahá'í beliefs relating to the view, purpose, direction and culmination of the course of history (Chapter 7); and the Bahá'í principle of the oneness of religion (Chapters 8 and 9). The concepts addressed in these chapters are profound and have the power to exercise a significant impact on the advancement of the Bahá'í Faith.

Chapter 6, *The Twofold Process and Growth,* provides a discussion centred on the workings of the twin processes of integration and disintegration operational in the course of history. These are of particular relevance to our turbulent and tumultuous times. Analogies from science serve as metaphors for explaining the phenomenon of 'newly emerging entities' – the new potentialities infused into creation through the Dispensations of the Twin Manifestations, the Báb and Bahá'u'lláh. In order to explain the optimism which the Bahá'ís have on the outcome of history and their assurance in an emerging new world order, two insightful metaphors on perception are offered for the readers' reflection. These are (i) through diagrams on 'hidden image', and (ii) the physiology of vision.

Chapter 7, *The Flow of History and Growth,* discusses the Bahá'í worldview on the course of history and its eventual culmination in the unification of the human race in a global civilization. This chapter discusses certain key questions in the philosophy of history. Several points based on the thesis of Arnold J. Toynbee about alternative fundamental views of history are represented through illustrations. The Bahá'í view of history is discussed through the use of a diagrammatic representation. The insights imparted through the metaphor of a chrysalis are explored and applied to the development of the world civilization within the chrysalis – the environment of the Bahá'í Faith.

Chapter 8, *The Paradigm of Oneness of Religion and Growth,* expounds on the role of religions in civilization. It presents the Bahá'í principle of the oneness of religion as an expanded paradigm of religion free from the faults of insistence on the finality of divine revelation and claim to exclusivity of salvation through its Prophet-Founder. The cogent analysis and discussion offered by Thomas Kühn on progression of scientific knowledge through paradigms set the backdrop for this discussion.

Chapter 9, *Progressive Revelation and Growth,* presents and discusses the essential features of the Bahá'í premise of continuing progressive revelation – as articulated by Bahá'u'lláh, and expounded by 'Abdu'l-Bahá and subsequently by Shoghi Effendi. This premise includes several fundamental convictions. It asserts that divine truth is absolute and that its revelation through the divine Educators is progressive over time. The discussion in this chapter offers two diagrams to draw attention to the two aspects of religions: the fundamental – that is, those eternal verities, the essential teachings which remain changeless; and the teachings which expand and evolve in response to the requirements of time, place and conditions of life. It emphasizes that divine revelation will continue into the future. At this particular point in the history of humankind all religions can come together in one common Faith. The chapter draws attention to the urgent need for an all-encompassing worldview that can explain and address religious multiplicity and diversity.

There are numerous other principles of the Bahá'í Faith of particular relevance to our times that are bound to influence its rate of growth but are not included in this book. Among these are the proposal for collective security put forth by Bahá'u'lláh in the nineteenth century toward the establishment of a world commonwealth,[34] the principle of harmony of science and religion, as well as several other precepts.[35]

Part 3

This part has one chapter, serving as the conclusion to this book.

Chapter 10, *The Worldwide Bahá'í Community and the Unification of World Society*, briefly discusses the replacement of the old world order with the new world order ushered in by Bahá'u'lláh. Herein, based on a statement from Bahá'u'lláh, the metaphor of a clay structure – unstable and prone to dissolution – is applied to the old world order.[36] This, in turn, evokes an image from the Book of Daniel in the Old Testament, of a seemingly majestic structure which rests on feet of clay.

The chapter discusses the emergence of *a new race of men* in relation to Francis Fukuyama's thesis expressed in *The End of History and the Last Man*. It offers for the readers' consideration the worldwide Bahá'í community as a community well suited for bringing about global unity. The Bahá'í community has a distinct identity; it is not limited to one patch of earth but is spread across the face of this planet and is dedicated to the oneness of the human race.

PART 1

1
THE NATURE OF GROWTH

> The Faith of God does not advance at one uniform pace. Sometimes it is like the advance of the sea when the tide is rising. Meeting a sandbank the water seems to be held back, but, with a new wave, it surges forward, flooding past the barrier which checked it for a little while. If the friends will but persist in their efforts, the cumulative effect of years of work will suddenly appear.
>
> *The Universal House of Justice*[1]

Introduction

The Bahá'í Faith, the youngest of the world's major religions – at this time over a century and a half since its founding – is in the earliest stage of its growth and is yet unknown to the overwhelming majority of the planet's inhabitants. As might be expected, smallness in the number of its adherents[2] – its avowed believers – is among those features that characterize a religion at such an early stage in its growth. The great British historian Edward Gibbon,[3] chronicler of the fall of Rome and the rise of Christianity, comments on the number of Christians during the first two centuries after Christ. Referring to estimations attempted in various sources, he observes that, although it is not possible to achieve an accurate measure of the number of Christians during this embryonic stage in the religion's development, one can surmise that the proportion of believers to the vast number of those under Rome's dominion must have been quite small.[4] It is clear that during this earliest phase of its growth, Christianity was obscure, with a limited spread and a sparse number of believers.

Despite the relatively small number of people who have thus far embraced it, the Bahá'í Faith has experienced impressive geographical spread for a religion now in its second century. Data from several sources[5] show that the worldwide expansion of the Faith has been noteworthy. The most recent available data on the number of Bahá'ís worldwide is reported variously at approximately five to five-and-a-half and to over six million, though higher numbers have been reported by other sources; these numbers are propitious considering the Faith's short history.

The remarkable growth of the Bahá'í Faith thus far has been achieved as a result of systematic action directed through a series of global plans devised by the successive world heads of the Faith and supported by the entire Bahá'í world community. Through such action, by 2005 the Faith had already spread to over 120,000 localities. It had been embraced by some 2,112 indigenous tribes, races, and ethnic groups, and had seen its writings translated into 800 different languages.[6] Impressive as they are, these statistics underscore the importance of continuing expansion of the Bahá'í community and its reaching out to permeate the consciousness of still larger segments of the world's population in order to spur societal change; this remains the Faith's critical objective.

The notable level of growth of the worldwide Bahá'í community can be attributed to three major factors.

First, like the other great religions of the world, the Bahá'í Faith contains a rich repository of those verities which every person craves deep within her or his inmost self – those profound truths answering life's most basic and troubling questions, fulfilling the deepest needs of the human soul, fostering spiritual development and ultimately enkindling the transformation of both individuals and society as a whole.

Second, the Faith's teachings have special relevance to the condition of society in our time. They are responsive to the urgent need for the establishment of world civilization and a truly global approach to the solution of the multitude of problems facing humanity and threatening the very survival of our planet.

Third, the strategy that has been employed to make the Faith known to the generality of humankind and to stimulate its expansion has followed an ingenious and systematic course. This strategy focused relentlessly, at an earlier stage of its history, on the Faith's global spread; it thus succeeded in establishing by the middle of its second century an expansive worldwide Bahá'í community encompassing every nation and territory on earth. This theme will be explored in greater depth in Chapter 3 of this book.

Although the estimated number of Bahá'ís worldwide is respectable considering the Faith's short history, it nevertheless constitutes a small percentage of the world's total population, at this time over seven billion.[7] This number is simply not commensurate with the magnitude of the Faith's claims and the depth and breadth of its mission as the begetter of a world civilization and culture. Accelerating the movement of populations toward the vision conceived by Bahá'u'lláh for humanity is the focus of the plans of the Bahá'í world and will continue to be the foremost challenge facing the Bahá'í Faith in the years ahead.

To meet this challenge, the worldwide community of Bahá'ís has, in recent decades – following the guidance provided in a series of global plans devised by the Faith's international governing body, the Universal House of Justice – been engaged in a massive coordinated effort to put into place systems that will not only foster such a large-scale expansion but will effectively bring on societal change and consolidate growth. Such consolidation must ensure that new believers and others who wish to participate are provided with the opportunities to develop their knowledge, spiritual insights and skills to contribute to the community-building process, thus creating a sustainable system for growth and development.

Throughout the world, the most advanced geographical units of growth known as 'clusters' (see the Glossary) show progress toward the goal of balanced expansion and consolidation. In thousands of neighbourhoods and villages there is evidence of a movement of populations towards Bahá'u'lláh's vision for a new society. Examples from one cluster in each of the four continents – Norte de Bolivar, Colombia in South America; Toronto, Canada in North America; Lubumbashi, Democratic Republic of Congo in Africa; and Bihar Sharif in India, Asia – are included in a documentary which was produced in recent years.[8] These attest to the vital role of the 'institute process' (see the Glossary) in community building through addressing the needs and cultural challenges which confront children, junior youth, youth and adults. Significantly, in all of these, the dynamic contributions of the youth is noteworthy (see also Chapter 3).[9] Thanks to this continuing effort, the Bahá'í community in the 21st century is making significant advances.[10]

There has therefore never been a better time to examine the dynamics of growth – to explore and thoughtfully consider the many factors that promote growth. These include:

1. Conditions and requirements essential for vital growth in any dynamic system.

2. Factors that enhance growth from within – the individual, the Bahá'í community and its institutions.

3. Factors that are unanticipated from 'without' – that is, they lie outside the direct influence of the individual, the Bahá'í community and its institutions, yet, when set in operation, can serve to greatly enhance the growth and advancement of the Bahá'í Faith.

This chapter, in common with every chapter in *The Dynamics of Growth*, makes use of metaphors and analogies to illuminate fundamental concepts. Most are derived from the natural sciences. Though metaphors and analogies have their limitations, when applied to processes that have a spiritual component they can be of great value. Many of the processes at work in the growth of the Bahá'í Faith adhere to principles with analogues in the sciences. Examples from science can impart important insights and engender empowerment.

This chapter will explore a few of the conditions and requirements that are essential for vital growth in any dynamic system. To do so, a number of **metaphors** and **analogies,** and a few **similes,** will be employed to elucidate key points.

A few definitions

Metaphors are used when one object is likened to another. Metaphors make implicit or implied comparison between two things that are unrelated, such as the physical sun for the spiritual Sun of Truth. ***Analogies*** are used to show a resemblance of properties – or a one-to-one relationship – between two things or concepts which have similar features. ***Similes*** express comparison or likeness between two different things, such as 'lovely as a rose'.

The use of metaphors and analogies is an essential component of discourse, as we make comparisons and relate things we know to things that are new to us. Though they are of immeasurable value in our attempts to understand the universe we live and move in, there are obvious limits to their application.

Despite their limitations, such devices can clarify and elucidate concepts, serving to stimulate further thinking and to expand understanding. Note the plenteousness of metaphors, analogies, similes and parables in the sacred literature of the world's religions: their abundance is proof enough that spiritual truths cannot be fully conveyed through the ordinary mechanisms of language.

Metaphors and analogies can be invested with both subtlety and power, often enwrapping a core truth in multiple layers of meaning and significance. Jesus Christ used parables to promulgate His teachings, employing deceptively simple stories to convey profound moral lessons. Bahá'u'lláh, the Manifestation of God for this age, makes extensive use of metaphors to illuminate the mystical dimension of life, that invisible realm of the spirit that surrounds us, infusing our acts with gravity and consequence. Metaphors employing the image of the sun to represent the centrality and incandescent power of truth – as in the 'Sun of Truth' – or the image of the ocean to represent the vastness and depth of divine revelation are found repeatedly in His writings. 'Abdu'l-Bahá, His eldest son and the authorized interpreter of His teachings, likewise makes use of such means, in many instances applying them to the contingent world.

In His lucid and supremely logical public addresses and talks, 'Abdu'l-Bahá often uses examples from nature – such as the cultivation of plants, the development of the seed and leaves in plants,[11] the development of a plant from a seed,[12] the development of embryos,[13] and numerous others – to convey a point or to make His argument more forceful. 'Abdu'l-Bahá invites us to reflect on these, encouraging us to plumb their depths for the insights to be found there: this clearly implies that beneath the surface of metaphors and analogies lies a treasure trove of wisdom just waiting to be brought to light.

It is in the spirit of 'Abdu'l-Bahá's invitation to such exploration that a number of metaphors and analogies are offered in these pages for the reader's thoughtful reflection. The application of examples from the natural sciences – such as the process of division in a living cell – to the growth of the Bahá'í Faith, which has an inseparable spiritual dimension, may seem at first overstretched and even incongruent. They are, however, offered in keeping with what 'Abdu'l-Bahá maintains in His talk on 'intelligible realities and their expression through sensible forms'.[14]

The Dynamics of Growth affirms the writer's belief that examples from the workings of the natural world can be applied to the processes that will surely be entailed in the present and future growth of the Bahá'í Faith. Put another way, the processes involved in the growth of a religion adhere to principles that correspond to the principles of science.

The metaphors and analogies employed in this chapter focusing on the conditions and requirements essential to growth in dynamic systems consist of the:

- germination of a seed in a milieu suitable for viable growth;
- multiplication of a population of cells in a tissue culture system;
- division of a single living cell into two.

The requisites of growth

By exploring how growth is customarily defined in the world of the natural sciences, we can obtain insights that will be of great value in furthering the growth and development of the Bahá'í community.

To substantiate from the scientific point of view that meaningful growth is present in any object of study, it must manifest the characteristics of ***vitality*** and ***sustainability***. Vital growth is the growth displayed by a living organism – that is, the capability of imparting continuation to its own life. Sustainable growth is characterized by endurance, perseverance and self-maintenance. Wherever these qualities are seen in an object of study, we have ascertained the existence of a living, growing organism – a dynamic system. Furthermore, the growth of a religion must have the added dimension of ***vibrancy***. Vibrant growth is energetic, enthusiastic, and vigorous; it is passionate. 'Vibrant' is a term often used in the messages of the Universal House of Justice.

Two essential dimensions of growth

The growth of a religion must also manifest the two essential characteristics of ***qualitative*** and ***quantitative*** growth. Qualitative growth signifies a demonstrable improvement in quality; quantitative growth denotes an increase in numbers. The two characteristics of qualitative and quantitative growth, like the two sides of one coin, are interrelated and inseparable. An object of study (such as the Bahá'í Faith) deficient in either of them will not be capable of mounting a growth that is vital, sustainable and vibrant.

Qualitative growth, here defined as the transformation of individuals and communities, is at the very core of the world's enduring religions; it is their hallmark, their *raison d'être*. The mission of every religion is to bring about a transformation in the character and conduct of individuals and, in so doing, to effect a regeneration of society. Quantitative growth in the case of a religion signifies an increase in the number of its followers. A religion must effectively reach out to a significant portion of the inhabitants of the planet, gathering within its fold large and diverse populations. These two facets of growth must advance hand in hand; neither without the other can hope to result in meaningful change.

The Bahá'í writings inform us that growth in numbers alone will not be sufficient to fulfil the Faith's mission:

> It is not sufficient to number the souls that embrace the Cause to know the progress that it is making. The more important consequences of your activities is the spirit that is diffused into the life of the community.[15]

> It is not enough to expand the rolls of Bahá'í membership, vital as that is. Souls must be transformed, communities thereby consolidated, new models of life thus attained. Transformation is the essential purpose of the Cause of Bahá'u'lláh.[16]

Shoghi Effendi calls attention to this point:

> Not by the force of numbers, not by the mere exposition of a set of new and noble principles, not by an organized campaign of teaching – no matter how worldwide and elaborate in its character – not even by the staunchness of our faith or the exaltation of our enthusiasm, can we ultimately hope to vindicate in the eyes of a critical and sceptical age the supreme claim of the Abhá Revelation. One thing and only one thing will unfailingly and alone secure the undoubted triumph of this sacred Cause, namely, the extent to which our own inner life and private character mirror forth in their manifold aspects the splendor of those eternal principles proclaimed by Bahá'u'lláh.[17]

Growth in numbers without a concomitant growth in quality may be likened to the growth of a weed which, over time, can choke vital and purposeful growth, driving the community away from the very spirit that had once animated and invigorated it. The Faith would, in consequence, become an empty shell of practices and rituals; it would survive as a form without a soul, a body without life, and would sink in time into a state of decadence and degeneracy.

As we have already seen, ***transformation*** of the individual and community is the essential purpose of the Bahá'í Faith and constitutes the ultimate measure of its success. 'Abdu'l-Bahá refers to the 'heavenly army' as 'those souls who are entirely freed from the human world, transformed into celestial spirits and . . . divine angels'.[18]

However, growth in quality – transformation – without a concomitant growth in the number of the Faith's adherents will not fulfil the Faith's mission. The Bahá'í Faith is a world religion whose teachings must reach large numbers of the inhabitants of this planet and whose spirit must permeate their consciousness to bring about *collective transformation* – a requisite for achieving worldwide acceptance of the oneness of the human race and the advancement, by a great quantum, of civilization. Just as the Faith is centred on the transformation of the individual, it is likewise centred on the transformation of the collective, of the entire human race.

The concern of the individual with the spiritual development of one's self may be personally satisfying; by itself, however, it can neither hope to transform the face of society nor effect lasting change in the world. A matter traditionally sparking much debate in the world's religious communities has been whether it is sufficient for a person of faith to be concerned with the transformation of his or her own soul exclusively – that is, in isolation from society and its concerns. Arguments on both sides of the matter have led, in some religious communities, to the evolution of two different and opposed branches of thinking about it. In extreme cases, one branch of thought has led some to renounce the world and to live as monks and ascetics. The Bahá'í teachings strongly discourage a cloistered life, lived in seclusion from society. 'O people of the earth!', Bahá'u'lláh exhorts us, 'Living in seclusion or practising asceticism is not acceptable in the presence of God.'[19]

In the Tablet of Bi<u>sh</u>árát, Bahá'u'lláh acknowledges the 'pious deeds' of monks and priests, but calls upon them to 'give up the life of seclusion and direct their steps towards the open world and busy themselves with that which will profit themselves and others'.[20]

In place of seclusion, Bahá'u'lláh calls humanity to a new form of religious life that requires creative *engagement* with the world as the path to spiritual development. The challenge of this age, He tells us, is to bring spirituality to bear, in a practical way, on the world's manifold problems. Further, He requires His followers to be employed in a useful profession or trade, raising the pursuit of excellence in one's calling – when it is performed in a spirit of service to humanity – to the level of worship. As 'Abdu'l-Bahá expresses it:

> All humanity must obtain a livelihood by sweat of the brow and bodily exertion, at the same time seeking to lift the burden of others, striving to be the source of comfort to souls and facilitating the means of living. This in itself is devotion to God.[21]

In sum, seclusion from the world cannot bring about satisfying growth and transformation in the individual, let alone society as a whole. On the contrary, the path to spiritual fulfilment – and to both personal and collective transformation – in this day lies in the individual's interactions with society. It is the individual's addressing of society's concerns and challenges that sets in motion the development and growth of both. The fulfilment of the mission of the Bahá'í Faith – understanding of the oneness of the human race and its establishment as a universally recognized truth – requires that large numbers of the inhabitants of this planet be imbued with this worldview.

Any system whose aim is vital, vibrant, and sustainable growth must address the two essential characteristics of growth; that is, growth in quality – or transformation – and growth in numbers. The concepts of qualitative growth and quantitative growth are woven into the fabric of the Tablets of the Divine Plan, that essential Charter for the worldwide growth and development of the Bahá'í Faith. They have been integral to the successive plans that have been outgrowths of that Charter.[22]

Dynamic relationship between the two dimensions of growth

The worldwide advance of the Bahá'í Faith can be attributed to a dynamic relationship between the two dimensions of growth – transformation and growth in numbers. Recognition of this dynamic relationship is essential to an understanding of the growth process and its anticipated outcome. Two illustrations may assist the reader in obtaining this recognition.

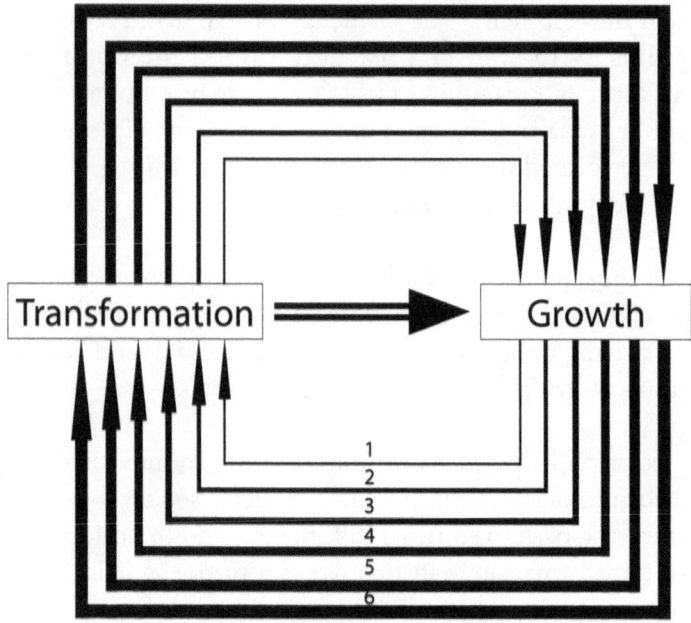

Figure 1. The dynamics of growth and transformation

Figure 1 shows the dynamic relationship between transformation and growth. Simply stated, *transformation begets growth in the number of the Faith's adherents and its active supporters; growth in the number of the Faith's adherents induces transformation at a yet higher level.* The process continues at ever-increasing levels (in the diagram, shown from one through six). Accelerated growth in the number of the Faith's adherents at each round results in an escalation in the level of individual and collective transformation; this, in turn, results in an increase in the number of the Faith's adherents. This continuous reciprocal process holds great promise for a large-scale growth that has vitality, vibrancy and sustainability. At the core, the heart of this process is the Covenant of Bahá'u'lláh, the force that sparks the whole dynamic process. The Revelation of Bahá'u'lláh is the impetus that drives it. The Covenant of Bahá'u'lláh is a unique heritage unprecedented in previous Dispensations. It assures the successorship in His Faith, and safeguards His revealed Word and the integrity and unity of the Bahá'í community.[23]

The transformation of individuals is bound to increase their vibrancy, as manifested by the dedication, consecration, and ardour that mark their conduct. Such vibrancy naturally attracts others to the Faith. The enthusiasm and zeal of the transformed impassions and galvanizes them to share their experience with their immediate circle of family and friends and, beyond that, with the larger community. It empowers them to effect the transformation of their fellow newly enrolled believers. Imagine the *enormous* possibilities for growth contained in this dynamic process. The interplay between transformation and growth holds the potential and the promise of escalating levels of vital, vibrant, and sustainable growth.

This dynamic relationship between the two dimensions of growth is also at work in the evolution of the key constituents of the Bahá'í community – namely, the individual, the community, and the institutions of the Faith at the local, national, and global (international) levels of organization, as depicted in **Figure 2**. Just as we have seen in the first illustration, the transformation of Bahá'í communities and institutions at various levels stimulates growth and furthers transformation in a reciprocal manner.

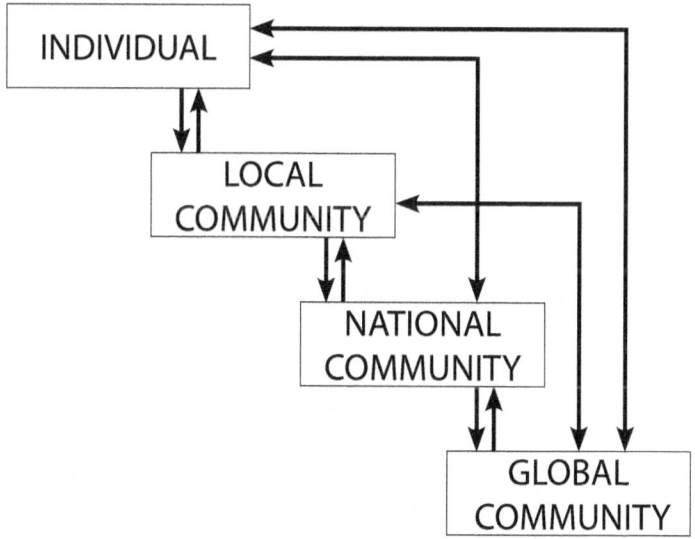

Figure 2. Dynamic reciprocal relationships at different levels of organization

Figure 2 shows these dynamic reciprocal relationships at different levels of organization:

* the individual's relationship with the local Bahá'í community
* the local community's relationship with the national Bahá'í community
* the national community's relationship with the global Bahá'í community

and, in every case, vice versa.

The figure illustrates the reciprocal relationships between the individual, the local, the national and global community; and the local community with the global community. This complex of reciprocal relationships and mutual interdependence makes possible a complete and sustainable system for mutual transformation. Thus it can be said that the Bahá'í Administrative Order both attracts and enables the operation of a *co-evolutionary* process. Once such a process takes hold, it can escalate transformation and growth to very high levels. **Co-evolution** will be discussed in Chapter 2.

Conditions essential to growth

To understand the dynamics of growth, it is helpful to consider, with the aid of knowledge gained from science, those conditions essential to growth for any living organism – that is, for any dynamic system.

A growth-inducing milieu

Examining the germination and cultivation of a plant is a good starting point. This phenomenon offers many insights into the processes of life and is a metaphor frequently used by 'Abdu'l-Bahá to convey significant spiritual verities. Conditions essential for the growth of a plant include an environment – or **milieu** – rich in nutrients and able to provide ample energy and water.

When a seed is planted in arid soil, it will not germinate. However, when the same seed is planted in soil rich in the requisite nutrients, it will germinate and will continue to grow into a vibrant plant, fulfilling its inherent potential. The same seed with the same genetic information encoded within its DNA (see the Glossary) germinates in fertile soil but not in arid soil. Why this difference in results? The answer, of course, is that fertile soil contains the nutrients and other conditions essential for the germination of the seed and the unfolding of its potential, while arid soil lacks them.

Besides soil nutrients, a seed has other requirements in order to ensure its development into a plant. These include energy from the sun and water supplied by rain or through man-made irrigation. Energy from sunlight is essential for photosynthesis, a natural process indispensable to plant and all animal life (see the Glossary for further explanation).

Similarly, the vital growth of the Bahá'í Faith requires a growth-inducing milieu that contains essential 'nutrients', together with sources of 'energy' and 'water'. As we have seen, the sun is frequently used in the sacred writings of the Bahá'í Faith as a metaphor for the source of spiritual energy radiating from the core of all the world's major religions – the succeeding revelations of Divine Truth. Clouds, which provide the earth with life-giving rain, serve in the context of growth as a metaphor to represent the source of divine confirmations and blessings. In the Bahá'í sacred writings, repeated reference is made to these factors:

> For the bounty of the cloud, the effulgence and heat of the sun and the breath of the vernal zephyrs can transform the tiny seed and develop it into a mighty tree.[24]

The requisites for the long-term growth of the Bahá'í Faith have been set forth in the series of plans presented to the Bahá'í community by the successive world heads of the Faith. Core activities such as study circles, devotional meetings, children's classes, and junior youth programmes, further discussed in Chapters 2 and 3, as well as other activities, contribute their share to a 'growth-inducing milieu', providing the rich nutrients essential for the germination and vibrant growth of the Bahá'í community. The systematic plans of the Bahá'í world ensure that these nutrients are continually supplied. The elements of the plans inspire and stimulate action and provide the means for connection to the Source of illumination and energy – to Bahá'u'lláh, through His sacred writings.

The characteristics of growth: Some considerations

Under the guidance of the plans of the Universal House of Justice, the Bahá'í community is making headway in its growth. Certain parameters applied to the growth and advancement of the worldwide Bahá'í community suggest significant advancement in the process of growth by both quantitative and qualitative measures.

Quantitative growth may be gauged by using certain fundamental indicators of growth. Among these are increases in the numbers of: clusters with programmes of growth, learning sites, core activities, trained human resources, youth and adults at the forefront, and friends and supporters engaged in the community-building endeavours. Qualitative growth may be gauged by certain parameters: enhancements in the devotional character of communities, development of a pattern of community life based on Bahá'u'lláh's teachings, spiritual empowerment of junior youth and children and the quality of the institute process. These are further discussed in Chapter 3.

Any sense of impatience its avowed believers may experience about growth must be attributed to the urgency they feel in making available the solutions – which only the Bahá'í Faith can offer – to the desperate needs of humankind.

It may be of value to reflect on characteristics which are inherent in growth of any dynamic system. Growth in such systems is often slow at first; at times, it may seem to have ceased altogether and a quiescent state been reached, leaving one with the impression that 'not much is happening'. But such is not the case. To understand why it appears so, it is necessary to examine features of growth in the natural world. Here again, the application of metaphors and analogies from the natural sciences will help to illustrate key points.

Lag periods

Examining the growth of a population of cells in a tissue-culture medium can provide us with a host of valuable insights. Living cells are grown outside the organism in a medium which includes essential nutrients and under conditions optimal for their growth. **Figure 3** shows the time curve of the growth of a population of cells in a culture medium containing the required nutrients. Characteristically, there is an initial period of no apparent growth. This phase is called the ***lag period***, during which the cells are becoming conditioned to the culture medium, their new environment.

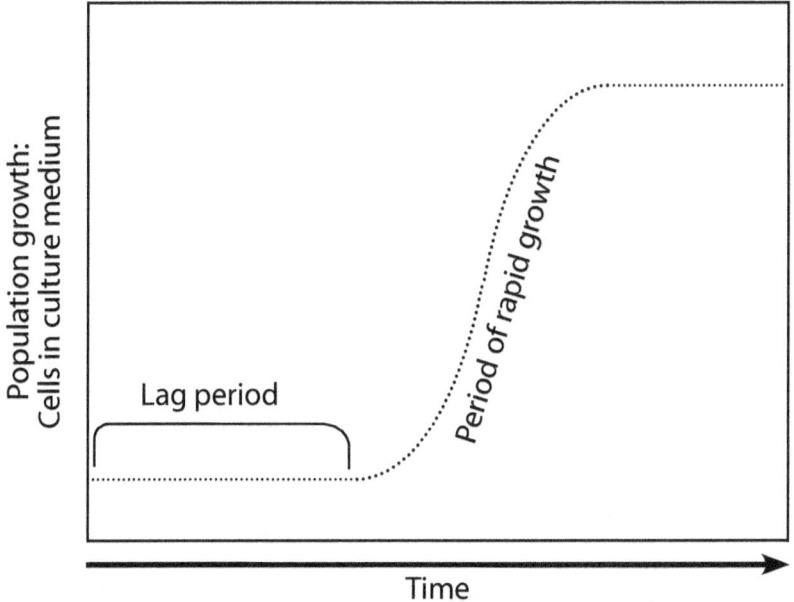

Figure 3. Characteristics of growth of a population of cells in a culture medium

What happens next can only be described as amazing. The lag period of no apparent growth is followed by a phase of rapid, *exponential* growth. Indeed, growth beyond this exponential phase can continue if the nutrients in the culture medium are replenished.

What might this phenomenon suggest about the growth of the Bahá'í Faith?

The worldwide development of the Bahá'í community has been guided ever since the years 1916–17 in accordance with 'Abdu'l-Bahá's Tablets of the Divine Plan addressed to the Bahá'ís of North America. All the subsequent plans devised by the successive world heads of the Faith can be accurately thought of as unfolding stages of that single divine Charter. The plans devised by the Universal House of Justice beginning in 1996 and continuing to the present have introduced novel strategies for accelerating the growth of the Bahá'í community. These strategies and their overall framework provide a new environment, a new milieu for growth.

As seen in the tissue-culture example, the community's exposure to the new environment may require a period of adjustment and *conditioning* – an initial 'lag period', a delayed period in the process of accelerated growth in certain regions and countries. Once the period of conditioning has taken place, once the Bahá'ís are accustomed to the new environment, it is to be expected that the current lag period will be followed by a period of rapid and exponential growth.

Furthermore, it must be noted that historically the pattern of growth of the Bahá'í community has experienced variations from time to time, from country to country, and from region to region. Periods of rapid growth have been followed by phases of lower rates of growth and vice versa. Some countries report a high level of growth in the number of avowed believers, whereas in other countries such growth has been less perceptible. Some clusters show advancement and growth by various measures used. It is likely that in some settings the period of adjustment and conditioning to the new environment is more rapid than in others.

Again referring to the tissue-culture example (Figure 3), in the aftermath of such a phase of exponential growth, the rate of growth may well plateau. To sustain growth, a continuing supply of essential nutrients will be necessary. The plans of the Universal House of Justice provide for continuing nourishment of the Bahá'í community. One such provision is in the system of study circles, composed of small groupings at the grassroots level and being replicated in hundreds of thousands of settings around the globe. These together with service, a major component of study circles, enable newly enrolled and veteran Bahá'ís, and also those imbued with the vision of Bahá'u'lláh for humanity, to access the 'foodstuffs' of their belief – the sacred texts of the Faith, endowed with nourishment rich enough to fuel the transformation of individual souls and communities.

Early growth can be imperceptible

Another analogy that can be made between natural processes and the growth of the Bahá'í Faith comes from scientific observation of a process which is known as the **cell cycle** and the ultimate division of one cell into two through a mechanism known as **mitosis.**

When a single cell divides in two, it undergoes what is called a *cell cycle* of varying time duration, depending on the type of cell. The cell cycle – or the *cell division cycle* – includes the events that occur from the time the cell initiates the process that leads to its actual division into two cells.

The cell division cycle

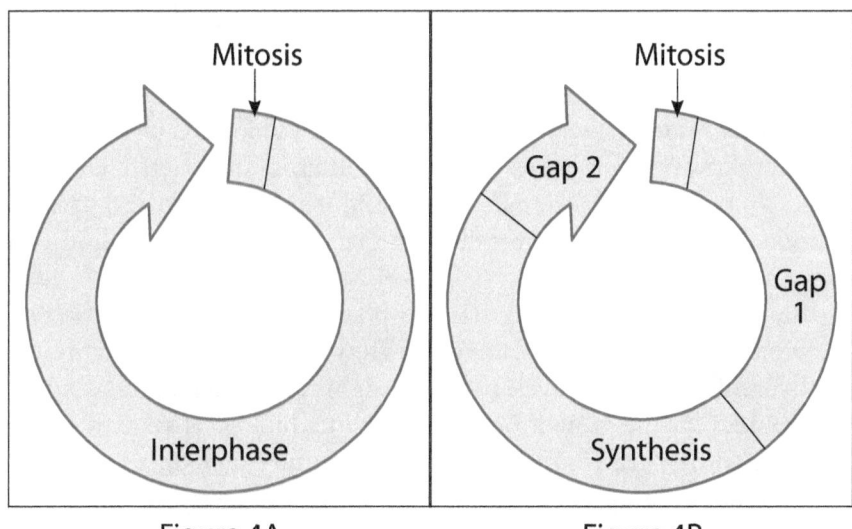

Figure 4A Figure 4B

Figure 4. Phases leading to cell division

Figure 4 consists of two diagrams showing the cell cycle. Figure 4A shows that the cell cycle is divided[25] into two major sequential periods – the lengthy **interphase** (see the Glossary) and the short **mitosis** – during which one cell visibly divides, giving rise to two daughter cells. Interphase is itself further divided into three phases, as shown in Figure 4B. The first phase follows mitosis and is called the **Gap 1** phase. This is followed by a second phase known as **synthesis,** in the course of which replication of the genetic material – DNA – takes place. Synthesis is then followed by a **Gap 2** phase, which precedes mitosis. The process of mitosis leads to the actual division of the cell into two visible cells.

The duration of the cell cycle is variable among different types of cells. The process of mitosis is only a short fraction of the entire cell cycle. As an example, should we take a duration of 24 hours for the cell cycle of a human cell, then mitosis takes about one hour. The remaining 23 hours are taken up by the interphase.

During interphase (Figure 4A) the cell appears quiescent, offering no visible sign of doubling. Yet the cell is actually quite active; measurements and assays show that all of the cell's resources – its molecular components – are doubling in preparation for its division into two daughter cells. Contrary to its appearance of quiescence, throughout interphase all of the fundamental requirements for the cell's growth and doubling are being effectively addressed.

It is also important to note that the interphase, besides providing for a build-up of resources, serves other important functions. Gap 1 and Gap 2 phases allow time for the cell to assess its internal and external environments to monitor and ascertain that conditions warrant proceeding with division. These phases ensure a division that can effectively result in two viable cells.

The cell cycle – including its Gap phases and mitosis – can serve, therefore, as an effective analogy for growth in dynamic systems. As the dynamics of the cell cycle include a significant phase of building up of resources for the growth of living cells in a biological system, so the dynamics of the growth of the Bahá'í community include a significant phase of building up of resources – building of capacity for expansion in the community of its avowed believers and others imbued with the vision of Bahá'u'lláh for humanity – in a system which is essentially spiritual. Notwithstanding the differences between the two, similarities in their processes and insights do apply.

The successive plans of the Universal House of Justice for expansion of the Bahá'í community, beginning with the Four Year Plan launched in 1996, are based on a novel infrastructure which employs balance between expansion and consolidation. The Bahá'í community has since been engaged in multiplying its resources. Though growth during this period may not always have been readily perceptible, measurements show that indeed a significant increase in resources has been taking place.[26]

The emphasis of the current plans of the Bahá'í world on the process of learning – how to empower individuals to build community in varied circumstances through consultation, action and reflection – has contributed much to the current progress, while laying the foundation for large-scale growth.

Adequate preparation and groundwork

Effective growth in a dynamic system requires:

- adequate preparation and groundwork;
- sufficient nutrients to support growth;
- a high level of coordination of activities.

Just as living cells require sufficient nutrients to accommodate an increase in their numbers, so will a supportive environment rich in spiritual nutrients be necessary for a significant growth in the community of the avowed believers of the Baháʼí Faith as well as other populations drawn to the vision of Baháʼuʼlláh. The successive plans devised by the Universal House of Justice provide for this supportive environment. A high level of coordination of activities at the local, national, and international levels will also be essential for large-scale growth of the Baháʼí community.

Growth takes place in phases

Each time a Manifestation of God appears in the world, powerful historical forces to reshape the world are set in motion that cannot be halted or prevented from achieving their ultimate aim. At most, we humans can only, through the exercise of choice in how we respond to them, either accelerate or retard their progress.

The progress of the Baháʼí Faith may well be characterized now and in the future, at times by periods of little visible growth, and at other times by periods of startling accelerated growth. Throughout, the Baháʼí community will continue to develop and to further Baháʼuʼlláh's vision of a unified, peaceful, and just world civilization, until it is realized in every detail.

Observation of the natural world confirms that growth does not take place at the same rate continuously but, rather, in phases. Some phases are rapid, others slow. There may even be periods of resistance to growth. The advance from one phase of growth to the next is, however, bound to stimulate still further growth. The meeting of resistance, of barriers – the *meeting with a sandbank* – will serve to energize new *surges forward*. As the Universal House of Justice has expressed it:

> The Faith of God does not advance at one uniform pace. Sometimes it is like the advance of the sea when the tide is rising. Meeting a sandbank the water seems to be held back, but, with a new wave, it surges forward, flooding past the barrier which checked it for a little while. If the friends will but persist in their efforts, the cumulative effect of years of work will suddenly appear.[27]

The Bahá'í community will continue to surge forward until it assumes universal dimensions:

> Some movements appear, manifest a brief period of activity, then discontinue. Others show forth a greater measure of growth and strength, but before attaining mature development, weaken, disintegrate and are lost in oblivion . . . There is still another kind of movement or cause which from a very small, inconspicuous beginning goes forward with sure and steady progress, gradually broadening and widening until it has assumed universal dimensions. The Bahá'í Movement is of this nature.[28]

The Bahá'í Cause is not an ordinary movement; it is a revelation from the divine Source, endowed with heavenly potential and destined to achieve universal dimensions.

Diversity of population and growth

Strategies for the growth of the Bahá'í community must take into account diverse populations – each with its own distinctive inclinations and degree of receptivity – in the geographic area in which they are invited to participate. We can think of these populations as forming a series of concentric circles, with the outermost circle being the population possessing only a modicum of familiarity with the Bahá'í Faith. The innermost circle would, by contrast, represent the population of Bahá'ís whose level of devotion to the Faith could only be called *consecrated*.

Figure 5 illustrates this concept. The levels shown are not official Bahá'í categories; this author uses them to describe a process of individual search for truth. Beyond the circle's circumference lies the population of the world at large – the population with least familiarity with the Bahá'í Faith. The next levels consist of those populations who are:

THE NATURE OF GROWTH

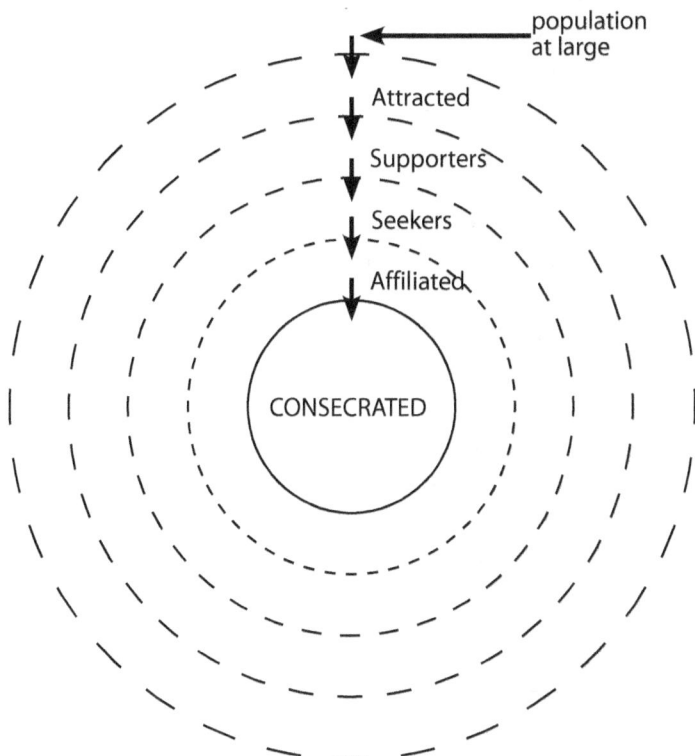

Figure 5. Varied populations, growth through implementation of plans

- attracted to Bahá'í principles;
- supportive of the Faith while choosing to remain unaffiliated;
- seeking out the truth of the Faith;
- affiliated with the Faith;
- consecrated to the Faith.

Those affiliated with the Bahá'í Faith are also seen to be at differing levels of understanding and commitment. At the innermost centre of the circle are the Faith's consecrated believers: those who remain steadfast in their conviction and manifest complete dedication even in the face of unpopularity, relentless persecution and other severe tests.

Bahá'u'lláh, in the Tablet of Aḥmad, alludes to these mystical ranks: the 'sincere ones', the 'believers in the Divine Unity', the 'severed ones', and the 'lovers'.

> He is the King, the All-Knowing, the Wise! Lo, the Nightingale of Paradise singeth upon the twigs of the Tree of Eternity, with holy and sweet melodies, proclaiming to the sincere ones the glad tidings of the nearness of God, calling the believers in the Divine Unity to the court of the Presence of the Generous One, informing the severed ones of the message which hath been revealed by God, the King, the Glorious, the Peerless, guiding the lovers to the seat of sanctity and to this resplendent Beauty.[29]

In *Gems of Divine Mysteries* Bahá'u'lláh talks about the station of the lover:

> When once the seeker hath ascended unto this station, he will enter the City of Love and Rapture, whereupon the winds of love will blow and the breezes of the spirit will waft ... At every moment he burneth with the fire of longing and is consumed by the onslaught of separation in this world . . . Thou findest him chill in the fire and dry in the sea, abiding in every land and treading every path. Whosoever toucheth him in this state will perceive the heat of his love. He walketh the heights of detachment and traverseth the vale of renunciation. His eyes are ever expectant to witness the wonders of God's mercy and eager to behold the splendours of His beauty. Blessed indeed are they that have attained unto such a station, for this is the station of the ardent lovers and the enraptured souls.[30]

That utmost level of consecration, the station of the true lover, is exemplified by detachment and sacrifice:

> Glory to Thee, O my God! But for the tribulations which are sustained in Thy path, how could Thy true lovers be recognized; and were it not for the trials which are borne for love of Thee, how could the station of such as yearn for Thee be revealed?[31]

Writing of the quality of consecration, Shoghi Effendi refers to those international pioneers of the Faith who possess:

> [T]he essential qualities of audacity, of consecration, of tenacity, of self-renunciation, and unstinted devotion, those who were

prompted to abandon their homes, and forsake their all, and scatter over the surface of the globe, and hoist in its uttermost corners the triumphant banner of Bahá'u'lláh.[32]

Elaborating on these characteristics as requirements for their stewardship of Bahá'u'lláh's Faith, the Guardian continually asks Bahá'ís to rise to 'higher levels [of] consecration and heroism'.[33]

Referring again to Figure 5, the ultimate aim of any strategy for the growth of the Bahá'í community should be to foster each population's journey toward the circle's core. Imagine how the Faith's growth could be accelerated: if a percentage of the population at large became familiar with Bahá'í principles; and the minimally aware population became attracted to the Faith; and the attracted population were inspired to become supporters; and if, in turn, supporters were inspired to become seekers and seekers to become affiliated. Imagine, further, the affiliated gradually progressing in their spiritual journey toward higher levels of conviction – ultimately becoming consecrated.

The successive plans of the Universal House of Justice and their core elements provide just such an impetus, as people are invited to participate in community-building activities regardless of whether they choose to become Bahá'ís or not. Additionally, the Universal House of Justice calls the attention of the Bahá'í community to neighbourhoods and villages.[34]

In one of its most recent messages, the Universal House of Justice called special attention to the fact that:

> a pattern of action that is able to embrace large numbers comes chiefly from working to bring more neighbourhoods and villages – places where the convergence of spiritual forces is effecting rapid change within a body of people – to the point where they can sustain intense activity. A core of individuals from within each is assuming responsibility for the process of building capacity in its inhabitants. A broader cross section of the population is being engaged in conversations, and activities are being opened up to whole groups at once – bands of friends and neighbours, troops of youth, entire families – enabling them to realize how society around them can be refashioned. The practice of gathering for collective worship, sometimes for dawn prayers, nurtures within all a much deeper connection

with the Revelation of Bahá'u'lláh. Prevailing habits, customs, and modes of expression all become susceptible to change – outward manifestations of an even more profound inner transformation, affecting many souls. The ties that bind them together grow more affectionate. Qualities of mutual support, reciprocity, and service to one another begin to stand out as features of an emerging, vibrant culture among those involved in activities.[35]

In this fashion others can be introduced to 'the vision of transformation they have themselves already glimpsed'.[36]

Such a focus provides avenues for expanding outreach to these populations. Moreover, the plans' emphasis on an 'outward-looking orientation' and 'open portals' encourage a continually wider outreach to populations in the larger community. They increasingly require us to rethink distinctions heretofore drawn between believers and non-believers and to remove barriers to effective communication and understanding. This is, of course, perfectly in keeping with every plan's ultimate purpose – *for the Bahá'í Faith aims for nothing less than the transformation of all humanity.*

Furthermore, the two lines of action introduced in the later plans of the Universal House of Justice[37] – specifically, engagement in social action and participation in the prevalent discourses of society – can spark familiarity and interest in the population beyond the circle's circumference: the population at large.

Organic growth

The concept of 'organic growth' merits in-depth reflection. The growth of the Bahá'í Faith is often described as fundamentally organic.[38] This characterization conveys that the Bahá'í Faith develops and grows as a living organism or as a viable organ within the body. Such analogies are thought-provoking and can impart important insights.

From the perspective of a biologist, either example can serve as a meaningful analogy for the organic growth of the Bahá'í Faith: that is, the development from an embryo into a living organism with multiple organs, each with specialized and complex functions; or the development of an organ from a few cells to a multicellular structure with appropriate and highly specialized functions. In explanation of the organic growth of the Bahá'í Faith, however, the simpler system – the development of an organ (***organogenesis***) – serves well for this discussion. Reflecting on this simpler analogy, biologists know that an organ develops initially from a few cells into a multicellular organ which becomes endowed with appropriate and highly specialized functions.

In this process, cell division, cell movements, and cell specialization play critical roles in attainment of its ultimate outcome. Additionally, certain 'inductive factors' are essential to induce and stimulate each phase of its growth and development. When this organ ultimately attains its appropriate structure, it then becomes invested with its full function – realizing its destiny.

The analogy of organogenesis brings to the forefront of our understanding two essential points which bear special relevance to the discussion of the growth and development of the Bahá'í Faith.

First, might the growth and development of the Bahá'í Faith, similar to the growth and development of an organ, be organic in all respects described above? Through the process of its growth might it not be destined to manifest its inherent destiny – the fulfilment of the purpose with which it had been invested?

Second, fundamentally, this understanding implies that the ultimate structure of that viable organ, elegantly suited to its purpose, is inherent within it from its very beginning; that is, at the level of those first potent cells. Such an organ develops gradually and systematically until its purpose – its destiny – becomes ultimately fulfilled and its function becomes operational.

It manifests that which was latent within it from the very beginning.

2

ENHANCING GROWTH FROM WITHIN

O ye beloved of the Lord! This day is the day of union, the day of the ingathering of all mankind. 'Verily God loveth those who, as though they were a solid wall, do battle for His Cause in serried lines!' Note that He saith 'in serried lines' – meaning crowded and pressed together, one locked to the next, each supporting his fellows.
'Abdu'l-Bahá[1]

Introduction

The pace of growth of the Bahá'í community has varied from time to time and from place to place. Though growth in some of the geographical regions known as clusters has been remarkable,[2] while in others the initial phase may have seemed slow and imperceptible, it should nevertheless be noted that historically the Bahá'í community has displayed wide variation in the process of its large-scale growth – from time to time, country to country and region to region.

In any assessment of the growth of the Bahá'í Faith to date, it should be appreciated that the community's currently perceived slow rate of growth in some regions may be a feature of the 'lag stage' in its evolution, as it increases its capacity to reach out to large populations to spur societal change.

The community must – with confidence rooted in a solid understanding of the nature of growth – continue imperturbably to test and refine its strategies for systematic expansion and consolidation. Rather than slacken its efforts during such lag periods, the community should forge ahead with strengthened resolve to raise up a world civilization, conscious that, as seen in Chapter 1, lag periods can and do precede periods of rapid and exponential growth.

The Universal House of Justice in a recent message refers to the 'heightened capacity of a worldwide community to assist populations to move towards the vision conceived by Bahá'u'lláh', expressing confidence in an advance in the process of large scale growth 'of a kind not experienced heretofore'.[3]

At the same time, however, the community must guard against complacency and an undue feeling of self-satisfaction, whatever the pace of growth and development in a given location. While variation in the rate of growth is characteristic of the nature of growth itself, the slower the process overall, the longer it will be before this Faith can exert its impact on the course of human history toward realization of Bahá'u'lláh's vision of a peaceful and just world. Even the most cursory survey of the world's condition will reveal humanity's desperate need for that ultimate outcome. Thus the Bahá'í community has a sense of urgency to act under the plans of the Bahá'í world.

Indeed, the cry for an international solution to the world's seemingly intractable problems is being increasingly heard from every corner. The apparent level of humanity's receptiveness to the unifying teachings of the Bahá'í Faith is simply not in keeping with the pressing needs of our time. The human and material resources which can be marshalled at this time are as yet insufficient to influence the thinking and conduct of the planet's billions of inhabitants.

The Bahá'í community is dedicated to the pursuit of systematic plans aimed at bringing about a significant acceleration in its growth, development and community-building processes, inviting all those who are willing to participate in this enterprise. The previous chapter provided an overview of factors essential to growth in dynamic systems. This chapter highlights several factors which, in this author's view and experience have proven to be growth-enhancing. Certain fundamentals, imperatives that hold potential for a significant enhancement in growth of the Bahá'í community – within the framework of the current plans – are offered for the reader's in-depth reflection.

Growth-enhancing factors

Those elements that hold the greatest potential for enhancement of growth – and over which the Bahá'í community *can* exert influence – include such powerful factors as: **vision, passion, ecstasy, individual action** and **collective action** of key participants. Metaphors and analogies from the natural sciences that can be applied to elucidate the workings of these factors hold powerful insights for expanding and enlightening our understanding of the process of growth. These include:

- the reflex arc of the nervous system
- the principle of coherence in the generation of the laser beam
- co-evolution
- phase transition

Vision

Vital to the accelerated growth of the Bahá'í Faith is the vision that Bahá'u'lláh has conceived for humanity's future: a vision centred on the oneness of the human family; a vision that foresees and lays down the fundamental precepts for the establishment of a global society and a spiritually based world order; a vision with enormous power to motivate action, dedication, and consecration.

This vision permeates Bahá'u'lláh's writings, a treasury of guidance for the advancement of civilization, a vast repository of truth wide in scope and illuminating every aspect of life. Inspired promulgation of Bahá'u'lláh's teachings and precepts can drive a vital, vibrant, and sustainable growth in the Bahá'í community. **Two fundamental principles** of the Bahá'í Faith derive from the vision Bahá'u'lláh has disclosed to humanity.

First is a conviction in the inherent nobility of man, hence the inherent nobility of the collective – that is, its perfectibility. Human society can evolve into a global civilization with noble characteristics.

Second, closely associated with the first, is faith in the outcome of history. History is progressive and is moving toward its ultimate goal, the unification of humankind.

The nobility of man

That humans are fundamentally spiritual beings created in the image and likeness of God and destined for eternal life – though perhaps expressed differently in each of their scriptures – is a central tenet of all the world's major religions: 'And God said, Let us make man in our image, after our likeness. So God created man in his own image.'[4]

The innate nobility of all humans is essential to the Bahá'í teachings.

'Man is the supreme Talisman . . . a mine rich in gems of inestimable value',[5] endowed with the potential for noble conduct; failure to develop that potential is the cause of abasement:

> O Son of Spirit!
> Noble have I created thee, yet thou hast abased thyself.
> Rise then unto that for which thou wast created.[6]

At the very heart of faith in humanity is the belief that man is a noble creation. Man's abasement is the consequence of his failure to arise to fulfil this inherent nobility – or, expressed another way, to convert the **potential energy to kinetic**:[7] that is, to convert the stored energy to motion. This in essence means to make manifest that which is hidden. This failure to arise results in a state conducive to abasement. Although the Bahá'í Faith does not believe in the doctrine of original sin, it nevertheless recognizes that the state of abasement can be calamitous; it can conduce to negative outcomes, as the absence of air and matter in vacuum or the absence of light in total darkness.

Whether we believe in original nobility or in original sin has implications that are of great consequence. The purpose of religion is to bring to vibrant life man's storehouse of potential nobility. As with all the Manifestations of God, Bahá'u'lláh's mission is to induce the actualization of nobility within the individual such that he or she will take action to advance human civilization.

Exactly how this concept of the nobility of man – and therefore of collective humanity – relates to the series of plans that have thus far directed the growth and development of the worldwide Bahá'í community is addressed by June Thomas in her seminal work, *Planning Progress*.[8] The individuals who, over the decades, have selflessly arisen to spread this Faith and to root it in the far-distant corners of the earth were impassioned by this vision. Those who are labouring today within the framework of the plans are inspired by this vision. They feel the pressing and inescapable need for large-scale growth of the Bahá'í community and of its society-building process if the Faith's mission for the future of humanity in a peaceful and just world civilization is to be fulfilled.

The course of history

Human history, as envisaged by Bahá'u'lláh, is moving slowly, gradually, but inexorably toward a glorious future – the transformation of the entire planet and its unification in a single world order, centred on the fundamental truth that humanity is one and upholding as its hallmark the principle of unity in diversity. This future is in accordance with the promises recorded in the sacred scriptures of the world's major religions.

It is the integration in their lives of this grand view of history that impassions Bahá'ís and empowers them to act – assured as they are in the inevitability of the outcome described by Bahá'u'lláh.

Passion

Passion is a powerful stimulus to growth. Passion induces action; its absence can bring growth to a standstill. Passion is the hallmark of a new religion in its earliest stages of development. It is the motive force that propels a new Faith's followers to act with exceptional dedication and courage in the face of daunting obstacles to its growth. Passion actuates those who willingly leave behind the security of their homes and set out for distant lands, placing their lives on the altar of sacrifice, to ensure that new populations are presented with their Faith's message and teachings.

The reflex arc

The reflex arc of the nervous system provides an analogue for passion-induced action. A reflex works by means of an arc, with an incoming sensory input and an outgoing motor output. It is automatic; integration at higher levels of the nervous system is not required.[9] An example of a simple reflex can demonstrate this point: touching a hot object results in withdrawal of that hand; thus the sensory stimulus to a limb, of heat or pain, results in automatic action – the rapid withdrawal of that limb. Thinking and decision-making are not involved. By comparison to a nervous reflex, passion would be the sensory input and the resulting action, the motor output. Reasoning is not required; passion fires action automatically.

An example from mysticism

The world's literary history is dotted with examples of mystics and poets making use of the metaphor of 'the moth and the flame' to describe passion – with the moth symbolizing a lover and the flame the beloved. Several passages in the Bahá'í writings evoke the imagery of the sacrifice of the 'lovelorn moth' to the flame, thus the imagery of moth and candle permits poetic licence for reflection on the following analogy.

The flame excites the moth, irresistibly drawing it to its brightness and heat. In its ardour, the moth 'circles around' the flame. The light of the flame, as sensory input, impassions the moth. The moth's response is a reflex; attracted to the flame, it circles ever and ever closer – ultimately to scorch its wings and become consumed by its heat. There is no reasoning involved; only the intense attraction of the moth to the flame, with outcome in the loss of its life. The response of the moth to the flame symbolizes a passion for the beloved so intense and all-consuming that life itself is sacrificed in its path.

In the Bahá'í writings, the extent of devotion of several individuals has been likened to that of the moth to the flame. One such personage was Bahíyyih Khánum, the daughter of Bahá'u'lláh, whose life exemplified utmost devotion and sacrifice. She 'fluttered so close about the lamp of the Faith as to scorch her wings'.[10] 'Abdu'l-Bahá writes about her, 'Moth-like she circled in adoration round the undying flame of the Divine Candle, her spirit ablaze and her heart consumed by the fire of His love . . .'[11]

The great Persian mystic and poet Rúmí[12] expresses this passion through these verses:

Moth-like he has seen the blaze of the light,
And fool-like has plunged therein and lost his life.[13]

Sa'di too, another great Persian poet, tells the story of the candle and the sacrifice of the moth in his moving verses. These inspired one Bahá'í to extend the analogy. Dr Youness Afroukhteh, who served as secretary to 'Abdu'l-Bahá in the prison city of Akka for several years and observed 'Abdu'l-Bahá's continual acts of self-sacrifice, writes of Him:

> I was reminded of the great Persian poet Saʻdi, who so movingly tells the story of the candle and the sacrifice of the moth. Oh, but the sacrifice of the moth is unworthy of mention when compared to the sacrifice and renunciation of the lighted Candle of this heavenly assemblage, for the sacrifice of the moth lasts but a moment, while the sacrifice of this Candle has lasted a lifetime, imparting the light of guidance while being consumed by the flame of love and renunciation.[14]

Mystics believe that self-sacrifice bespeaks the clarity of perception of the truth embodied by the beloved.

Acts of passion have been a powerful impetus to growth in the evolution of the world's religions. Passion fires immediate, spontaneous, sacrificial action. It is marked by an indescribable state of ecstasy. The passion of the world's martyrs – whether through their defiance of death or through their acts of sacrificial living – have time and again throughout religious history provided a powerful stimulus to growth. Such martyrs, dedicated to their ideals and true to their conscience, accept suffering and death at the hands of their oppressors; thus they bear witness to the validity of their convictions. These martyrs are distinguished by their gentleness and love for fellow humans. They do not shed the blood of others; rather, for the love of humanity, they place their own lives on the altar of sacrifice.

Ecstasy

In the realm of religion, ecstasy is vital to growth. It is the state of spiritual attraction – ecstasy generated by the discovery of divine mysteries – that drives sacrificial acts. In one of His Tablets, ʻAbduʼl-Bahá asks a believer to supplicate for ecstasy:

> Thank thou God that thou hast stepped into the arena of existence in such a blessed Age and hast opened thine ears and thine eyes in such a Promised Day. The Splendor of the Sun of Truth thou hast beheld and the divine Call thou hast heard. To thine ultimate desire thou hast attained and from the sweetness of the love of God thou hast tasted. Consequently, supplicate ardently for spiritual attraction and ecstasy.[15]

We have before seen that the state of ecstasy characterizes the acts of martyrs. 'Abdu'l-Bahá refers to the martyrs in these words:

> Those who had seeing eyes found the Most Great Glad-tidings, began to cry the call, 'O blessed are we! O blessed are we!' – and have beheld the reality of things in themselves, have discovered the mysteries of the Kingdom, were released from superstition and doubts, perceived the lights of Truth and became so intoxicated with the cup of the love of God, that, wholly forgetting themselves and the world while dancing, they ran with utmost joy and ecstasy to the city of Martyrdom, sacrificing their minds and their lives upon the altar of Love.[16]

The Guardian of the Bahá'í Faith, Shoghi Effendi, refers to true mysticism through the acts of the martyrs:

> ... the Spirit of God reaches us through the souls of the Manifestations. We must learn to commune with Their Souls, and this is what the Martyrs seemed to have done, and what brought them such ecstacy of joy that life became nothing. This is the true mysticism, and the secret, inner meaning of life which humanity has at present drifted so far from.[17]

Individual action

Transformation

Action founded on such level of individual transformation can bring about a change of great magnitude in human character. Humanity's long quest for a method to convert base metals into precious gold came to be known as the 'science' of alchemy. Bahá'u'lláh applies the metaphor of alchemy to the transformation that can be induced through contact with the Word of God; this He names the divine Elixir 'through whose potency the crude metal of human life hath been transmuted into purest gold'.[18] Again, He informs us that:

> No more than a mere handful, however, hath been found willing to cleave to His Cause, or to become the instruments for its promotion.

> These few have been endued with the Divine Elixir that can, alone, transmute into purest gold the dross of the world, and have been empowered to administer the infallible remedy for all the ills that afflict the children of men.[19]

Far greater than the transmutation of base metals into gold is the transformation of the human soul through the potency of the Word of God:

> Is it within human power, O Ḥakím, to effect in the constituent elements of any of the minute and indivisible particles of matter so complete a transformation as to transmute it into purest gold? Perplexing and difficult as this may appear, the still greater task of converting satanic strength into heavenly power is one that We have been empowered to accomplish. The Force capable of such a transformation transcendeth the potency of the Elixir itself. The Word of God, alone, can claim the distinction of being endowed with the capacity required for so great and far-reaching a change.[20]

The individual believer is the prime agent in the growth of the Bahá'í Faith. As the Universal House of Justice has expressed, the power of action 'is unlocked at the level of individual initiative'.[21] Elsewhere they write:

> Every individual believer – man, woman, youth and child is summoned to the field of action; for it is on the initiative, the resolute will of the individual to teach and to serve, that the success of the entire community depends.[22]

This is, of course, consistent with Shoghi Effendi's characterization of the matter:

> [It is] primarily the individual believer on whom, in the last resort, depends the fate of the entire community. He it is who constitutes the warp and woof on which the quality and pattern of the whole fabric must depend. He it is who acts as one of the countless links in the mighty chain that now girdles the globe. He it is who serves as one of the multitude of bricks which support the structure and ensure the stability of the administrative edifice now being raised in every part of the world.[23]

Collective action

In the final analysis, the growth of the Bahá'í Faith depends on the action of the individual. By itself, however, individual action is not of sufficient force to bring about large-scale accelerated growth. A force of greater magnitude is essential – as that which can be generated through collective action.

The laser beam

The generation of a laser beam is an apt and a striking metaphor for such collective action. When applied to large-scale growth of the Bahá'í community, the metaphor illustrates how the power of action unlocked by the individual believer can escalate at the collective level to a force powerful enough to accomplish extraordinary tasks. The metaphor of the laser beam contains certain properties that merit in-depth consideration on the part of Bahá'ís engaged in large-scale growth. Key among these properties are **coherence, direction, focus** and **alignment**.

Coherence. Let us first consider the principle of coherence. Light, in general, consists of many different, tiny packets of waves – **quanta** – of differing wave lengths. In ordinary light, these quanta are out of step (*out of phase*) with one another. When connected to a power source, however, under appropriate conditions, a property referred to as 'coherence' can be induced – that is, the out-of-phase quanta, which by themselves were without much power, are rendered *in phase* (of the same wave length) and coherent. Consequently, a laser beam can be generated of a power and intensity capable of performing a wide variety of tasks.

In the view of this writer, the phenomenon of coherence – the rendering *in phase* – may bear a conceptual relationship to the achievement of 'coherence' addressed in the 2010 message of the Universal House of Justice as contributing to 'the movement of populations towards Bahá'u'lláh's vision of a prosperous and peaceful world civilization'.[24]

The essential requirements for the generation of a laser beam include an external source of energy and an **active medium** enclosed under specific conditions in an optical cavity.[25] The energy from that external source stimulates the active medium, pumping the atoms in the medium to an excited state.[26] Ultimately, a laser beam is generated with the specific properties of ***monochromaticity, coherence*** and ***directionality***.

The generated beam is monochromatic in that it is of one specific wavelength.[27] In the context of the metaphor this can stand for oneness of purpose in dedication to the mission of Bahá'u'lláh for humanity. Further, the beam is coherent, in that its photons are 'in step' with one another and thus can be launched in unison. Finally, the beam is directional in that it is organized; it is strong and concentrated, rather than weak and diffuse. The generated laser beam can be of a power commensurate with any desired task, whether it is surgery or the welding of metals.

Insights derived from coherence. The metaphor of the laser beam provides several insights into the dynamics of growth.

In the generation of the laser beam, connection to a source of power is an absolute requirement for exciting and energizing the active medium. Through its influence, the excited quanta are rendered in phase and coherent. Without a source of power, the generation of coherent quanta is impossible.

Applying the same principles to spiritual matters, we see that connection to a source of spiritual power, a generator, is essential for stimulating the active medium. In the context of this metaphor, 'active medium' stands for the human soul; in contrast to other life forms, the human soul can become activated and transformed.

Energy from the source of spiritual power, the Revelation of Bahá'u'lláh, induces transformation of the human soul, exciting it to a higher state of being. As in the example of the laser beam, it generates a collective force with the properties of coherence and directionality.

Further, in the case of the laser beam, in the process of building up of power, as more and more out-of-phase quanta are rendered in phase (that is, of the same wave length), they lock into each other. The result is the generation of a beam of a desired quality and of a power equal to the designated task. Surely this can provide a profound insight into spiritual matters; consider for example the following excerpt from the words of 'Abdu'l-Bahá:

> O ye beloved of the Lord! This day is the day of union, the day of the ingathering of all mankind. 'Verily God loveth those who, as though they were a solid wall, do battle for His Cause in serried

lines!' [Qur'án 61:4]. Note that He saith 'in serried lines' – meaning crowded and pressed together, one locked to the next, each supporting his fellows.

He explains:

> To do battle, as stated in the sacred verse, doth not, in this greatest of all dispensations, mean to go forth with sword and spear, with lance and piercing arrow – but rather weaponed with pure intent, with righteous motives, with counsels helpful and effective, with godly attributes, with deeds pleasing to the Almighty, with the qualities of heaven. It signifieth education for all mankind, guidance for all men, the spreading far and wide of the sweet savours of the spirit, the promulgation of God's proofs, the setting forth of arguments conclusive and divine, the doing of charitable deeds.[28]

Collective transformation. A third insight to be gleaned from the metaphor of the laser beam has to do with the spiritual matter of collective transformation. As the dynamics involved in the creation of a laser beam follow their natural course, a state of coherence is reached. Expressed in scientific terms, as more and more out-of-phase quanta are rendered in phase, they lock into each other until a certain critical level – referred to as the 'threshold level' – is reached. At this level, the number of particles in an excited state exceeds the number of particles in a lower energy state. As a result, a most remarkable phenomenon occurs. The quanta that are in phase and have locked into each other form a laser beam. The quanta that remain out of phase are of no consequence – they cancel each other out.[29] The laser beam predominates.

Similarly, in the development of a religion, might collective transformation – and, hence, **collective empowerment** – take effect when acceptance of the religion rises above a certain critical level? Might we speculate that, in the case of the Bahá'í Faith, once that certain yet-to-be-discovered critical level is reached – perhaps, for example, at the global level, when a significant share of the population become avowed followers of the Bahá'í Faith, having made contact with the Revelation of Bahá'u'lláh in the 'excited' state – empowerment ensues? This premise may also be extended to the level of smaller geographical zones known as clusters. There are indications that such a process may be at work in some regions[30] and that the impact of empowerment may be extending well beyond those directly involved. Might such collective empowerment spark a surge in growth?

The phenomenon of threshold level, or 'critical level', is also a point when – whether in the world of matter or in the realm of social events – the momentum for change becomes unstoppable. This same phenomenon is described in a number of systems as 'boiling point' or 'critical mass'.[31] Still another term, of recent coinage, is 'tipping point', which describes the moment trends catch on and become enormously popular.[32]

To sum up, insights garnered from the dynamics involved in the generation of a laser beam may be effectively applied to the growth of the Bahá'í Faith. This metaphor underscores the essential importance of critical elements fundamental to growth – that is, individual transformation, its progression to collective transformation, and its outcome in collective action. As the Universal House of Justice has expressed:

> The power of action in the believers is unlocked at the level of individual initiative and surges at the level of collective volition.[33]

Meaningful action

Once the laser beam is generated, its successful use requires that a few conditions be met:

- The task at hand must be clearly identified and defined.
- The beam must be directed to the task.
- The beam must be focused on the task.
- Individuals and institutions must be in perfect alignment in carrying out the task.

The Universal House of Justice calls attention to the importance of planning in the Bahá'í Faith – its role as well as its unique nature. The plans of the Bahá'í world are systematic; they identify objectives to be achieved and decisions for achieving them, striving to align the work of the Cause with the processes that are steadily unfolding in the world: 'The challenge to the Administrative Order is to ensure that, as Providence allows, Bahá'í efforts are in harmony with this Greater Plan of God.'[34]

Thus these systematic plans require: identification of specific tasks, direction of action, focus on the tasks, as well as alignment of the individual and communities with the institutions of the administrative order of the Bahá'í Faith.

Identifying and defining the task. Whether the task is surgery, the welding of metals, or promoting the large-scale growth of the Bahá'í Faith, a laser beam can accomplish a task only after it has been properly identified and defined.

The efforts of the Bahá'í community to achieve large-scale growth are directed through a unique system of governance firmly grounded in Bahá'u'lláh's teachings and fundamental to His vision of world civilization. The institutions of this system identify and define particular tasks to be accomplished through the orderly and systematic activity of the community.

Directing to the task. The elected institutions of the Bahá'í Faith – which function at the local, national and global levels together with the appointed institution – the institution of Counsellors[35] – assess the needs, identify and define the tasks, and direct and align the focused action of the 'laser beam'; that is, the faithful and devoted collective action of the Bahá'í community.

About the importance of direction, the Universal House of Justice has had this to say:

> ... actions, untempered by the overall direction provided by authorized institutions, are incapable of attaining the thrust necessary for the unencumbered advancement of civilization.[36]

> To realize its highest purpose, this power needs to express itself through orderly avenues of activity.[37]

Focus on the task. Powerful as a laser beam may be, it cannot fully manifest its potential nor exert its effect until it is focused on the task. 'Abdu'l-Bahá uses the metaphor of a lens to emphasize the importance of focus:

> One cannot obtain the full force of the sunlight when it is cast on a flat mirror, but once the sun shineth upon a concave mirror, or

on a lens that is convex, all its heat will be concentrated on a single point, and that one point will burn the hottest. Thus it is necessary to focus one's thinking on a single point so that it will become an effective force.[38]

Maintaining focus is critical to the advancement of the series of plans that continue to direct the long-term growth and development of the Bahá'í community.

Alignment. The institutions of the Bahá'í Faith are central to – indeed, they direct – the focused action of that laser-beam-like force at the individual and collective levels. To be successful, concerted action requires that both individuals and the community, coherent as a 'serried line',[39] be aligned with their institutions. Such an alignment requires being in complete harmony. The alignment must be based on trust.

So basic is the element of mutual confidence and trust that it underlies the viability and vitality of all systems. Francis Fukuyama, the noted political scientist, provides convincing arguments in establishing his thesis that trust underlies success in all endeavours, even the creation of prosperity and the viability of an emerging global economic order.[40]

That essential alignment – that relationship of genuine and sustained cooperation and mutual confidence and trust between individual believers and the institutions that guide and govern their activities – is the cause of harmonious and effective functioning in the work of the Bahá'í community.[41]

The Bahá'í Faith has no clergy; its affairs are conducted under the guidance and supervision of elected institutions that operate at the local, national, and global levels. Alignment with these institutions of the Faith's administrative order and in accordance with their periodic and systematic plans is imperative for the community's effective growth and development. The Bahá'í administrative order – 'the nucleus and pattern' of the World Order of Bahá'u'lláh, in the words of the Faith's Guardian, Shoghi Effendi – is a system of governance unprecedented in the world's religious history. Because it is firmly anchored in and derives its existence from the sacred writings of the Faith's Central Figures, it can be thought of as a channel through which the Faith's vivifying spirit flows. It relies on a unique, redefined concept of the principle of consultation.

To qualify as Bahá'í consultation, the deliberations of these bodies must fulfil a number of conditions, as here described by 'Abdu'l-Bahá:

> The first condition is absolute love and harmony amongst the members of the assembly. They must be wholly free from estrangement and must manifest in themselves the Unity of God, for they are the waves of one sea, the drops of one river, the stars of one heaven, the rays of one sun, the trees of one orchard, the flowers of one garden ... Should they endeavour to fulfil these conditions the Grace of the Holy Spirit shall be vouchsafed unto them, and that assembly shall become the centre of the Divine blessings, the hosts of Divine confirmation shall come to their aid, and they shall day by day receive a new effusion of Spirit.[42]

Cohesive bonds

Basic to the vitality of the Bahá'í administrative system is the nature of the bonds of attraction, love, and unity among its members. Strong cohesive bonds are prerequisites for growth at all levels. As we have seen, 'Abdu'l-Bahá identifies fellowship and love among the believers as a condition for success in growth.[43]

> Such a love among 'all the members of human society' makes them 'a single great assemblage, even as individual drops of water collected in one mighty sea ... as birds in one garden of roses, as pearls of one ocean, as leaves of one tree, as rays of one sun'.[44]

The achievement of such high levels of love, unity, and harmony can produce miraculous results. Implicit in such transcendent love is the transformation and transmutation of the collective body into one entity – into a new creation. The analogy of chemical bonds can help us understand this.

Chemical bonds. The bonds that hold atoms together in a compound are such that a new entity is formed with properties which were not present in its constituent parts. As an example, the properties of a molecule of water – composed of two molecules of hydrogen and one molecule of oxygen – are quite different and distinct from the properties of either oxygen or hydrogen. Water is an entirely new structure with unique properties. Furthermore, such bonds are not easily dissociated. The highest level chemical bonds that form between atoms – the strongest bonds that keep atoms together in a molecule – are not easily broken.

To truly realize their potential, the bonds of unity among the individuals composing Bahá'í institutions must be of such strength as to transform and transmute those consultative bodies into *whole new entities* – just as seen in the highest level chemical bonds that form between atoms in the molecules of a compound.

The ideal unity to which the institutions of the Bahá'í Faith aspire is such that the collective is more than the sum of its parts; it has been transformed into a new being. Such *transubstantiation* is a powerful enhancer of growth.

Evolution and maturation. The institutions of the Bahá'í Faith are in the process of evolving and maturing. Shoghi Effendi affirms that these institutions will be emerging *gradually and organically*, and that as they 'begin to function with efficiency and vigour', they can 'assert [their] claim and demonstrate [their] capacity to be regarded not only as the nucleus, but the very pattern of the New World Order destined to embrace in the fullness of time the whole of mankind'.[45]

The Bahá'í community's successive plans for accelerated growth are bound to serve as an impetus to the evolution and maturation of these institutions. The challenges and needs that emerge from this process, together with the learning and insights that will be gleaned, will stimulate and induce the evolution of these institutions in a remarkable and reciprocal manner – through a *co-evolutionary* process. The dynamic process of co-evolution holds enormous potential for enhancement of growth.

Co-evolution

While it may not have been identified as such, the idea of co-evolution was implied in the work of Charles Darwin as far back as 1859.[46] The term was coined by Ehrlich and Raven through their widely acclaimed work in 1964, and the developed concept is often credited to these scientists, whose research focused on ecologically intimate organisms.[47]

Co-evolution refers to the mutual evolutionary impact of species that are intimately linked and dependent on one another; it is the dynamic process that brings about reciprocal evolutionary changes in such species. Put another way, through the process of co-evolution, the evolution of one species influences the evolution of other species to which it is intimately linked. This dynamic process has continuing mutual effects on each of the component entities; it progressively augments the evolution and maturation of them all. The implications of co-evolution can range from biological species to molecular evolution[48] to the evolution of systems on the grand scale of galaxies[49] and beyond.

The process of co-evolution can thus be applied to a system composed of several closely linked entities, such as A, B, C, D, E and more. Evolution of the entity A to a higher level is bound to carry with it – and escalate to higher levels – entities B, C, D, and E. Similarly, the subsequent evolution of any of the other entities, such as entity B, will carry with it and escalate to yet higher levels the entities A, C, D and E. We can therefore reasonably expect that perpetuation of this process will result, at each round, in the evolution and maturation of all. The co-evolutionary process holds the potential for a progressive acceleration in the rate of evolution of all its intimately linked entities.

With constituent elements that are interdependent and tightly linked to one another, the Bahá'í administrative order provides a natural framework for the workings of co-evolution of the individual, the local community and the various levels of its administrative system. Indeed, success of the plans of the Bahá'í community for growth depends on the evolution, maturation, and coherent actions of three key protagonists – the individual believer, the Bahá'í community and Bahá'í institutions at several levels of organization. The Universal House of Justice speaks of 'the widening impact of the dynamism flowing from the interactions between the three participants . . .'[50]

The Bahá'í system thus encompasses several key entities which must be intimately connected through strong and indissoluble bonds of love and unity, generated and assured through staunchness in the Covenant of the Bahá'í Faith. Through the cohesive power of their spiritual forces, the network is able to function as a single dynamic unit. This is fundamental to the Bahá'í administrative order.

The relationships between the individual believer, the Bahá'í community and Bahá'í institutions are reciprocal, tightly linked and interdependent; the continuing evolution of one will dramatically enhance the continuing maturation of the others. One caveat, however, is that for the process of co-evolution to work, these closely linked entities must be in perfect *alignment* with one another and with the guidance derived from the Covenant (see the Glossary). Co-evolution can then serve as a powerful enhancer of growth; its constituent elements will coevolve at unimagined and unprecedented rates.

As to the critical role of the individual in this process, it should be emphasized that the action of the individual believer is pivotal. Individual believers' high level of dedicated involvement in the plans of the Bahá'í world can induce a unique state akin to that which the noted psychologist and author Mihalyi Csikszentmihalyi identifies as 'flow'.[51]

The state of flow is that optimal experience described in peak performance of champions. Studies of the brain of individuals in this unique state show changes in their brain waves. In such state of peak performance, the individual is able to transcend self. The self disappears; what remains is the act – mastered and exquisitely performed.

Phase transition

A classic example of phase transition – water's transition from liquid to steam – may serve as an insightful analogue for transition in phase of the Bahá'í community. Regarding water, its transition entails a change in the state of the water molecules from the aqueous to gaseous phase; this requires a significant amount of heat under constant pressure. Increasing the water's temperature to 100° C causes it to boil; next follows a period with no observable change in state, but this is followed by a sudden conversion of molecules from liquid to steam. At first there is resistance to change; this is followed by an abrupt change in the state and behaviour of the system. It should be noted that the phase transition of water from aqueous to steam is dependent on pressure in addition to heat; increase in pressure on the system accelerates its transition from an aqueous to gaseous state.

Boundary conditions

Here consideration of the phenomenon of 'boundary conditions' is of special interest. The boundary between two levels – such as water and steam – is characterized, on one hand, by great resistance to change

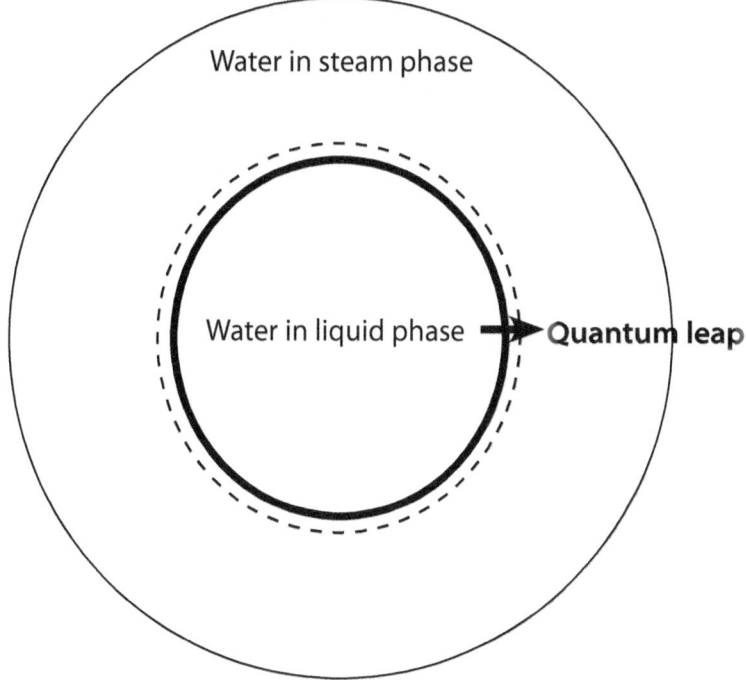

Figure 1. Overcoming boundary conditions: Quantum leap into a new phase

and, on the other hand, by a significant transformation in state. Much activity takes place at the boundary between the two phases; there is resistance to be overcome, but when it is, a sudden and major transition into the next phase can occur- a transition tantamount to a *quantum leap*.

Figure 1 is on overcoming boundary conditions. The solid inner line illustrates resistance at the boundary between the two phases – water in liquid phase and water in steam phase. The dashed line signifies overcoming the resistance, thus prompting a quantum leap, into the steam phase of water.

The characteristics of phase transitions can be applied to the transition taking place in the Bahá'í community. It is important to note that as a transition in phase is taking place at this time at the level of the culture of the Bahá'í community, another transition is also taking place in the course of human history: the events of the world are exerting pressure, impelling humanity toward a higher level of consciousness

– global consciousness. Can the synergy between these two transitions bear on the growth and advancement of the Bahá'í Faith?

The evolution and maturation of the Bahá'í community is propelled by successive systematic plans bound to advance it to a new phase, a new culture. These plans revolve around two essential and inseparable facets of growth: growth in quality refers to individual and collective transformation; growth in quantity refers to enlarging the number of the Faith's adherents as well as those populations that are imbued with the vision of Bahá'u'lláh for humanity. Both facets of growth were discussed at some length in Chapter 1.

Plans of the Bahá'í world induce transition in phase

The novel approaches of the current plans of the Bahá'í world place emphasis on capacity building and community building in collaboration with surrounding populations. These play a significant role in bringing about the transformation of the Bahá'í community and its transition into the next phase.

The plans of the Bahá'í world should be viewed as periodic and incremental measures designed to advance the overarching Divine Plan of 'Abdu'l-Bahá set out in the Tablets of the Divine Plan addressed to the Bahá'ís of North America in 1916 and 1917.

The plans directed by the Universal House of Justice from 1996 to date,[52] and beyond to 2021, consist of the:

- Four Year Plan (1996–2000)[53]
- One Year Plan (2000–01)[54]
- First Five Year Plan (2001–06)[55]
- Second Five Year Plan (2006–11)[56]
- Third Five Year Plan (2011–2016)[57]
- Fourth Five Year Plan (2016–2021)[58]

This series of unfolding stages of the Divine Plan launches a new phase in the development and growth of the Bahá'í Faith. These plans introduce a novel system of organizational units known as 'clusters' and a prescribed set of community activities commonly referred to as the 'core activities'. Devised to address the Faith's need for sustainable and balanced expansion and consolidation, this system has given the Bahá'í community a new language, a new mindset and novel tools. Taken together, these plans akin to phase transition discussed above are propelling the transition of the Bahá'í community into a new culture. In several messages, the Universal House of Justice refers to changes which have taken place in the culture of the Bahá'í community.[59]

A new phase of growth

A new phase of growth of the Bahá'í community was launched by the Universal House of Justice in 1996 with the inauguration of the Four Year Plan. Its approach was community building through addressing the imbalance between expansion and consolidation. This plan was directed at bringing about a turning point of epochal significance in the community's patterns of action by introducing it to a new mindset characterized by systematic capacity building and an attitude of learning through experience and reflection. A strategy was subsequently introduced based on the organizational structure of geographical constructs designated as 'clusters', and the set of core activities consisting of study circles, devotional meetings, children's classes and junior youth empowerment programmes. These key elements of the series of succeeding plans hold promise for enhancement in growth – both qualitative growth, or transformation, and quantitative growth, or numerical expansion.

Significantly, the core activities provide settings for engaging larger segments of society in the community-building process regardless of whether the participants choose to affiliate with the Bahá'í community or not.

Let us visualize the multiplication of such core activities through a model of small units – hundreds of thousands across this planet – and reflect on the enormous power they can wield; through enlarging their circles of influence they can reach out to the world society at large. Taken together, the programmes of core activities hold incalculable society-building potential. Their outreach to populations in every segment of humanity can bring about a transformation global in scope. Such a level of transformation can serve as preparation for the raising up of a 'new race of men' fit for the rebuilding of human civilization – at present a 'broken world . . . caught in a spiral of crisis'.[60] These vital features of the plans will be further discussed in Chapter 3.

All of the elements of the successive plans of the Bahá'í community for large-scale growth hold immense potential for the building of capacity and increase in human resources, with the purpose of serving the wider community. The current series of plans devised by the Universal House of Justice are being strenuously pursued; these serve as powerful means for enhancing growth within the community. These plans include strategies that provide ***portals of entry***, ***open networks*** and increase in ***social surface*** with the general population. An outward-looking orientation will continue to be critical to the growth of the Bahá'í community.

Portals of entry

'Firesides' – small informal gatherings held in the homes of believers to introduce the Faith to friends, neighbours and coworkers – have served the Bahá'í community long and well by expansion of their circle through inclusion of others in the work of the community. The core activities introduced through the series of plans since 1996 serve as effective portals of entry. By including others in the community-building efforts of the Bahá'ís, service can be extended to include the wider community.

Open networks

The concept of open networks is employed by Rodney Starke, to describe networks that are open to and inviting of all. In his book *The Rise of Christianity*, Starke, an American sociologist of religion, provides a compelling discussion on the pivotal role which such networks played in the growth and development of Christianity in its earliest centuries.

Wherever they are infused with genuine love and all-embracing acceptance, the programmes of growth of the Bahá'í community provide open networks to all, whether they are affiliated with the Bahá'í Faith or not. These welcoming portals of entry to the Bahá'í community, open to and inviting all, are bound to attract and expand the number of those with a special affinity for the Faith's purpose, aims, and teachings. In this manner, the barrier between those who have chosen to enrol as Bahá'ís and those who have not will steadily become more fluid, promoting growth.

Social surface

Social surface is another term aptly used by Starke to point to a significant factor which contributed to the growth of Christianity.[61] The expression refers to the ratio of the number of believers to the number of nonbelievers, and is the interface for contact and interaction between the two.

Consideration of social surface is especially relevant to the growth of the Bahá'í Faith. An increase in the number of those associated with the Bahá'í community, whether enrolled believers or not, is bound to increase the Faith's social surface with the population at large, significantly increasing the likelihood of the average person's encounter with the Faith and hence its influence on society.

With a social surface of one believer to the vast numbers of nonbelievers – based on current estimates for the size of the worldwide Bahá'í community and the world's population of over seven billion and increasing – the Faith's impact on society must be quite small. When the numbers are small, outreach becomes specially challenging. An analogy may serve to further illustrate this point.

Let us consider the dilution of a substance such as sugar in a medium that also contains a second substance in vastly greater abundance. Assume the sugar molecules represent the community of Bahá'ís and the molecules of the second substance represent the world population. The sugar molecules are diluted over a thousand times – mirroring the current ratio of distribution of Bahá'ís among the inhabitants of the world. The probability of an encounter between the scarce sugar molecules and the rest of the molecules in the medium is quite low; in the same way, the interactions of one Bahá'í with the majority of the other inhabitants of the world for the purpose of disseminating the Bahá'í teachings will be infrequent, if not rare.

This poses a significant challenge, at this time, to the efforts of the Bahá'í community to achieve widespread outreach – a challenge all the major religions of the world faced in the early stages of their growth. With each increase in the number of a Faith's adherents, however, the social surface expands.

The number of avowed believers and other populations imbued with the vision of the Bahá'í Faith is not sufficient, at this time, for the Bahá'í community to exert a significant influence on the heart and psyche of humankind. As we have seen, the question of accelerated large-scale growth has become an imperative.

Technological innovations – specifically the digital revolution – are bound to have considerable impact on social surface. Programmes for effective outreach which tap into such systems will significantly increase the social surface of believers with others worldwide.

The Major and Minor Plans of God

At present, the Bahá'í community is at the boundary between two phases of development and in transition to a new level of growth guided and invigorated by the Minor Plan of God. In 1996 the Universal House of Justice informed the Bahá'í community that it was 'engaged in an immense historical process that is entering a critical stage'.[62] One facet concerns the 'Minor Plan', while the other is concerned with the 'Major Plan' of God.[63] The Major Plan relates to the course of human civilization throughout history. The Minor Plan relates to the deliberate work of the Bahá'í global community toward the fulfilment of the vision of Bahá'u'lláh for humankind. The Major and Minor Plans of God go hand in hand.

The Major Plan of God. Shoghi Effendi refers to the Major Plan of God in these words: 'the theatre of whose operations is the entire planet, and whose ultimate objectives are the unity of the human race and the peace of all mankind'.[64] The Universal House of Justice further explains that the operation of the Major Plan of God will continue, 'gathering force and momentum, until the human race has been united in a global society that has banished war and taken charge of its collective destiny'.[65] The Major Plan of God is at work throughout the world, hastening the disintegration of the old order as the new one unfolds. God's Major Plan is for ***transformation*** of human society.[66] Its purpose and fulfilment are the eventual establishment of His Kingdom on earth.

The Minor Plan of God. The working of God's Major Plan proceeds mysteriously in ways directed by Him alone, but the Minor Plan that He has given the Bahá'ís to execute, as their part in His grand design for the redemption of mankind, is through 'the orderly and well-known processes of a clearly devised Plan . . .'⁶⁷ It is to this work – the execution of the Minor Plan of God – that the Baháʼís devote their energies.

The transition of the Baháʼí community into a new phase and a new culture through the plans of the Baháʼí world is, on the whole, salutary. The transition of the course of history to a new phase of global consciousness through the Major Plan of God is turbulent. The operation of these two processes is bound to affect the growth of the Baháʼí Faith and its transition to a new phase and culture – bound to revolutionize all aspects of Baháʼí community and to bear its impact on society.

Further discussion on the growth of the Baháʼí community under the flow of guidance through these plans – the unfolding stages of the Divine Plan – will be the focus of the next chapter.

Summary and conclusions

For eight decades, the Baháʼí community, through the series of plans carefully crafted by its Guardian, Shoghi Effendi, and today by its supreme governing body, the Universal House of Justice, has been engaged in a systematic process of growth and development. These plans can be thought of as periodic and incremental measures designed to advance the overarching Divine Plan of ʻAbdu'l-Bahá detailed in the Tablets of the Divine Plan addressed to the Baháʼís of North America in 1916 and 1917.

The plans address two basic facets of the growth of the Baháʼí community: *qualitative* growth – meaning the moral and spiritual transformation of individuals and of communities; and *quantitative* growth – meaning growth in the number of the Faith's enrolled adherents as well as other populations imbued with the vision conceived by Baháʼu'lláh for humanity. The essential importance of qualitative growth and quantitative growth was emphasized in the previous chapter. Through the Baháʼí community's faithful and assiduous efforts to carry out these plans, the Faith has achieved – without resort to coercion of any sort – a remarkable spread, with a presence distributed across the face of the globe.

Prospects for the future

The 120,000 localities throughout the world where Baháʼís reside can be thought of as focal points of growth. They can be likened to the minute centres of growth in a solution about to undergo crystal formation. Crystallization takes place in phases, leading to the emergence of that most unique structure, the crystal, possessing not only beauty of form but remarkable purity. In similar fashion, the worldwide Baháʼí community is crystallizing into a structure displaying beauty and purity of character. The phenomenon of crystallization will be discussed in Chapter 4.

Widespread transformation

As these new truths for a new age increasingly permeate human consciousness, a sweeping transformation in the character and mindset of the individual and society will be effected, extending its life-changing influence to every sector of society, to people of all races, ethnicities, cultures, nationalities and religious backgrounds. This change in the consciousness of the earth's inhabitants will serve as a prelude to the installation of a new world order and to the eventual efflorescence of a unified, spiritually based civilization embracing the entire planet, fulfilling the grand vision Baháʼuʼlláh articulated a full century and a half ago, in the darkest days of His exile and imprisonment. *Under such conditions a spiritual renaissance was given birth.*

3

THE FLOW OF PLANS AND GROWTH

And O, Ye heralds of the Golden Age!
Promise of Prophets, dream of every sage,–
The Master calls ye. Rise ye up and go
To spread the news, that all the world may know!

Joseph Hannen[1]

The worldwide growth and advancement of the Bahá'í community, inspired by the vision of Bahá'u'lláh for the transformation of society, have been guided by the flow of a sequence of coherent and systematic plans directed by the successive world heads of the Bahá'í Faith.

Phases in the growth of religions

In general, the growth of religions advances through several distinct phases. The earliest phase marks the ***critical period***. Similar to the development of a human embryo, it is the time for laying down the foundation of essential structures in order to develop in time into systems which can assure its continuing viability. It is a period of extreme vulnerability as well as of enormous possibilities.

In comparison to the growth of a plant, a religion must during its critical period germinate and send out roots. The succeeding phases must address the establishment of a more extensive root system as well as the upward growth of shoots and production of buds toward the consummation of its mission, in fruition. The outward growth of a religion implies significant outreach – expansion in geographical spread and increase in the population of those devoted to its beliefs and principles. In time, these must culminate in the fulfilment of its mission – the transformation of society and advancement of civilization.

Essential to all these phases is that growth in quality be sustained, thus assuring that the religious community remains faithful to its central vision and the spirit that must continue to animate it.

The earliest phase: The period of revelation

The earliest phase in growth of religions is the period of revelation. It is associated with the heroic Figure of its Prophet-Founder who announces His mission as the bearer of Truth from a higher realm. Like a magnet, He attracts the first group of devoted disciples and followers. His awesome claim brings on intense persecution, imprisonment, exile and martyrdom directed at Himself and also at His followers.

This period is characterized by drama, zeal, fervour and ardour; those converted become transformed and enkindled with love and devotion. At first, increase in the number of its adherents may be small; passion, however is at a high point – attracting in turn hostility. New rounds of persecution spur higher levels of dedication and consecration, unleashing powerful forces – a major impetus to growth. Action is heroic, dedicated and focused; sacrifice in the path of the new religion is the hallmark. The early phase in growth of all religions including Judaism, Christianity, Islam, and the Bàbi and Baha'i Faiths attests to the adage that 'the blood of martyrs waters the growth of the tree of religion'.

The period of revelation of the great religions of the world has been of varying duration; in Christianity three years, in Islam twenty-three years, in the Bábí Faith six years and in the Bahá'í Faith thirty-nine years. The period of revelation associated with the Dispensations of the Twin Manifestations, the Bàb, the forerunner to Bahá'u'lláh, and Bahá'u'lláh, the Prophet Founder of the Bahá'í Faith, spanned respectively a period from 1844 to 1850 and from 1853 to 1892,[2] an expanse of time unprecedented in the annals of world religions.

The first century: The phase of early growth

The first century in the history of religions marks the period of their initial expansion.[3] In its first century Christianity spread to a limited number of localities surrounding the Mediterranean Sea.[4] The initial phase of expansion of Islam had its beginning during the lifetime of Muhammad; it continued with the advance of Islam to the West and culminated in the invasion of the Iberian Peninsula in 716 AD, eighty-six years after the death of Muhammad in 630 AD.[5] The Bahá'í Faith, by the end of its first century,[6] had already expanded far beyond the land of its birth to countries in the Eastern and Western hemispheres and including the Northern and Southern hemispheres.[7]

The second century: The phase of continuing growth

An extensive discussion which compares the growth of the Bahá'í Faith to all other major religions of the world is neither the intent nor within the scope of this book. In the following discussion the growth of the Bahá'í Faith is compared to that of Christianity – the predominant religion in the West. In drawing such comparisons one should be mindful that rapid travel and communication – conditions of our times – must have influenced the growth of the Bahá'í Faith. Such conditions have been significantly different from those entailed in the growth of Christianity. On one hand such factors can augment the rate of growth of the Bahá'í Faith; on the other hand they also increase the 'noise' – distractions – produced by a plethora of groups and movements, thus making it more difficult to see, to discern the genuine.

The growth of Christianity and the Bahá'í Faith during their second century may be compared in two respects: geographical spread and increase in the number of their adherents. The expanse and extent of the growth of the Christian Faith during this period can be used for comparison to the growth of the Bahá'í Faith, now in its second century, since 'the formal assumption of Bahá'u'lláh of His Prophetic Office' in 1863.[8]

Geographical spread. In the second century of the Christian era, the spread of Christianity remained limited to a small number of localities in the Roman Empire, whose boundaries were set in the west by the Atlantic Ocean, in the north by the Rhine and Danube rivers, in the east by the Euphrates river and in the south by Arabia and Africa.[9] These early communities were called 'home churches', as they met in homes.[10] Compared to Christianity, over the same span of time the spread of the Bahá'í Faith across the globe is noteworthy. Furthermore, it is of particular interest that a vast majority of these Bahá'í communities also meet in the homes of believers rather than in structures devoted to congregational gatherings.

Several sources provide data on the Bahá'í Faith and compare these to statistics on the 2,000 years of Christianity and the 1,400 years of Islam.[11] More recent statistics published in 2005[12] show that Bahá'ís reside in over 120,000 localities and that there are 236 countries and dependent territories where the Bahá'í Faith is established. These figures, when compared to the number of localities and countries opened to the Bahá'í Faith by 1921[13] when Shoghi Effendi became its Guardian, highlight an increase of over sixfold in the number of localities, and a significant increase in the number of countries and dependent territories where Bahá'ís reside. It can be reasonably surmised that the worldwide spread achieved by the Bahá'í Faith in the approximately 160 years since its founding has been exceptional. The Bahá'í Faith includes within its fold a wide diversity of indigenous tribes, races and ethnic groups; its sacred texts have been translated into over 800 languages.[14] These measures point to propitious conditions for its continuing growth as it endeavours under the plans of the Bahá'í world to diffuse the message of Bahá'u'lláh throughout the world.

Number of adherents/avowed believers. Accurate statistics are not available on the number of Christians during the mid-second century of the Christian era.[15] According to the testimony of Origen,[16] 'the proportion of faithful was very inconsiderable when compared to the multitude of an unbelieving world'.[17] Notwithstanding the paucity of data, several sources have deduced estimates of 40,500 for the number of Christians 150 years after Christ and 60 million for the population of the Roman Empire.[18] Should we choose to use these figures, the number of Christians constituted approximately 0.068 per cent of the population of the Roman Empire. As the spread of Christianity was limited to the Roman Empire, this percentage would be significantly smaller if it were possible to take into account the total population of the world, albeit much of it unknown and yet undiscovered at that time.

Data from several sources provide variable estimates on the total number of Bahá'ís worldwide in approximately 160 years of the Bahá'í era.[19] It should be noted that these figures for the number of Bahá'ís are at best approximations. The statistic for the total number of Bahá'ís is based on registered members. There are reasons to believe that there are significant numbers who view their convictions in line with the Bahá'í Faith and may consider themselves Bahá'ís though not formally registered. This may explain the larger number of Bahá'ís reported by some sources.

In any case, using the lower estimate of 5–5.5 million for the number of registered Baháʼís throughout the world, and the current world population of 7.4 billion, Baháʼís constitute approximately 0.07 per cent of the entire world's population; this is comparable to the percentage of Christians of the population of the Roman Empire in the early years of Christianity. Notwithstanding this favourable comparison, the number of Baháʼís is nevertheless a small percentage of the entire world population.[20]

The current strategies of the plans of the Baháʼí world involve the participation of populations who are registered Baháʼís as well as those who are attracted to the vision of the Baháʼí Faith but not registered at this time. One can surmise the likelihood of significant influence in growth – over time – through the 'cohort effect' of such populations. The term 'cohort effect' is used in a number of disciplines on the study of populations defined by some shared temporal or common life experience. The cohort effect is relevant to this discussion in that it is the effect of all those – whether registered Baháʼís or not – who have the common experience of participating in and supporting the community-building efforts of the Baháʼís. Thus, the cohort effect can serve as a powerful path to growth, transformation and advancement of the Baháʼí Faith (see the Glossary).

Expansion and growth of Christianity beyond the second century

The significant acceleration in growth and expansion of Christianity can be attributed to several key factors – state support, military conquest, and trade and colonization. These led to its large-scale geographical expansion and mass conversions. In these, conversion by force and or by decree were important contributing factors.

A turning point. The support of Emperor Constantine I[21] – who was baptized on his deathbed in 337 AD – was a pivotal event that brought about a turning point in the growth and expansion of Christianity in its fourth century. Furthermore, Eusebius of Caesarea,[22] court prelate during the reign of Constantine I, played a significant role in formulating what is known as the 'image' doctrine; that is, Christianity and the Roman Empire were complementary and indeed a good fit – made for each other. This image dominated the mindset in the fourth century, thus identifying Christianity with the political and social order of the Roman Empire.[23] To be identified as a Christian conferred prestige. Emperor Theodosius the Great[24] in 380 AD declared Christianity the only legitimate religion of the Roman Empire. Hence, Christianity was transformed from a persecuted minority to elite status, paving the path to becoming a 'dominant majority'. It became fashionable to be a Christian; such incentive was deplored a century later by Augustine, Bishop of Hippo.[25]

The continued expansion of Christianity in the European continent over the following millennium through conversion of the masses – often through conquest, as in Scandinavia and Muslim Spain – led to almost the whole of Europe becoming officially Christian.[26] Colonial and trade adventures of mainly Spain and Portugal in the late fifteenth century – through the voyages of Christopher Columbus in 1492, Vasco da Gama in 1497 and other explorers – led to the discovery of the world then unknown to Europeans. These resulted in the spread of Christianity beyond Europe and the Christianization of the masses. It was not until 1800 AD that Christianity spread throughout the globe and became worldwide.[27]

The future growth of the Bahá'í Faith

Military conquest and conversion by decree, although important factors in the growth of Christianity and Islam, are not consistent with the explicit teachings of Bahá'u'lláh. In the growth of the Bahá'í Faith, other factors come into play.

The use of the sword was incompatible with the teachings of Jesus Christ, as He urged His followers to be gentle and meek:

> But I say unto you, That ye resist not evil: but whosoever shall smite thee on thy right cheek, turn to him the other also.[28]

Jesus commanded them to put away their swords:

> Then said Jesus unto him, put up again thy sword into his place: for all they that take the sword shall perish with the sword.[29]

Nonetheless, the following verses from the New Testament may have provided an excuse to justify the use of sword for conquest and conversion.

> Then said he unto them, But now, he that hath a purse, let him take it, and likewise his scrip: and he that hath no sword, let him sell his garment, and buy one.[30]

In another passage Christ warns His followers, 'Think not that I am come to send peace on earth: I came not to send peace, but a sword.'[31]

This was the excuse Pope Urban II [32] used when he raised the call of the First Crusade against the Muslims. Such misuse of religion for acts of aggression and brutality – invasions, conquests, and the coercive conversion of those conquered and subjugated – abound throughout major periods in the course of the history of Christianity. The Crusades of 1096–1270 AD are notable examples.[33]

It is inconceivable that any course that the Bahá'í Faith may follow for its growth and expansion could include the use of force, coercion or oppression. This assertion can be argued in respect to several fundamental considerations.

First, the use of sword for promotion of the Bahá'í Faith is explicitly forbidden. Holy war, jihad, is an anathema unequivocally prohibited by Bahá'u'lláh Himself:

> O people of the earth! The first Glad-Tidings which the Mother Book hath, in this Most Great Revelation, imparted unto all the peoples of the world is that the law of holy war hath been blotted out from the Book. Glorified be the All-Merciful, the Lord of grace abounding, through Whom the door of heavenly bounty hath been flung open in the face of all that are in heaven and on earth.[34]

And then again:

> Beware lest ye shed the blood of any one. Unsheathe the sword of your tongue from the scabbard of utterance, for therewith ye can conquer the citadels of men's hearts. We have abolished the law to wage holy war against each other. God's mercy hath, verily, encompassed all created things, if ye do but understand.[35]

Bahá'u'lláh replaced the power of the sword with the power of the metaphorical sword of utterance – speech. He has ordained that His Cause be taught through the power of men's utterance, and not through resort to violence.[36]

> Arise for the triumph of My Cause, and through the power of thine utterance, subdue the hearts of men.[37]

Second, conquest and the use of force for promotion of the Bahá'í Faith is at variance with its fundamental principles. Bahá'u'lláh in His summons to the kings and rulers introduced principles of collective security for a lasting peace.[38] These preclude the use of force by any of its component entities.

Third, the fundamental principle of the Bahá'í Faith on independent investigation of truth precludes the use of sword and coercion for conversion.

In addressing the next phase of its growth, the Bahá'í Faith must employ approaches and strategies that affirm its animating spirit. Over 150 years into its history, this Cause is now well positioned to address its large-scale expansion and accelerated growth, remaining confident in its ultimate victory. Guidance for the worldwide expansion and systematic growth of the Bahá'í Faith is enfolded within its Divine Plan.

The Divine Plan: Tablets of the Divine Plan

Fourteen letters, known collectively as the Tablets of the Divine Plan, compose the charter for the worldwide growth of the Bahá'í Faith. They were written in 1916 and 1917 by 'Abdu'l-Bahá, the appointed successor to Bahá'u'lláh, and addressed to the believers in North America; this was only 23 years after the Bahá'í Faith had reached the Western hemisphere.[39] All plans of the Bahá'í world are unfolding stages of the Tablets of the Divine Plan. These Tablets hold the guidance for growth and worldwide spread of the Bahá'í Faith. In them, 'Abdu'l-Bahá called upon the American and Canadian believers to assume the role of leadership in establishing the Cause of Bahá'u'lláh throughout the planet,[40] and to take the message of Bahá'u'lláh to areas of the globe where it had not yet been heard. In the words of Shoghi Effendi, the Divine Plan holds, 'within it the seeds of the world's spiritual revival and ultimate redemption'.[41]

The unveiling

The Tablets of the Divine Plan were unveiled at the end of the First World War in 1919, from 26 to 30 April, at the Eleventh Annual Convention and Bahá'í Congress in Hotel McAlpin in New York City.[42] This gathering was designated by 'Abdu'l-Bahá as the Convention of the Covenant. 'Let this be the Convention of the Covenant,' He had cabled.[43]

It is noteworthy that during the same time period when the call of 'Abdu'l-Bahá was being raised for taking the message of Bahá'u'lláh for the redemption of humanity to various tribes, races and inhabitants in distant parts of the world, another gathering, the Paris Peace Conference which had convened at the end of the World War, was in session across the Atlantic Ocean. The intent of that gathering was to address the political, social and economic problems of post-world-war Europe in order to assure its future peace and tranquillity.[44] 'Abdu'l-Bahá warned, however, that the outcome of that peace treaty would plant the seeds of a more severe conflagration.[45]

These two events – these two calls – and their anticipated outcomes compel reflection. One planted the seeds for the more severe Second World War; the other planted the seeds for the crystallization of the Bahá'í community – toward the fulfilment of the vision of Bahá'u'lláh for the oneness of humankind, a lasting peace and a global civilization.

The Convention of the Covenant had a large attendance of Bahá'ís as well as other dignitaries. It commenced with an elegant reception in the immense banquet hall of the Hotel – a setting surrounded by jubilation with music, poetry and eloquent talks. Joseph H. Hannen had composed a soul-stirring poem for the occasion, 'The Call', wherein he referred to those responding to the call of the Master as the 'Heralds of the Golden Age', 'Heralds of the Lord of Lords', urging them to set out throughout the world and unfurl the banner of Bahá'u'lláh. He concluded with these rousing words:

> The great new charters of the world are read!
> The Word hath spoken – now thy feet must tread,
> From north to south, from east to west, the word,
> Till far and near His banner is unfurled! [46]

The language of 'Abdu'l-Bahá in the Tablets of the Divine Plan was poetic, uplifting, encouraging and ennobling. He called upon the Bahá'ís to arise and fulfil their noble potential as 'apostles of Bahá'u'lláh',[47] as an 'Israfil of life'.[48] He empowered the believers, designating them as the heavenly army, assuring them of ultimate victory and likening 'each one as unto a regiment'.[49] He reminded them of their high destiny recalling the station of the apostles of Christ:

> Consider! The station and the confirmation of the apostles in the time of Christ was not known, and no one looked on them with the feeling of importance – nay, rather, they persecuted and ridiculed them. Later on it became evident what crowns studded with the brilliant jewels of guidance were placed on the heads of the apostles . . .
> The range of your future achievements still remains undisclosed.[50]

'Abdu'l-Bahá expressed his fervent hope 'that in the near future the whole earth may be stirred and shaken by the results of your achievements'.[51]

At the same time that 'Abdu'l-Bahá called the believers to immediate action, he also gave an understanding that this process would take centuries, drawing parallels to the growth of Christianity:

> Throughout the coming centuries and cycles many harvests will be gathered. Consider the work of former generations. During the lifetime of Jesus Christ the believing, firm souls were few and numbered, but the heavenly blessings descended plentifully that in a number of years countless souls entered beneath the shadow of the Gospel.[52]

The response

Although the Divine Plan would 'be held in abeyance' until the system necessary to its execution had been brought into being,[53] a few believers responded passionately and sacrificially to the call raised by 'Abdu'l-Bahá to take the lead in the launching of the enterprise to unfurl the banner of Bahá'u'lláh throughout the globe. The focused and vigorous action of the 'Heralds of the Golden Age' during the subsequent stages of the unfoldment of the Divine Plan resulted in the dispersion of the Bahá'í Faith throughout the world and the ***diffusion***[54] of its light.

The unfolding stages of the Divine Plan

The flow of guidance through the Tablets of the Divine Plan

The Tablets of the Divine Plan hold the guidance for the ensuing plans of the Bahá'í world. Their injunction to go out and spread the message of Bahá'u'lláh is centred on transformation:

> If they arise to teach My Cause . . . they must let the breath of Him Who is the Unconstrained, stir them, and must spread it abroad on the earth with high resolve, with minds that are wholly centered in Him, and with hearts that are completely detached from, and independent of, all things, and with souls that are sanctified from the world and its vanities . . .[55]

At the heart of all of the plans of the Bahá'í Faith for growth is detachment and purity of character. 'Abdu'l-Bahá calls on the believers to become sanctified and purified:

> Therefore, rest ye assured in the confirmations of the Merciful and the assistance of the Most High; become ye sanctified above and purified from this world and the inhabitants thereof; suffer your intention to work for the good of all; cut your attachments to the earth and like unto the essence of spirit become ye light and delicate.[56]

The Tablets of the Divine Plan – the major impetus to the growth and expansion of the Bahá'í Faith – are the well-spring of guidance from which have streamed forth the successive plans of the Bahá'í world.

After the passing of 'Abdu'l-Bahá, the unfolding stages the Divine Plan were directed by Shoghi Effendi and subsequently by the Universal House of Justice. The systematic strategy of these plans devolved in periodic and incremental measures – through phases.

During the first phase, dispersion was of foremost importance; sharp focus was placed primarily on the global spread of the Bahá'í community. This phase emphasized the primacy of diffusing the message of Bahá'u'lláh throughout the areas of the world where it was not yet known. The later phases place special focus on advancing the process of entry by troops – large-scale growth – through the spiritual empowerment of individuals and communities and a vast increase in the number of adherents and supporters of the Bahá'í Faith, including registered Bahá'ís and others. Furthermore, during these phases emphasis is also placed on geographical spread of activities, albeit in the smaller units of culture, in villages and neighbourhoods. The aim of all the plans is to lay down the spiritual foundation for the transformation of society toward the construction of a world civilization.

Emphasis on global spread to establish the structural basis of Bahá'u'lláh's World Order

'Abdu'l-Bahá's Tablets of the Divine Plan issued the mandate for global dispersion. They called the believers to take the message of Bahá'u'lláh to those places in which it had not permeated. Emphasis was placed on detachment:

> Now is the time for you to divest yourselves of the garment of attachment to this world that perisheth, to be wholly severed from the physical world, become heavenly angels, and travel to these countries . . .[57]

The focus on global dispersion was of foremost importance. Fundamental to the growth of the Bahá'í Faith was the command of Bahá'u'lláh to each believer – to teach His Faith.[58]

Those dedicated and selfless individuals who responded to the call raised by 'Abdu'l-Bahá acted passionately, regardless of the obstacles of meagre resources, advanced age or poor health. They abandoned material comforts and, armed with the sword, 'the power of utterance', set out for distant parts of the world. They relied on divine confirmation; thus each, as promised by 'Abdu'l-Bahá, became 'as unto a regiment'.[59]

Shoghi Effendi, in *The World Order of Bahá'u'lláh*, praised the achievements of these 'intrepid heralds of the Faith of Bahá'u'lláh' who responded to the clarion call raised by 'Abdu'l-Bahá:

> Forsaking home, kindred, friends and position a handful of men and women, fired with a zeal and confidence which no human agency can kindle, arose to carry out the mandate which 'Abdu'l-Bahá had

issued. Sailing northward as far as Alaska, pushing on to the West Indies, penetrating the South American continent to the banks of the Amazon and across the Andes to the southernmost ends of the Argentine Republic, pressing on westward into the island of Tahiti and beyond it to the Australian continent and still beyond it as far as New Zealand and Tasmania, these intrepid heralds of the Faith of Bahá'u'lláh have succeeded by their very acts in setting to the present generation of their fellow-believers throughout the East an example which they may well emulate.[60]

In this document, Shoghi Effendi rejoiced that the Cause of Bahá'u'lláh had 'encircled the globe':

Its light, born in darkest Persia, had been carried successively to the European, the African and the American continents, and was now penetrating the heart of Australia, encompassing thereby the whole earth with a girdle of shining glory.[61]

Global plans directed by Shoghi Effendi

Dispersion continued under the plans launched by Shoghi Effendi, the appointed successor to 'Abdu'l-Bahá and the Guardian of the Bahá'í Faith. Numerous national teaching plans were set in place throughout the Bahá'í world; next, through a systematic and sequential approach, communities and their National Spiritual Assemblies were prepared for upcoming enterprises of increasing complexity and wider scope. Implicit in the approach of Shoghi Effendi to growth were capacity building and community building, albeit in large geographical regions of the globe.

Some of the later plans of Shoghi Effendi encouraged international cooperation among several National Spiritual Assemblies – developing their capacity in preparation for the launching of global plans of transnational and transcontinental scope. An extensive coverage, albeit brief, of the accomplishments under these plans is beyond the scope of this book.

The First Seven Year Plan, the Second Seven Year Plan, the Africa Plan and the Ten Year Global Crusade continued the primary focus on global dispersion to establish the structural basis of Bahá'u'lláh's World

Order. The First Seven Year Plan (1937-1944) placed its focus on expansion and consolidation of the Bahá'í community in the Western hemisphere. The Second Seven Year Plan (1946-1953)[62] and the Africa Plan (1951-1953)were followed by the launching of a decade-long world-embracing plan (1953-1963) – the Ten Year Global Crusade, named a 'Spiritual Crusade'. Here the term 'Crusade' implies spiritual conquest and not a military one: in the words of Shoghi Effendi, 'the aim of this spiritual crusade is the conquest of the citadel of men's hearts'.[63]

The **First Seven Year Plan was** launched in 1937 to culminate in 1944, the centenary of the Declaration of the Báb. In this Plan Shoghi Effendi urged the American Bahá'ís:

> Would to God every state within the American Republic, and every Republic in American continent might ere termination of this glorious century embrace the light of the Faith of Bahá'u'lláh and establish structural basis of His World Order.[64]

The focus on worldwide spread continued with the **Second Seven Year Plan** launched in 1946 to culminate in 1953, the centenary of the intimation to Bahá'u'lláh of His Prophethood in the Síyáh-Chál.[65] This Plan placed its emphasis on transatlantic service, to specific areas in post-Second World War Europe. In this Plan Shoghi Effendi evoked a God-given mandate addressed by the Exalted Báb in the Qayyúmu'l-Asmá' to the peoples of the West to 'issue forth' from their cities and aid His cause.[66]

In January of 1947, Shoghi Effendi appealed to the North American Bahá'ís:

> Impelled to plead afresh to ponder responsibilities incurred in transatlantic field of service . . . Initial stage of colossal task undertaken in European continent still in balance. Urge stress for entire community extreme urgency to reinforce promptly, at whatever cost, however inadequate the instruments, the number of volunteers, both settlers and itinerant teachers, whom posterity will rightly recognize as vanguard of torch-bearers of Bahá'u'lláh's resistless, world-redeeming order to despairing millions of diversified races, conflicting nationalities in darkest, most severely tested, spiritually

depleted continent of globe. Prayerfully awaiting response by all ranks of community to supreme call to fuller participation in glorious enterprise.[67]

It should be noted that the accomplishments of these plans must also be credited to the support of several other Bahá'í communities and National Assemblies throughout the world that prepared the foundation for such enterprises by expanding the base of the Administrative Order. The Universal House of Justice has commented:

> Once again, the North American Bahá'í community was summoned to assume a demanding responsibility, one that essentially built upon and developed the achievements of the earlier Plan. The great difference, however, was that several other Bahá'í communities were now in a position to participate. Already in 1938, the Bahá'ís of India, Pakistan and Burma had set out on a plan of their own. As international hostilities gradually came to an end, the National Spiritual Assemblies of Persia, of the British Isles, of Australia and New Zealand, of Germany and Austria, of Egypt and the Sudan, and of Iraq – freed from the limitations imposed on them by the war – embarked on projects of various durations to expand the base of the Administrative Order, settle pioneers in goals both at home and abroad, and multiply the available Bahá'í literature.[68]

The **Africa Plan** which the Guardian launched in 1951 is especially noteworthy as it was the first teaching plan to draw on the combined efforts of several National Spiritual Assemblies. It led to international cooperation among these five Assemblies, paving the way for the forthcoming global plan. Furthermore, it prepared the communities for dealing with increasingly more complex enterprises. The hour had struck, Shoghi Effendi explained, for a 'meritorious enterprise undertaken primarily for the illumination of the tribes of East and West Africa, envisaged in the Tablets of the Centre of the Covenant revealed in the darkest hour of His ministry'.[69] A future worldwide plan was foreshadowed in his cable of January 1951:

> Fervently praying participation British American Persian Egyptian National Assemblies unique epochmaking enterprise African

continent may prove prelude convocation first African teaching conference leading eventually initiation undertakings involving collaboration all National Assemblies Bahá'í world thereby paving way ultimate organic union these assemblies through formation international House Justice destined launch enterprises embracing whole Bahá'í world . . .[70]

Shoghi Effendi linked the sacrificial completion of this teaching plan to creation of new capabilities.

> So magnificent an achievement [completion of the British Six Year Plan] has . . . endowed the entire community . . . with tremendous potentialities, empowering it to launch on the first stage of its historic overseas mission destined to bring that community into closer and more concrete association with is sister communities in North America and Egypt, for the purpose of promoting the Faith in the vast virgin territories where its banner is still unraised. . .[71]

This was a remarkable preparation for the launching of the Ten Year Global Crusade *whose field of action would encompass the entire planet.*

When Shoghi Effendi was appointed Guardian in 1921, the total number of countries in which Bahá'ís lived was 35; by 1952, the countries opened to the Faith (between 1844 and 1952) were at a total of 128.[72]

The Ten Year Global Crusade was launched in 1953 to culminate in 1963, the centenary of the declaration of Bahá'u'lláh in Baghdad.[73] Shoghi Effendi impassioned the Bahá'ís, calling upon them to scatter far and wide, by evoking the words of Bahá'u'lláh:

> 'Light as the spirit,' 'pure as air,' 'blazing as fire,' 'unrestrained as the wind' – for such is Bahá'u'lláh's own admonition to His loved ones in His Tablets, and directed not to a select few but to the entire congregation of the faithful – let them scatter far and wide, proclaim the glory of God's Revelation in this Day, quicken the souls of men and ignite in their hearts the love of the One Who alone is their omnipotent and divinely appointed Redeemer.[74]

In this first truly global plan Shoghi Effendi continued the emphasis

– with a yet greater intensity and passion – on the worldwide dispersion of the Bahá'ís. He called this majestic Plan a 'world-encompassing Crusade', 'world-girdling crusade',[75] whose theatre of operation was the entire planet.

This Plan was unlike the Crusades launched by the Christians in the Middle Ages against the Muslims in order to regain the city of Jerusalem – in which the sword was used, cruelty was inflicted and much blood was shed. The juxtaposition of the Ten Year Global Crusade called forth by Shoghi Effendi against the infamous Crusades between the Christians and Muslims is illuminating. The Ten Year Crusade was a campaign for the spiritual regeneration of this planet. The sacred grounds it aimed to conquer were the citadels of the human heart – the seat of God's Revelation. Its army was the 'army of life', invested with the shield and armour of Covenant, and armed with the sword, the power of utterance, whose potency was derived from its Sacred Writings. This army of life forged ahead not to shed the blood of others but to place its own life on the altar of sacrifice! This Crusade had many Lionhearts. Shoghi Effendi was at the helm – inspiring, motivating, invigorating and galvanizing the Bahá'í world community.

Shoghi Effendi evokes soul-stirring images in the following passage:

> Let there be no mistake. The avowed, the primary aim of this Spiritual Crusade is none other than the conquest of the citadels of men's hearts. The theater of its operations is the entire planet . . . Its Marshal is none other than the Author of the Divine Plan . . . Its legions are the rank and file of believers . . . The charter directing its course is the immortal Tablets that have flowed from the pen of the Center of the Covenant Himself. The armor with which its onrushing hosts have been invested is the glad tidings of God's own message in this day, the principles underlying the order proclaimed by His Messenger, and the laws and ordinances governing His Dispensation.[76]

This Plan had a multitude of objectives, among them the establishment of the Bahá'í Faith in 131 additional countries and territories, together with the formation of 44 new National Spiritual Assemblies; the incorporation under national legislation of 33 of these; a vast increase in Bahá'í literature; and the expansion of the number of Local Spiritual

Assemblies around the world to a total of 5,000, of which 350 were to be incorporated under the national law of their respective countries.[77] Such a large-scale mandate resulted in further diffusion of the light of Bahá'u'lláh throughout the globe.

The Ten Year Global Crusade took place in several phases. The first phase,

> which lasted from 1953 to 1954, witnessed the planting of the banner of Bahá'u'lláh's Revelation in no less than one hundred additional countries, territories and islands of the globe . . .[78]

In the second phase, a quick succession of victories was chronicled by Shoghi Effendi in his *Messages to the Bahá'í World*:

> The opening months of the second phase of the Ten-Year Plan have witnessed, on the American, the European, the African, the Asiatic and the Australian fronts, a succession of victories rivalling, in their variety, rapidity and significance, the prodigious efforts exerted, and the superb exploits achieved, during the first twelve months of the Global Crusade, by the mighty company of the stalwart Knights of Bahá'u'lláh in well nigh a hundred virgin territories scattered over the face of the planet.[79]

In his Riḍván 1957 Message, the Guardian informed the Bahá'í world that there were 4,200 localities throughout the world where Bahá'ís resided.[80]

> He himself was immensely heartened and pleased over the victories won during the first half of this Holy Crusade, and characterized this five year period as one of marvellous progress achieved in so vast a field in so short a time by a small band of heroic souls.[81]

Phenomenal progress was made during the last five years of the Crusade. By 1963, the end of the plan, all the goals were won! The number of countries opened to the Bahá'í Faith reached 254, while the number of localities had increased to 11,210.[82] The Bahá'í world was jubilant: Bahá'u'lláh had anticipated the planting of His message in distant lands, contrasting this with the hardship and repression in the land of its birth.[83] Now, the victories of 'the unique, brilliant and spiritually glorious Ten Year Crusade' had 'implanted the banner of Bahá'u'lláh throughout the planet'.[84]

When we review the remarkable accomplishments of the Ten Year Global Crusade, we are struck by the extent and scope of its achievements. The Crusade was the culmination of Shoghi Effendi's global planning; it entailed the coordination of the activities of National Spiritual Assemblies, the consolidation of all new territories opened to the Bahá'í Faith, and also the opening of the remaining chief 'virgin' territories on the planet – places where no Bahá'ís had previously resided.[85] The Bahá'í community had proceeded, under the command of Shoghi Effendi, to win goals spread across the face of this planet, extending from pole to pole in distant lands and islands. The Ten Year Global Crusade marked a ***turning point*** in the fortunes of the Bahá'í Faith – its expansion from a limited geographical spread to a worldwide community, barely over a century since its founding by Bahá'u'lláh.

A veritable turning point. Shoghi Effendi had on several occasions referred to 'turning points' in the growth and spread of the Bahá'í Faith. On the occasion of the celebration of the centenary of the first century of the Bahá'í Era, he rejoiced in the spread of the Bahá'í Faith, referring to it as a 'great turning point in the history of our Faith' when 'a spiritual front extending the entire length of the Western Hemisphere' had been established, when 'the crowning act of an entire century had been accomplished'.[86]

In several of his messages referring to the Ten Year Global Crusade, Shoghi Effendi also used the term 'turning point'. In its first months he called attention to the fact that this 'decade-long global Crusade must mark a veritable turning point in American Bahá'í history'.[87] He referred to the opportunities of the 'world-encompassing Crusade' as a turning point in the fortunes of the Faith of Bahá'u'lláh.[88] Again, in 1956, he praised the victories of the Ten Year Crusade, on which the army of the Lord of Hosts had so joyously and confidently embarked, as 'a major turning point in the history of its marvelous unfoldment'.[89]

The character, expanse and panorama of the Ten Year Global Crusade qualify it as a ***defining moment*** in the fortunes of the Bahá'í Faith. A community subjected to intense persecution had spread well beyond the land of its birth to distant continents – even to the 'midmost heart of the ocean', recalling the poetic image foreshadowed by Bahá'u'lláh:

Should they attempt to conceal its light on the continent, it will assuredly rear its head in the midmost heart of the ocean, and, raising its voice, proclaim: 'I am the life-giver of the world!'[90]

The Ten Year Global Crusade led to the establishment of the framework of Bahá'u'lláh's World Order for bringing about the oneness of humankind and a lasting peace. Shoghi Effendi pays tribute to those whose dedication and sacrifice generated a global Bahá'í community.[91] The Bahá'í world owes much gratitude to those 'heralds of the Golden Age', the heroines and heroes who set out to spread the message of Bahá'u'lláh' for the redemption of humankind.

The systematic worldwide emphasis resulted at an early stage for the Bahá'í Faith to succeed in developing roots in thousands of localities throughout the globe; thus had been established the 'structural basis of His World Order'. Such expansive spread required a vital administrative system for the continuing growth and increasing viability of the Bahá'í Faith.

The Administrative Order: Fundamental to worldwide growth of the Bahá'í Faith

The Bahá'í Administrative Order is the 'nucleus and pattern' of the New World Order of Bahá'u'lláh, as Shoghi Effendi explains:

> This Administrative Order . . . will, as its component parts, its organic institutions, begin to function with efficiency and vigour, assert its claim and demonstrate its capacity to be regarded not only as the nucleus but the very pattern of the New World Order destined to embrace in the fullness of time the whole of mankind.[92]

The unique and novel features of the Bahá'í administrative system address the essential needs of the Bahá'í community at several levels of organization.

The institution of the House of Justice

Governance in the Bahá'í Faith rests with the institution of the House of Justice:

The institution of the House of Justice consists of elected councils which operate at the local, national and international levels of society. Bahá'u'lláh ordains both the Universal House of Justice and the Local Houses of Justice in the Kitáb-i-Aqdas . . . 'Abdu'l-Bahá, in His Will and Testament, provides for the Secondary (National or Regional) Houses of Justice and outlines the method to be pursued for the election of the Universal House of Justice.[93]

Shoghi Effendi points out:

It should be carefully borne in mind that the local as well as the international Houses of Justice have been expressly enjoined by the Kitáb-i-Aqdas; that the institution of the National Spiritual Assembly, as an intermediary body, and referred to in the Master's Will as the 'Secondary House of Justice,' has the express sanction of 'Abdu'l-Bahá; and that the method to be pursued for the election of the International and National Houses of Justice has been set forth by Him in His Will, as well as in a number of His Tablets.[94]

Spiritual Assemblies: The bedrock

In 1924, Shoghi Effendi affirmed that the Local and National Spiritual Assemblies constituted 'the bedrock upon the strength of which the Universal House of Justice is in future to be firmly established'.[95] In 1951, he further emphasized this point through a cablegram: 'FUTURE EDIFICE UNIVERSAL HOUSE OF JUSTICE DEPENDING FOR ITS STABILITY ON SUSTAINING STRENGTH PILLARS ERECTED DIVERSIFIED COMMUNITIES EAST WEST.'[96]

Local Spiritual Assemblies are the firm foundation for the National Spiritual Assembly in their country. They are instituted annually and directly elected, in every city, town, and village where nine or more adult believers over the age of 21 are resident.[97] Local Spiritual Assemblies are responsible for supervising all Bahá'í matters in their areas.[98]

National Assemblies – the 'pillars' to sustain the weight of the Universal House of Justice – are elected at the national level.[99] At the passing of 'Abdu'l-Bahá in 1921, there were no National Spiritual Assemblies, as their election required a sufficient number of Local Spiritual Assemblies in any given country or region. In 1953, at the outset of Shoghi Effendi's Ten Year Global Crusade there were twelve National Spiritual Assemblies; two years later Shoghi Effendi called for the election of thirteen more, bringing the total number formed during his ministry to twenty-six.[100] After the passing of Shoghi Effendi, in 1957, the Hands of the Cause (see the Glossary) succeeded in ensuring that the Crusade's objectives were achieved and that the necessary foundation was in place for the erection of the Universal House of Justice.[101]

During the six years after the passing of Shoghi Effendi, the entire contingent of the Hands of the Cause including the Custodians (see the Glossary) increased the number of National Spiritual Assemblies to fifty-six by the end of the Ten Year Global Crusade.[102] These fifty-six established regional and national bodies – 24 in the Western hemisphere and 32 in the Eastern hemisphere[103] – formed the initial **pillars** for the erection of the Universal House of Justice – the supreme governing body of the Bahá'í community, created by Bahá'u'lláh. These pillars, which were to sustain the weight and strength of the Universal House of Justice, were in turn reared upon the firm foundation of Local Spiritual Assemblies.

In elucidating the fundamental importance of these local and national administrative bodies to the election of the Universal House of Justice, Shoghi Effendi often referred to the structure of the resting-place of the Greatest Holy Leaf, Bahíyyih Khánum, the daughter of Bahá'u'lláh. He emphasized that the steps of her holy resting-place represent Local Spiritual Assemblies, the columns – the pillars – symbolize the National Spiritual Assemblies, while the dome represents the Universal House of Justice, which in accordance with the Master's Will and Testament must be elected by the secondary Houses of Justice – the National Spiritual Assemblies of East and West.[104] Thus the foundation and the pillars must be strong and firm.

In sum, over the first two decades of the twentieth century, through the loving care of 'Abdu'l-Bahá the spiritual and administrative foundations necessary to the World Order of Bahá'u'lláh were established. After the passing of 'Abdu'l-Bahá, Shoghi Effendi devoted himself, during the thirty-six years of his ministry, to refining the administrative instruments needed to carry forward the Divine Plan, culminating in the successful establishment of the Universal House of Justice, first elected on 21 April 1963 and celebrated at the Jubilee of the centenary of the Declaration of Bahá'u'lláh's prophetic mission. The institution of the Hands of the Cause played an essential role in the erection of that dome – the Universal House of Justice.[105]

It is fitting, at this point, to pause and reflect on the lessons learnt through the succession of plans under the guidance of 'Abdu'l-Bahá and Shoghi Effendi, so that we may apply the insights therein to the ensuing plans directed by the Universal House of Justice.

Success under the plans: Lessons learnt and insights imparted

The establishment of the framework for the World Order of Bahá'u'lláh as anticipated by Shoghi Effendi has been successfully achieved.[106] Such accomplishment – in face of many obstacles – must be attributed to several factors.

First, the response to the plans was enthusiastic, passionate and sacrificial, notwithstanding the dire conditions of the world: during the difficult periods following the First World War; or the outbreak of Second World War in 1939, two years after the launching of the First Seven Year Plan; or the ever continuing chaos and turbulence of a declining world order. Notwithstanding such ominous disturbances, those who responded to the call raised by the Divine Plan remained focused, undeviated by the changes and chances in world events.

Second, those heroes and heroines remained resolute. Poignant losses suffered by the Bahá'í world did not dampen their action; response to the call continued. After the passing of 'Abdu'l-Bahá in 1921, those who responded to His call acted sacrificially with renewed ardour. After the passing of Shoghi Effendi in 1957, less than midway in the Ten Year Global Crusade, the Crusade continued; by 1963 all the objectives had been met. The accomplishments were astonishing. All the goals were won before the culmination of each plan. Each plan had its heroes and heroines, its honour roll.

Third and foremost was firmness in the Covenant. Its loyal followers succeeded in establishing the framework for Bahá'u'lláh's World Order. Fundamental to their success was staunchness in the Covenant. 'Abdu'l-Bahá had identified firmness in the Covenant as the first prerequisite of success. The Covenant assured dedication and continuation of response to the plans. It was steadfastness in the Covenant after the passing of 'Abdu'l-Bahá that sustained the dedicated response to the plans under the direction of Shoghi Effendi and its continuation under the Custodians. This quality will assure continuation of response to the plans of the Bahá'í world under the direction of the Universal House of Justice.

Reflection on the history of the Bábí and the Bahá'í Dispensations bears out that calamitous events have neither deterred action nor dampened enthusiasm. No force has been able to bring to a halt the commitment of those heroes and heroines. Within the Bahá'í Faith is a reality – fundamental to all the great religions of the world – that drives its growth. Shoghi Effendi attests:

> [T]he Faith that had been the object of such monstrous betrayals, and the target for such woeful assaults, was going from strength to strength, was forging ahead, undaunted and undivided by the injuries it had received. In the midst of trials it had inspired its loyal followers with a resolution that no obstacle, however formidable, could undermine. It had lighted in their hearts a faith that no misfortune, however black, could quench. It had infused into their hearts a hope that no force, however determined, could shatter.[107]

The outcome of the passionate and dedicated response of those 'Heralds of the Golden Age' was the establishment of a widespread global framework mobilized for the growth and crystallization of the World Order of Bahá'u'lláh.

With such accomplishments under the Ten Year Global Crusade, the Bahá'í world did not become complacent. Plans continued. The future direction was set. The flow of guidance that had streamed forth from the Divine Plan of 'Abdu'l-Bahá through the plans of Shoghi Effendi continued under the directives of the Universal House of Justice, elected in 1963 as the succeeding world head of the Bahá'í Faith.[108]

Plans under the guidance of the Universal House of Justice

Shoghi Effendi had anticipated the continuation of the unfolding stages of the Divine Plan – the 'launching of worldwide enterprises destined to be embarked upon, in future epochs of that same [Formative] Age, by the Universal House of Justice'.[109]

Plans were launched successively: the Nine Year Plan (1964-1973), the Five Year Plan (1974-1979), the Seven Year Plan (1979-1986), the Six Year Plan (1986-1992) and the Three Year Plan (1993-1996). The messages of the Universal House of Justice chronicle the extraordinary advances in proclamation, expansion and consolidation of the Bahá'í community through these plans, reaching a climax in the last two years of the Seven Year Plan with the Bahá'í Faith's **emergence from obscurity**.[110]

The **Three Year Plan**, launched in 1993 to culminate in 1996, continued the focus on expansion and the 'task of spreading the Message to the generality of mankind in villages, towns and cities'. This plan called for 'greatly developing the human resources of the Cause'.[111] It emphasized consolidation and proclamation, 'enhancing the vitality of the faith of individual believers, greatly developing the human resources of the Cause, and fostering the proper functioning of local and national Bahá'í institutions'.[112] The Three Year Plan paved the way for the ensuing plans of the Bahá'í world.

Later stages of the unfoldment of the Divine Plan

The stages directed through subsequent plans of the Universal House of Justice to date, are the Four Year Plan (1996-2000),[113] the Twelve Month Plan (2000-2001),[114] the first Five Year Plan (2001-2006), the second Five Year Plan (2006-2011), the third Five Year Plan (2011-2016), and the fourth Five Year Plan (2016-2021) to culminate in the hundredth anniversary of the passing of 'Abdu'l-Bahá, an event which had signalized the beginning of the Formative Age of the Bahá'í Faith.

The **Four Year Plan (1996-2000)** marked another turning point, a decisive moment in the approach of the Bahá'í world to growth. As the surge in expansion experienced in previous plans had to be sustained, balance was introduced between **expansion** and **consolidation**.[115] This was the outcome of the learning gained from previous plans of the Bahá'í world, wherein massive expansion had not been followed by sufficient consolidation.

The document *Century of Light* recounts earlier experiences of the Bahá'í world community with expansive growth which were not followed by successful consolidation.[116] During two decades the Bahá'í community experienced remarkable growth in its global undertakings.

This included an increase in the number of Local Spiritual Assemblies, ethnic and cultural diversity in membership, and receptivity to the Bahá'í message in villages and rural areas. The result of these global enterprises was outreach to indigenous populations in numerous countries – among them Uganda and several other countries in Africa, Bolivia and most other regions of Latin America, Indonesia, India, islands of the Pacific, Alaska, the native peoples of Canada, and the rural African-American population of the southern United States. Tens of thousands of new Bahá'ís were enlisted throughout Africa, Asia and Latin America.[117]

Collective teaching and proclamation projects were launched. Tens of thousands responded, becoming hundreds of thousands. The Bahá'í youth – in the tradition of the heroic youth of early Bábí and Bahá'í history – arose in the thousands to proclaim the message of the Bahá'í Faith throughout all continents and the scattered islands of the globe, often using their skills and talent in music, drama and the arts.[118]

These enterprises resulted in surges in new enrolments. Such bursts, however, were accompanied by challenges which overwhelmed the available resources of Bahá'í communities. Efforts toward addressing expansion and consolidation did not reap anticipated outcomes; hence discouragement set in.[119] Consequently, the initial rapid rise in enrolment rates slowed significantly in many countries, creating setbacks. Additionally, numerous challenges and questions emerged – including the establishment and functioning of Local Spiritual Assemblies and deepening of the newly enrolled. These critical challenges posed by the earlier plans provided the essential learning which was implemented through the design of the Four Year Plan (1996–2000).

The Four Year Plan placed its fundamental emphasis on the building and development of capacity in participants. Consequently, the 'institute process' (see the Glossary) was inaugurated. This process had proved its effectiveness in various parts of the world, resulting in valuable learning.

In subsequent plans, the institute process became central to the creation of a *sustainable pattern* of expansion and consolidation. The two essential movements: steady flow of participants through the sequence of training institute courses, and the movement of clusters along a continuum of development, propel sustainable growth. The institute process is thus aptly viewed as the 'engine of growth'.

The Four Year Plan addressed 'sustained growth of the Bahá'í community on a large scale'.[120] It introduced 'a new state of mind', a 'new culture', setting the Bahá'í community on a new course.

The goal of the Four Year Plan, its 'single-minded aim', was 'advancing the process of entry by troops' (see the Glossary). This plan introduced a new phase in the growth of the Bahá'í community. Systematization became a central factor in several respects in the roles of the individual, the institutions and the local community as they were 'summoned to arise to meet the requirements of this crucial time in our community and in the fortunes of all humankind'.[121] The Four Year Plan with its focused approach and **core activities**[122] has generated a new environment – an enriched milieu for growth.

In this phase, the novel structure of geographical units, known as clusters, and vital core activities introduced in the Four Year Plan and the first of the current series of Five Year Plans are aimed at building capacity and human resources, thus making available the essential provisions for an accelerated growth and expansion:

> The goal of advancing the process of entry by troops became the single-minded aim of the enterprise. The lessons that had been learned during earlier Plans now placed the emphasis on developing the capacities of believers – wherever they might be – so that all could arise as confident protagonists of the Faith's mission.[123]

Strategies of the current plans of the Bahá'í Faith for growth

The current plans of the Bahá'í Faith are centred on core activities and two intimately linked approaches at the grassroots level: **community building** and **capacity building.** Furthermore, the 2010 Riḍván message of the Universal House of Justice places its emphasis on neighbourhoods and villages, and on children and youth.[124]

The core activities

The core activities are central to the framework for action; they thus hold incalculable potential for growth and transformation.[125]

Core activities include study circles, devotional meetings, children's classes and a programme for the empowerment of junior youth – the critical stage of adolescence between the ages of 11 and 14; these activities address the two essential facets of growth: qualitative growth, or transformation, and quantitative growth, or numerical expansion. Thus the key elements of the series of plans that have followed can bring about enhancement in growth which has viability, vitality, and sustainability. The institute process is fundamental to growth. This point was emphasized once again in the 2014 Riḍván message of the Universal House of Justice: 'the two essential movements which continue to propel the process of growth' are 'the steady flow of participants through the sequence of training institute courses and the movement of clusters along a continuum of development'.[126]

Study circles. The institute process is carried out primarily through study circles. These are informal gatherings designed to assist participants to develop the knowledge, spiritual insights and skills needed to contribute to the betterment of their community. They provide a means for methodical group study of the history and fundamental verities of the Baháʼí Faith and include an essential service component, in order to learn through action, using a standard curriculum of training materials rich in excerpts from the Faith's sacred writings. As before observed, they ensure that new believers and others who wish to participate are provided with the opportunities to develop their capacity to contribute to the community-building process, thus creating a sustainable system for growth and development. Study circles have proved attractive to many others who wish to engage 'in systematic study of the Creative Word in an environment that is at once serious and uplifting'.[127]

Devotional meetings. Devotional meetings provide Baháʼís and others with a means to 'respond to the inmost longing of every heart to commune with its Maker', and to carry out 'acts of collective worship in diverse settings, uniting with others in prayer, awakening spiritual susceptibilities, and shaping a pattern of life distinguished for its devotional character'.[128] In devotional meetings Baháʼís can acquaint friends and neighbours with the character of worship in the Baháʼí Faith; all can share, in a relaxed and welcoming atmosphere, selections from the sacred and inspired writings of diverse traditions.

Children's classes. These classes offer children and parents, usually neighbourhood by neighbourhood, an all-embracing form of moral and spiritual education founded on Bahá'í teachings and unabashedly making reference to them as the source of the virtues, freedom from prejudice, and ideals for world citizenship they strive to inculcate.

Junior youth spiritual empowerment programme. Young people aged 11-14 form a special focus of the recent plans of the Bahá'í world.[129] Any plan aimed at creating the nucleus of a global civilization must embrace, nurture and serve these vital populations. The aim of the programmes for the spiritual and moral development of junior youth is to empower them during a crucial and decisive stage in their lives. This programme, which is not in the nature of religious education, offers junior youth a moral compass and practical training in skills for navigating through the confusion and temptations of our times.

Junior youth are positioned at an important juncture in their lives; they can make significant contributions to the construction of a better world. This programme views them as a valuable part of society and aims to instil in them 'the sense of a twofold moral purpose, to develop their inherent potentialities and to contribute to the transformation of society'.[130] Furthermore, the junior youth spiritual empowerment programme 'engages their expanding consciousness in an exploration of reality that helps them analyse the constructive and destructive forces operating in society and to recognize the influence these forces exert on their thoughts and actions, sharpening their spiritual perception, enhancing their powers of expression and reinforcing moral structures that will serve them throughout their lives'.[131]

In sum, the core activities of the Faith's current plans, concomitant with walking a path of service, provide a significant framework – an environment for transformation. They present settings for engaging larger segments of society in a community-building process regardless of whether the participants choose to affiliate with the Bahá'í Faith or not.

Capacity building and community building

The current plans of the Bahá'í Faith address two ingenious approaches to growth: **capacity building** and **community building** at the grassroots level in neighbourhoods, villages and throughout the localities in a cluster.

Capacity building. The Universal House of Justice describes the ongoing capacity-building efforts as 'a process that seeks to raise capacity within a population to take charge of its own spiritual, social and intellectual development'.[132] A framework that includes the core activities provides a dynamic system for promoting the essential dimensions of growth – in the Baháʼí community as well as its surrounding populations – toward the transformation of society. As transformation diffuses outward to the neighbourhood and beyond, it can **penetrate**[133] into collective consciousness, to bring about the fulfilment of the mission of Baháʼuʼlláh for humankind – the raising of a new race of men and women. The Universal House of Justice in its Riḍván message of 2009 envisions a 'glimpse of that race of beings, consecrated and courageous, pure and sanctified, destined to evolve over generations under the influence of Baháʼuʼlláh's Revelation'.[134]

Community building. In its Riḍván message a year later, the Universal House of Justice called attention to community building, describing the

> activities that drive this process, and in which newly found friends are invited to engage in: meetings that strengthen the devotional character of the community; classes that nurture the tender hearts and minds of children; groups that channel the surging energies of junior youth; and circles of study, open to all, which enable people of varied backgrounds to advance on equal footing to explore the application of the teachings to their individual and collective lives . . .[135]

Community building at grassroots level is an effective approach to society building, an important goal of the plans of the Baháʼí world. Neighbourhoods and villages provide ideal settings for learning about community building; they constitute ingenious models in several respects:

- These small units of culture, surrounded with relatively few distractions, are well contained and suitable environments. Thus they can serve effectively as laboratories for learning about growth.

- Knowledge obtained from focus on the smallest level of culture can be applied to the larger unit.

- These small settings contain multitudes of foci for growth. Transformation can expand in a dynamic fashion to bring about collective regeneration, just as a spark can ignite a blaze.

- The sheer numbers of such foci hold enormous possibilities for an ever-expanding process of community enrichment.

- Furthermore, focus at the grassroots level holds the prospect for universal participation in the affairs of a respective community.

The Universal House of Justice affirms:

> If the friends persist in their efforts to learn the ways and methods of community building in small settings in this way, the long-cherished goal of universal participation in the affairs of the Faith will, we are certain, move by several orders of magnitude within grasp.[136]

Continuing emphasis on advancing the process of entry by troops

At the end of the Four Year Plan, the Universal House of Justice wrote:

> The Five Year Plan that follows will initiate a series of worldwide enterprises that will carry the Bahá'í community through the final twenty years in the first century of the Faith's Formative Age. These global Plans will continue to focus on advancing the process of entry by troops and on its systematic acceleration.[137]

Thus all subsequent plans of the Universal House of Justice up to year 2021 are centred on learning to ***advance the process of entry by troops***.[138]

At the same time the Universal House of Justice calls on the Bahá'ís to reach out and influence the masses of humanity, through a 'high standard of excellence, pure and chaste lives, and rectitude of conduct',[139] emphasizing that these plans prepare for the 'rebuilding of a broken world' and the advancement of civilization.[140]

The Universal House of Justice emphasizes the importance of 'the process of learning that, through four successive global plans, has steadily gathered momentum, enhancing the capacity of the friends to engage in grassroots action',[141] pointing to the several-fold increase in capacity built in Bahá'í communities.[142]

Summary: Growth under the plans of the Bahá'í World

A panoramic survey of the growth of the Bahá'í community from the passing of Bahá'u'lláh in 1892 to the present day highlights several salient points. In 1892, all adherents of the Bahá'í Faith lived in fifteen countries in Asia and Africa.[143] A landmark year, 1893,[144] merely one year after the passing of Bahá'u'lláh, signifies the date when the Bahá'í Faith was first mentioned in the Western hemisphere – the beginning of enlisting followers in the West.

The Bahá'í Faith continued its growth under the plans of the Bahá'í world. In response to the call raised in the Tablets of the Divine Plan, a handful of dedicated believers set out for distant parts of the world to spread the message of Bahá'u'lláh. As the result of continuing response to the unfolding stages of the Divine Plan, the Bahá'í Faith has become widespread across the planet with significant increase, since Shoghi Effendi assumed Guardianship, in the total number of countries as well as localities where Bahá'ís now reside.[145]

Progress under the current plans of the Bahá'í world has been noteworthy in the advanced clusters.[146] The House of Justice in its Riḍván message of 2015 envisions bright prospects for the worldwide growth of the Bahá'í Faith, as expressed through these words: 'The paths that lead to sustained large-scale expansion and consolidation are being followed with firmer footsteps, valiant youth often setting the pace.'[147] It continues:

> Indeed, in an increasing number of settings the movement of a population towards Bahá'u'lláh's vision for a new society appears no longer merely as an enthralling prospect but as an emerging reality.[148]

And, despite the upheavals taking place in the world today,

> Yet there is reassurance in the knowledge that, amidst the disintegration, a new kind of collective life is taking shape which gives practical expression to all that is heavenly in human beings.[149]

Invigorated with immense confidence and assurance, the Bahá'í world community forges ahead to bring to the attention of the people of the world – in these critical times, amidst the disintegration of the present world order – the society-building influence of the Bahá'í Faith.

Reflections

As this chapter shows, the guidance that directs the growth of the Bahá'í world community is channelled through the plans of the Bahá'í world – the unfolding stages of the Divine Plan. The approaches to growth are evolutionary, coherent and systematic.

Specific historical circumstances. The Universal House of Justice summarizes the series of approaches over time to the growth of the Bahá'í community, starting from the cradle of the Bahá'í Faith in Iran about 160 years ago to its systematic spread under the direction of Shoghi Effendi. They signify that each approach was suited to its specific historical circumstance and emphasize that the growth of the Bahá'í community must yet evolve still further in complexity and sophistication once it has taken root in a cluster, demonstrating its inherent 'society building power'.[150]

A layering. The strategy of growth may be described as a *layering*. In a new phase, certain essential elements of growth are introduced cautiously and gradually in a timely manner, and in incremental measures, on top of an established structure – to be more fully disclosed and expanded in subsequent phases while retaining their fundamental focus. This layering may be viewed as a phased approach – a gradation. A stratum is first introduced and subsequently expanded in a stepwise manner, while at the same time retaining the stability and strength of its foundation.

Such *layering* is a dynamic process. One can appreciate such progression in the plans of the Bahá'í world. In the earlier phase, the global plans placed their primary focus on geographical spread. The next phase received increasing focus on consolidation: development of capacity and human resources. In 2010, the Universal House of Justice, prior to the launching of its subsequent Five Year Plan, introduced the elements of **social action** and **engagement in discourse on issues of society**.[151] These were introduced gradually. May we look to their further development in future plans?

The future growth of the Bahá'í Faith: Challenges and opportunities

At this point in time, as the Bahá'í community addresses its future growth, it is faced with conditions unique and hitherto unprecedented in the course of human history. On one hand these conditions pose special challenges; yet on the other hand they hold unimagined opportunities for its accelerated rate of growth and worldwide expansion.

Challenges to growth. The mission of the Bahá'í Faith – oneness of the human race and the establishment of a world civilization – requires extensive outreach to the inhabitants of this globe. Thus the principal challenge facing the Bahá'í community is to achieve a growth of sufficient magnitude, not through coercion, military conquest or colonization, but rather through the conquest of human hearts. Moreover, this rate of growth must take into account the rate of increase in the population of the world.[152]

Opportunities for growth. On the other hand, our times hold unique opportunities for growth. Rapid communication, ushered in by the advent of the Bàb in 1844, and signalized by the first telegraphic code, have generated possibilities favourable to the growth of the Bahá'í Faith.[153]

The pace of communication has since escalated. Shoghi Effendi, in the 1930s – at a time when such possibilities were unimaginable – foreshadowed a world inter-communication system:

> A mechanism of world inter-communication will be devised, embracing the whole planet, freed from national hindrances and restrictions, and functioning with marvellous swiftness and perfect regularity.[154]

The prediction of Shoghi Effendi is now a reality. Rapid spread of knowledge and enhanced interactions among the diverse inhabitants of this planet can facilitate the coming together and the unification of the entire human race. Such remarkable systems of rapid communication and innovations in this digital age can serve as powerful instruments for the spread and expansion of the Bahá'í message toward realization of the mission of Bahá'u'lláh for humankind. This is in fulfilment of the counsel of the Báb – in the mid-nineteenth century – that a system of swift communications should be established so that the entire world might hear the news of the coming of Bahá'u'lláh.[155] Such unique possibilities of this global age are the outcome of the new forces unleashed, the new creativity infused into the world system. This theme will be further discussed in Chapter 6.

It must be pointed out however that on one hand, the expansive spread of the Bahá'í world community in a relatively short period of time may be credited to advances in science and technology which have annihilated distance. Nonetheless, on the other hand, such astonishing technological advances can also pose impediments to growth. They serve to amplify the background and foreground 'noise' levels, introducing excessive distractions. Such noise includes the many spurious activities and movements which have also spread at astounding rates and compete for attention. The spread of multitudes of ideologies have added to the confusion of our times; these in turn can create obstacles to the discernment of reality amidst the profusion of contending voices, making it difficult to discriminate between the true and the false, the significant and the trivial, the authentic and the counterfeit. Shoghi Effendi attests to 'the noise and tumult of a distracted age . . .'[156]

Notwithstanding these challenges, our times provide opportunities for growth. Rapid transportation and communication together with mass migrations continue to bring into close proximity diverse populations. Communities composed of multi-national, multi-racial, multi-religious, multi-cultural and multi-ethnic populations constitute a suitable foundation for welding the bonds of oneness among the members of the human race. The Bahá'í Faith has already demonstrated its capability in creating models of unity from such rich diversity. This is a testament to its relevance and efficacy for forging such bonds at the global level – as a prelude to the establishment of a viable world civilization.

Under the guidance of the unfolding stages of the Divine Plan – directed by the successive world heads of the Bahá'í Faith – the Bahá'í worldwide community is well positioned to address its large-scale growth and crystallization. The crystallization of the Bahá'í community will be discussed in the next chapter. *Our times are opportune for widespread transformation and phenomenal growth.*

4

CRYSTALLIZATION AND GROWTH

> Though the Revelation of Bahá'u'lláh has been delivered, the World Order which such a Revelation must needs beget is as yet unborn. Though the Heroic Age of His Faith is passed, the creative energies which that Age has released have not as yet crystallized into that world society which, in the fullness of time, is to mirror forth the brightness of His glory.
>
> *Shoghi Effendi*[1]

Introduction

Crystallization, as inferred from several passages in the Bahá'í writings, signifies a process which proceeds gradually to culminate in fulfilment of anticipated objectives – the maturation of the institutions of the Bahá'í Faith and the advancement of the Bahá'í community – toward the realization of the vision of Bahá'u'lláh in a new world order.

The premise set forth in this chapter is that the advancement of the Bahá'í worldwide community to date and the prospect for its large-scale growth in the years to come must be credited to the plans directed by the successive world heads of the Bahá'í Faith. These plans have followed a coherent course by centering their focus on a sequence of stages. During an early stage in its history, global spread was unrelentingly pursued while at the same time remaining mindful of increase in the number of its adherents. During the subsequent stage, its primary aim was advancing the process of 'entry by troops' (see the Glossary) by developing and nurturing capacity in the community of its adherents and supporters – while at the same time attentive to its geographical spread. In particular, in this current stage of its development special focus is placed on the smallest level of society and culture, in neighbourhoods and villages.

This chapter is centred on crystallization.[2] It reasons that several salient features of the growth of Bahá'í community can be likened to the scientific process of crystal formation. The discussion that follows will first look at the systematic approach of the Bahá'í community to its development and advancement. Next, its focus will be placed on crystallization by: referring to this concept in Bahá'í writings; explaining the science of crystallization, as a metaphor for the growth of the Bahá'í community; discussing the process of crystal formation and its relevance to the crystallization of the Bahá'í community; and sharing the understandings gleaned from this metaphor.

Insights imparted by the metaphor of crystallization will be applied to the advancement of the Bahá'í community under the current plans of the Bahá'í world toward that ultimate objective, the fulfilment of Bahá'u'lláh's vision for humanity.

Growth and development of the Bahá'í community: A systematic approach

This chapter maintains that the plans of the Bahá'í Faith have placed their primary focus systematically and sequentially on two stages of growth: (i) ***worldwide spread*** and (ii) ***increase*** in the number of the adherents and supporters of the Bahá'í Faith – building and nurturing in them capacity to effect individual and societal change. The sequence in which these two stages are implemented is fundamental to vital and sustainable growth.

Visualized images

In the interest of explaining this thesis, the reader is asked to visualize two images, each representing a map of the world showing a pattern of the worldwide distribution of Bahá'í communities.

The first visualized image represents the distribution of Bahá'í communities by the year 1919 – the date of the unveiling of the Tablets of the Divine Plan – when the call of 'Abdu'l-Bahá was raised for taking the message of Bahá'u'lláh to areas of the world where no Bahá'ís yet resided. In this image we can envision a few thousand dots, representing the estimated number of Bahá'í communities in existence by the year 1919. Though accurate information on the number of all Bahá'í communities of that time is not available, it is not likely that the number exceeded a few thousand by much. In his Riḍván message of 1957, Shoghi Effendi stated that there were then 4,200 localities throughout the world where Bahá'ís resided, 'representing an increase of no less than a thousand centres in the course of the last two years'.[3] This figure, together with other statistics before this date, lend credence to the view that in 1919 the number of localities must have been in the very low thousands. These localities were of variable sizes – small, medium and large representing the proportionate sizes of the respective Bahá'í communities. The largest dot stands for the Bahá'í community in Iran, the birthplace of the Bahá'í Faith; medium-sized dots stand for communities of medium size in various countries or regions, notably the Bahá'í communities in the Caucasus and Central Asia where at the end of the 19th century many Persian Bahá'ís had found refuge from persecution in their native land and where the first Bahá'í House of Worship had been erected, in Ishqabad.[4] Smaller dots could stand for small communities throughout Europe and the North American continent – the United States, Canada and Greenland – as well as several countries in Asia, including Japan. In this first visualized image the dots are widely spaced, as a consequence of the sparse worldwide distribution of Bahá'í communities.

The second visualized image represents the present-day worldwide distribution of Bahá'í communities, the outcome of the response to the unfolding stages of the Divine Plan. In this image we can envision approximately 120,000 dots, each dot standing for a Bahá'í community;[5] these dots are more closely spaced than the dots in the first image. The vast increase in numbers of localities in this second image should be credited to the guidance provided through the plans of the Bahá'í world. At an early stage, primary and undeviated attention was placed on global spread; thus the efforts of the Bahá'í community were focused unrelentingly on global dispersion – that is, increase in the number of localities worldwide wherein the seeds of the message of Bahá'u'lláh were to be sown. The Bahá'í community was thus placed in an opportune situation for the next stage in its large-scale accelerated growth. It must be noted that concomitant with the increase in geographical spread, the number of avowed believers also increased.

A reverse scenario

In support of the thesis of this chapter, we can entertain the reverse scenario; that is, the consequence of a strategy which had placed its primary focus at an early stage on increase in the number of Bahá'ís in each locality. The outcome of such a strategy might have, by this time, increased the total number of Bahá'ís in these localities, but at the cost of a significant decrease in the worldwide expansion of the Bahá'í Faith, as it would have compromised its spread to other localities and regions of the world.

We can reflect on the possible outcome of such a scenario. On the positive side, each community would be larger and possibly more firmly established. The sparsity of communities worldwide, however, would have presented serious drawbacks. First, significant loss in diversity could have compromised the viability of the Bahá'í Faith; the coming together of diverse nationalities, races, tribes, cultures, ethnicities, and religions forms the cornerstone of the mission of Bahá'u'lláh. Second, the isolation, confinement and persecution of certain key Bahá'í communities, which were also the largest, would have significantly jeopardized the worldwide spread of the Bahá'í Faith.

From its early history the Bahá'í Faith has experienced suppression, intense persecution and confinement in several parts of the world, including Caucasus and Central Asia under the communist government of the Soviet Union as well as in Egypt and Iran. The hardship, restrictions and repression to which all religious communities, including the Bahá'í community, were subjected under the Soviet Regime in 1928–1929[6] led to the (re)migration of many Bahá'í families back to Iran. Most persistent and insidious are the ongoing persecutions that continue to the present day in the land of its birth, Iran. These have escalated in recent times in scope as well as in severity. The suppression of the Iranian Bahá'í community and the persecution and execution of its members have resulted in the isolation of Iran's largest and most significant religious minority. The Bahá'í population in Iran has suffered extreme forms of repression, among them denial of rights of citizenship, access to higher education, and earning a livelihood.

One can only speculate on the dire consequences of such acts on the spread and viability of the worldwide Bahá'í community if the geographical spread of the Bahá'í Faith had remained limited as in 1919 but the total number of its adherents had nevertheless increased. In this situation its worldwide growth would have been significantly stifled and jeopardized. Such a scenario would have had deleterious effects, placing the Bahá'í Faith in a precarious position and its continuing growth and viability at serious risk.

As it is, restrictions, confinement, isolation and persecution of Bahá'í communities in any part of the world – now in Iran – have not succeeded in restraining its growth. On the contrary: in one respect the dedicated acts of the Iranian Bahá'ís reverberate through the entire Bahá'í worldwide network, impassioning and invigorating it. At another level, accounts of those sacrificial deeds call the attention of the world community to the plight of the Bahá'ís in Iran and to the edifying mission of a Faith that can inspire such noble and selfless acts. The fortitude of the persecuted and suppressed Bahá'ís in face of opposition continues to strengthen and galvanize the Bahá'í community. Shoghi Effendi attests:

> The utmost its avowed and secret enemies could hope to achieve was to retard its growth and obscure momentarily its purpose. What they actually accomplished was to purge and purify its life, to stir it to still greater depths, to galvanize its soul, to prune its institutions, and cement its unity. A schism, a permanent cleavage in the vast body of its adherents, they could never create.[7]

In sum, the current worldwide spread of the Bahá'í community – the outcome of its systematic plans in the 20th century – places it in a salutary position, with prospects propitious for its large-scale growth as it continues to advance in the 21st century. Thoughtful reflection on the spread of the Bahá'í world community highlights certain conditions favourable to expansive growth. First, the large number of localities where Bahá'í communities reside enhances diversity and contributes to building models of unity in a microcosm of humanity. Second, assaults directed at certain key communities cannot have a drastic effect; rather, they serve to inspire and animate the entire Bahá'í world.

Possibility for the butterfly effect. Importantly, the widespread distribution of localities where Bahá'ís reside – envisioned through the second image – can heighten the probability for its worldwide advancement;

in one respect, this may be attributed to the 'butterfly effect'. Such an effect, initially infinitesimal, can under favourable conditions become operative to exert an enormous impact on its growth. This can be likened to that spark which sets a system ablaze. The butterfly effect, first shown in the field of meteorology, is a significant implication of the science of Chaos and will be discussed in the next chapter. It is conceivable that at any one time, any one of these localities may meet the requisite condition, thus increasing the probability for its occurrence. We can reasonably surmise that the greater the number of these localities, the higher the probability for the butterfly phenomenon to take hold.

Hence, at an early stage, the Bahá'í world – guided and directed by the Tablets of the Divine Plan of 'Abdu'l-Bahá and the plans of Shoghi Effendi – achieved a remarkable global spread whereby the seeds of this Faith were planted throughout the globe. This accomplishment now places the focus of Bahá'ís worldwide on the major thrust of the current plans of the House of Justice. These plans address large-scale development of human resources and building of capacity for effecting individual and societal change. Each one of the multitude of localities where Bahá'í communities are now established can serve as a focal point for growth and transformation of society.

It is now opportune to turn to the fascinating and insightful process of crystallization as it applies to its analogue – the crystallization of the worldwide Bahá'í community.

Crystallization

Crystallization in the Bahá'í writings

Crystallization denotes, 'to bring to definite and permanent form'.[8] This concept abounds in Bahá'í authoritative texts; it refers to an anticipated outcome – a world culture and civilization through realization of the vision of Bahá'u'lláh for humanity.

Shoghi Effendi, in *The World Order of Bahá'u'lláh*, foreshadows the crystallization of its institutions, the hallmark of the administrative system of the Bahá'í Faith:

> The onrushing forces so miraculously released through the agency

of two independent and swiftly successive Manifestations are now under our very eyes and through the care of the chosen stewards of a far-flung Faith being gradually mustered and disciplined. They are slowly crystallizing into institutions that will come to be regarded as the hall-mark and glory of the age we are called upon to establish and by our deeds immortalize.[9]

In reference to the Formative Age (see the Glossary), Shoghi Effendi again evokes the image of crystallization:

... that Formative Period which is to witness the gradual crystallization of those creative energies and the consequent emergence of that World Order for which those forces were made to operate.[10]

The Universal House of Justice, at the close of the first Five Year Plan of the current series, referred to crystallization of a structure, a *framework*:

The elements required for a concerted effort to infuse the diverse regions of the world with the spirit of Bahá'u'lláh's Revelation have crystallized into a framework for action . . .[11]

Crystallization, conveyed through these passages, is a process that progresses toward a glorious outcome – a viable structure, a framework for action toward the emergence of the World Order of Bahá'u'lláh.

Crystallization is a dynamic process with a multitude of facets and dimensions; each holds profound insights inviting reflection. Two Bahá'í authors, Hooper Dunbar and Craig Loehle, have looked at the concept of crystallization and its application to the Bahá'í Faith.[12] In this chapter, one other facet of crystallization grounded in natural sciences will be explored. The discussion in the previous chapter, *The Flow of Plans and Growth*, is fundamental to the thesis presented in these pages. It provides an overview of the stages in the development and advancement of the Bahá'í community under the guidance of sequential and systematic plans directed by its successive world heads.

The science of crystallization: Metaphor for growth of the Bahá'í community

Crystallization follows scientific principles. It is a method used by chemists for purification of solids.[13] Crystallization advances through two sequential phases – a slow phase of *nucleation* and a rapid phase of *crystal formation* to give rise to the desired product – a crystal with distinctive properties.

Briefly, the formation of a crystal, such as sugar in a solution, proceeds through these two phases: first appear numerous nuclei as foci of growth; next these continue to grow until a crystalline structure of highest purity is formed.

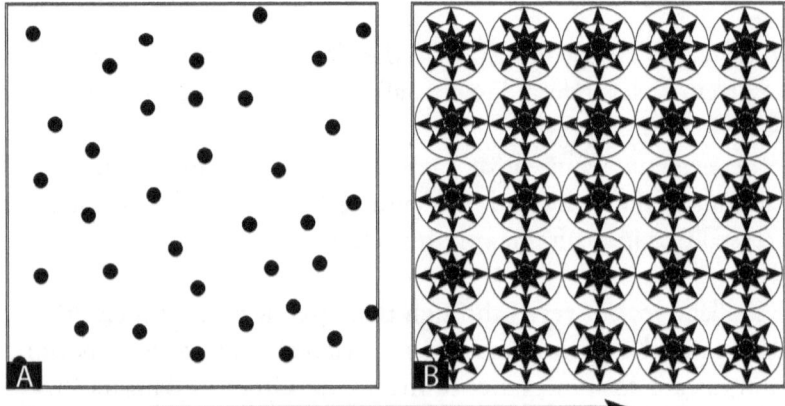

Figure 1. Growth of focal centres of crystallization

Figure 1 (A and B) is offered to illustrate the crystallization process. Crystallization of a substance is governed by certain conditions and specific requirements. In reference to the familiar example of crystallization of sugar in a solution, a critical concentration of the sugar molecule is needed before the process of crystallization sets in.

During the phase of nucleation, at a certain critical level of the sugar molecule numerous minute focal centres of growth – nuclei – form throughout the medium; these continue to grow in size as shown in Figure 1A until a threshold level is reached. Once this level is surpassed, the second phase of crystallization sets in; these centres of crystal formation continue to grow until the structure takes form and becomes crystalline, as shown in Figure 1B.

Crystallization of the Bahá'í community

The growth of the Bahá'í community is a dynamic process which may be likened to its analogue, the formation of a crystal in a solution. Crystallization is a metaphor infused with rich insights and poetic imagery which may be applied to the development of the Bahá'í community. Its salient features provide analogues to the dynamic process of the advancement of Bahá'í Faith and those elements which can promote it.

The current plans of the Bahá'í world are aimed at large-scale growth – advancing the process of 'entry by troops', as described in previous chapters. Special focus is placed on increase in the size of the Bahá'í community itself as well as of the number of its supporters and those imbued with the vision of Bahá'u'lláh for humanity. Transformation of the individual and the collective are implicit in this approach. Each locality where Bahá'ís reside serves as a focal centre of growth and transformation. As these continue to progressively increase in size, in turn they give rise to other localities. Together all these serve as centres of growth. Thus is set in motion the process of ***crystallization*** of a dynamic worldwide community – destined to crystallize into a world culture and civilization – in fulfilment of the vision of Bahá'u'lláh in a new world order.

In the context of the current plans of the Bahá'í world, the analogy of crystallization provides several insights whose depths invite exploration and reflection. The analogy can further enrich understanding and appreciation of growth at several levels: at one level, the development of geographical units designated as clusters in the recent plans of the Bahá'í world; at another level, the crystallization of the worldwide Bahá'í community; and yet at another level, the crystallization of a world civilization, the mission of the World Order of Bahá'u'lláh. Fundamental to all is the individual. Focal centres of growth in the crystallization process may be likened to 'expanding nucleus of individuals' that can 'generate a movement towards the goal of a new World Order'.[14]

Insights gleaned from the metaphor of crystallization

Reflection on the metaphor of crystallization imparts further insights on the crystallization of the Bahá'í community.

Specific requirements. A crystallization process has specific requirements which can be applied to the growth and development of the worldwide Bahá'í community. As before mentioned, crystallization of a substance such as sugar requires a *critical concentration* of the sugar molecules. By comparison, a critical number of adherents and supporters of the Bahá'í Faith will be essential for the process of crystallization of the Bahá'í community to take hold. Additionally, certain factors and structures induce and promote crystal formation.

Inducers of crystallization stimulate and advance crystal formation. By comparison, factors that induce the crystallization of the worldwide Bahá'í community include the essential elements of the current plans of the Bahá'í world – the core activities. These include study circles, devotional meetings, children's classes and junior youth empowerment programmes, as discussed in Chapters 2 and 3. These activities are operating at grassroots level in hundreds of thousands of small gatherings – often in homes – in neighbourhoods and villages spread across the face of the globe. They hold transformative power to induce the crystallization of a new entity, a *new race of men and women*[15] for bringing about that precious 'end product' – a world civilization.

Structures that promote crystallization serve as scaffolding for crystal growth. It is known that the presence of supporting structures (such as strings in the medium) enhance the crystallization of sugar; as ***scaffolding,*** they promote crystal formation. In the context of the current plans of the Bahá'í world, the ***framework of the institute process*** serves to fortify and sustain the crystallization of the Bahá'í community.

An autocatalytic process. The Universal House of Justice alludes to the outcome of the institute process[16] – an increase in numbers of those participating in and facilitating the essential elements of capacity building, the core activities. Reflection on this process characterizes it as self-catalyzing and may thus be viewed as autocatalytic (see the Glossary); it progresses continuously. An autocatalytic process[17] gathers speed with time; in this manner very high levels of growth can be achieved. The implication of such a process is considered further in Chapter 5.

The Universal House of Justice highlights the increase in participation in core activities as indicators of increased capacity in the Bahá'í community; referring to this system of developing human resources as 'an instrument of limitless potentialities', they point out that 'it is possible for an expanding nucleus of individuals to generate a movement towards the goal of a new World Order'.[18] Such ever-expanding nuclei hold the prospect for construction of a global civilization. We can envision a dynamic system wherein the incremental growth of such nuclei, once set in motion, holds enormous potential for the advancement of the Bahá'í Faith. The process of crystallization of the Bahá'í community is bound to bring forth a system wide in scope and world-embracing.

Insights gleaned from the crystal – the ultimate product of crystallization

Figure 1B calls attention to the outcome of the crystallization phase. The crystal, its end product, has the requisite properties of structure and order; its hallmark is *purity*. As a metaphor, the crystal holds rich insights which can be applied to its analogue – the ultimate product of development and crystallization of the worldwide Bahá'í community. Such a process must result in an entity characterized by order, structure and *purity of character*. Transformation – at the heart of all religions – is at the foundation of Bahá'u'lláh's Revelation, imperative to the crystallization of the Bahá'í community. This process is bound to bring forth that much sought after product – a community whose hallmark is purity, a transformed world society with moral and spiritual character, and a world civilization through the World Order of Bahá'u'lláh.

Reflecting on the growth and advancement of the Bahá'í Faith and the insights gleaned from the science of crystallization, the Bahá'í community may wish to note that the initial phase of crystallization – the phase of nucleation – is slow, but its subsequent phase, crystal formation, is rapid. Might we liken this to the crystallization of the Bahá'í community? Might we, with confidence and assurance, look beyond the slow phase of *nucleation* to the next phase – that rapid phase of *crystal formation*?

Once set in motion, factors yet unanticipated can bring about an accelerated rate of growth of the Bahá'í Faith and the advancement of civilization to its next level, a *vital and transformed world culture*.

5

THE SCIENCE OF CHAOS AND THOUSANDFOLD GROWTH

> . . . a day which, viewed in its proper perspective, will be the prelude to that long-awaited hour when a mass conversion on the part of these same nations and races, and as a direct result of a chain of events, momentous and possibly catastrophic in nature and which cannot as yet be even dimly visualized, will suddenly revolutionize the fortunes of the Faith, derange the equilibrium of the world, and reinforce a thousandfold the numerical strength as well as the material power and the spiritual authority of the Faith of Bahá'u'lláh.
>
> *Shoghi Effendi*[1]

Introduction

At this particular point in the course of history, humanity finds itself on the brink of a new phase, as foreshadowed by several noted philosophers and scholars.[2] The Bahá'í community can anticipate that transition to this new phase will be accompanied by forces and conditions bound to exert their influence on society, with the outcome of significant acceleration in its rate of growth and worldwide advancement. The following excerpt from a letter written on behalf of Shoghi Effendi, the Guardian of the Bahá'í Faith, conveys that promise.

> For it is only when the spirit has thoroughly permeated the world that the people will begin to enter the Faith in large numbers. At the beginning of spring only the few, exceptionally favoured seeds will sprout, but when the season gets in its full sway, and the atmosphere gets permeated with the warmth of true springtime, then masses of flowers will begin to appear, and a whole hillside suddenly blooms. We are still in the state when only isolated souls are awakened, but soon we shall have the full swing of the season and the quickening

of whole groups and nations into the spiritual life breathed by Bahá'u'lláh.[3]

At the present time, however, that quickening spirit of the Bahá'í Faith has not yet sufficiently permeated the world; its adherents are not numerous enough to exert an impact on collective consciousness. Increase in its membership and influence will be essential. The Universal House of Justice in its message of Riḍván 1990 highlights the need for a vast expansion in membership.

> The Order brought by Bahá'u'lláh is intended to guide the progress and resolve the problems of society. Our numbers are as yet too small to effect an adequate demonstration of the potentialities inherent in the administrative system we are building, and the efficacy of this system will not be fully appreciated without a vast expansion of our membership. With the prevailing situation in the world the necessity to effect such a demonstration becomes more compelling.[4]

As discussed in previous chapters, the worldwide advancement of the Bahá'í Faith is addressed through strategic and systematic plans, directed by the supreme governing body of the Bahá'í Faith, the Universal House of Justice; these plans inspire, guide and focus the action of the Bahá'í community, aligning it with the institutions of their administrative system. Furthermore, these plans have launched an effective approach for assisting populations to move toward the vision of Bahá'u'lláh for humanity – whether these populations are at this time registered Bahá'ís or not. The plans of the Bahá'í world spark collective transformation and societal change – the ultimate objective of the Faith of Bahá'u'lláh. Such a change is bound to bring in time, 'when the season gets in its full sway', vast numbers into its fold and the 'quickening of whole groups and nations into the spiritual life breathed by Bahá'u'lláh'.[5]

The question of the growth of the Bahá'í Faith should be examined in light of several key factors. These include:

- the characteristic features and essential conditions for growth in dynamic systems, discussed in Chapter 1;

- the impact of growth-inducing and growth-enhancing factors internal to the Bahá'í community. Over these factors, the three key protagonists in the growth of the Bahá'í Faith – the individual, the community and the institutions – can exert direct influence to enhance the effect of 'the growth-inducing milieu'.[6] Several of these factors were discussed in Chapter 2; and

- those unforeseen and unanticipated growth-enhancing factors which lie beyond the direct influence and control of the three key protagonists of growth. Discussion of some of these factors is the focus of this present chapter.

These unforeseen factors, external to the Bahá'í community itself, under opportune conditions hold such power as to spur a sudden increase of *a thousandfold* in the growth of the Bahá'í Faith. The statement from Shoghi Effendi, which launched this chapter, foreshadows such a glorious prospect.[7]

Unanticipated growth-enhancing factors

Comprehension of the full scope and magnitude of the breathtaking vision of Bahá'u'lláh for the oneness of the human race and its actualization in a sustainable global civilization lies beyond human ken. The Revelation of Bahá'u'lláh provides the impulse for transformation toward the fulfilment of this grand vision. However, in view of the prevailing world scene and the complexities entailed in the construction of 'the nucleus of a glorious global civilization . . . one that will demand centuries of exertion by humanity to bring to fruition',[8] the hope that such a monumental task can be accomplished by a handful of Bahá'ís spread across the face of this planet is not plausible.

The Universal House of Justice addresses these concerns in its Riḍván message of 2010, emphasizing that the construction of such a civilization will not be achieved by Bahá'ís alone. Other groups, organizations and agencies will also contribute to the process of civilization building.

The impact of those unforeseeable forces external to the Bahá'í community must be taken into account. When operative, these factors can wield a power of incalculable measure, enhancing the rate of growth and 'the spiritual authority of the Faith of Bahá'u'lláh'.[9] While the individual, the community or the institutions of the Faith cannot exert direct influence over these forces, they can nonetheless play their role in promoting favourable conditions. Through their state of preparedness, they can stand mobilized to garner the results once these factors are set in motion.

When these forces become operational, they hold the power for phenomenal influence on the worldwide recognition of the Bahá'í Faith, with outcomes of such magnitude as to bring about a momentous acceleration in its rate of growth. Those growth-enhancing factors addressed in this chapter include:

- the process of Chaos of the science of Chaos;
- the 'butterfly effect' of the science of Chaos;
- singular points in history;
- the chain of events in the course of history; and
- unforeseen and unanticipated developments in science and technology.

The process of Chaos

The following prophetic words of Bahá'u'lláh – chilling, yet thrilling and exhilarating – launch and illuminate the discussion in these pages on the science of Chaos:

> The world's equilibrium hath been upset through the vibrating influence of this most great, this new World Order. Mankind's ordered life hath been revolutionized through the agency of this unique, this wondrous System . . .[10]

This pronouncement of Bahá'u'lláh attributes the disequilibrium in the world system to the influence of the new world order introduced through His Revelation. It evokes key features of the science of Chaos. The destabilizing impact of the emerging new world order introduced through the Revelation of Bahá'u'lláh is the cause of turbulence, disequilibrium and disorder in the prevailing world system. Moreover, His statement 'Soon will the present-day order be rolled up, and a new one spread out in its stead'[11] confers the assurance that in time a new order will replace the present-day order. Instability, disequilibrium and apparent disorder are all features associated with the process of Chaos out of which will emerge a new order. Our times display the characteristics of a true Chaotic process.

The science of Chaos

A few definitions. In common usage, the term 'chaos' is applied to systems that are disorderly. However, the science of Chaos tells us that there is a process which appears disorderly on the surface but camouflages an emerging order. It should be noted, however, that not all patterns which appear disorganized qualify as a true process of Chaos – that is, with an emerging order. It is therefore important to be cognizant of two types of 'chaos': (i) a process which is disorderly – with no emerging order – but becoming progressively more disorganized and ultimately disintegrating; and (ii) a process which appears disorderly but results in emergence of order. In this writing, 'Chaos' with a capital C refers to the second type (ii). Such a process can give rise to a higher level of order and is distinguished by its mathematical feature of fractals.[12]

At this point a brief introduction to the science of Chaos is fundamental to the discussion in this chapter and to the following chapters. A more extensive study of this theme can provide a greater depth of appreciation of its relevance to the actualization of the vision of Bahá'u'lláh for humanity.

Along with relativity and quantum mechanics, the science of Chaos was one of the major theories of science in the 20th century.[13] The process of Chaos was predicted early by the physicist James Clerk Maxwell, a Nobel laureate. His essay contains the essential idea of modern Chaos theory: 'sensitive dependence on initial conditions', that is, a very small change under appropriate conditions can have a very large outcome.[14]

The science of Chaos confers perspective and significance on the tempo and tenor of our times. Chaos enhances understanding of the operation of forces and factors which are at work. It imparts a sense of hope and optimism to human destiny and the outcome of history. Its poetic imagery, the 'butterfly effect', bears fascinating relevance to the thesis of this chapter – significant acceleration in the growth of the Bahá'í Faith. Its effects are sweeping. Chaos is implicated in the workings of the twin processes of disintegration and integration (to be discussed in Chapter 6).

Insights shed by the science of Chaos on the course of human history and the attainment of a global civilization are especially illuminating and will be discussed in Chapter 7.

In a truly Chaotic process, order is camouflaged as disorder. When one views the system, on the surface it may appear disorderly; yet an inherent order is in process of emergence. Thus systems that display apparent disorganization with an emerging order follow the science of Chaos.

Edward Lorenz,[15] a pioneer in the field of Chaos, is credited as the first to identify this process. Chaos is ubiquitous; research has shown that it prevails in many systems and in numerous fields.[16] Among these are the chemical reaction, the laser beam, the physiology of the heartbeat and other biological systems, as well as in areas as diverse as the stock market, epidemiology and notably in the generation of the universe 13.8 billion years ago with the Big Bang. Increasingly, systems are found to have the characteristics of the science of Chaos.

Fractal: A characteristic feature of the science of Chaos. Fractal is a mathematical feature of Chaos. The term is derived from the word 'fractional'; it signifies any pattern, or property that displays self-similarity across all scales or levels of magnification. Simply put, fractal is repetition of a feature at all levels of enlargement. Thus the same attribute is repeated at each level.

In nature, fractal is seen, to name few examples, in the branching of trees, the pattern of the fern leaf, and the outline of coastlines. In biological systems it is evident in the folding of chromosomes, in the organization of blood vessels that branch out continuously, in the branching of air passageways within the lung, and in other living systems. Fractal is also a feature in epidemiology and financial markets and may extend to the social sciences as well as to numerous other fields. The feature of self-similarity at each level of enlargement can be discerned in each of these systems.

Chaos is associated with turbulence. Turbulence has a number of implications in the field of physics. As it relates to the discussion in this book, it is a key feature of the process of Chaos. Turbulence introduced into a system causes it to behave in a seemingly highly disorganized manner. Importantly, it leads to the building up of energy, capturing and holding a force sufficiently powerful for the creation of a higher-level order.[17] Turbulent flow is chaotic.

A Chaotic process is non-linear. In a non-linear system the output is not proportional to the input. Small changes in one part of the system can have complex effects throughout (see the Glossary).

An analogy to elucidate Chaos. Let us consider a stream of water in a river bed in whose path are a few rocks. At a low rate of flow, the current appears organized as it runs around and over the rocks. At this low rate, the pattern of flow around the rocks can be anticipated as orderly – following physical and mathematical principles.

With significant acceleration in the rate of flow of water in the river, it will be difficult to predict or to discern any order in its course as it surges, cascades and gushes over and around the obstructing rocks. The pattern has become chaotic, disorderly and torrential due to the significant **turbulence** introduced into the system. Nevertheless, the flow of water under this condition is still subject to the same physical and mathematical laws and orderly principles. The pattern has become turbulent due to significant acceleration in its rate of flow; nonetheless, an underlying order still prevails. Amidst the apparent chaos and disorganization an organized process is emerging; this turbulent flow, similar to the slow flow of water in the river bed, also follows the laws and principles of physics and mathematics. Order is emerging out of apparent disorder; that is, out of Chaos.

It is of special interest that Bahá'u'lláh, in the following passage from *Sahífiy-i-Shattiyyih* (Book of the River) refers to the analogy of the river, its natural flow and the outcome of disruption in that flow:

> Similarly, ponder upon the mysteries of divine decree and destiny. Whatever hath appeared or will appear is like this river. Each thing moveth or reposeth in its proper place. But if something contrary to this natural flow of events is manifested, the order of the world becometh gravely disrupted . . .[18]

The flow of water in a river bed is an apt metaphor for the course of events in our times. Since the mid-19th century, advances in science, technology and innovations have surpassed those of previous centuries. Consequently, the accelerated rate of change has escalated that course to a torrential level – to the *rapids of change*. Such monumental change has affected all dimensions of human affairs. The rapids of change, like the rapid flow of water in a river bed around and over the obstructing rocks, has introduced turbulence into the world system. Its outcome is tumult, disequilibrium, and apparent disorganization. Nonetheless, orderly principles do prevail; the system may appear haphazard and disorderly, yet like that rapid flow of water, an underlying *order is emerging out of apparent disorder.*

The extension of the analogy of the flow of water to the process of history is compelling. We may attribute the disorganization, disruption and Chaos readily discernible in our world to the significant acceleration of forces moving toward globalization. The cause of such momentous increase in the rate of flow we ascribe to the forces which have been released through the Revelations of the Twin Manifestations, the Báb and Bahá'u'lláh. This point warrants exploration and will be discussed in Chapter 6.

The butterfly effect: A powerful accelerator of growth

An important implication of the process of Chaos, the 'butterfly effect', bears relevance to the theme of this chapter. The butterfly effect was first demonstrated in the field of meteorology. This expression was used in 1972, by Edward Lorenz,[19] to show that a weak current generated by the flapping of the wings of a butterfly in one part of the world, under appropriate conditions, can escalate to a tornado-like impact in a distant part of the world.

The butterfly effect is an intriguing implication of the science of Chaos; Chaotic systems are sensitive to small initial forces, with an outcome of great magnitude. When turbulence and instability set in, small fluctuations are introduced into the system; these escalate to exert their enormous impact.

This analogy can also be extended to the process of history and the disruptive and chaotic events of our times. The workings of the butterfly effect should be taken into thoughtful consideration; as an unanticipated factor it has the power – once in operation – to induce significant acceleration in the advancement of the Bahá'í Faith.

Systems that show turbulence and instability are especially prone to the workings of the butterfly phenomenon. Systems that are in equilibrium are stable and balanced. Systems that are near equilibrium are slightly out of balance, so that small changes in energy produce small changes in the system. However, systems that are far from equilibrium are significantly out of balance; they are significantly unstable. In such systems a very small amount of additional energy can cause a very large change and even a complete reorganization of the system. As the present world order is markedly out of balance, an initial force under appropriate conditions can bring about a momentous reorganizing outcome – a major revolutionizing change to shake 'the foundation of all things'[20] and generate an outcome of tremendous magnitude.

At its highest level, this evokes the revolutionizing impact of the Word of God on history. This effect resonates in Handel's *Messiah* through these impassioned words from the Hebrew Bible: 'Yet once, a little while, and I will shake the heavens, and the earth, the sea, and the dry land, all nations – and the desire of all nations shall come.'[21]

On the surface, such a revolutionizing effect may appear catastrophic; upon further reflection, it holds the promise of an auspicious event. In the Dispensation of Bahá'u'lláh, that promise is for the transformation and complete reorganization of the world's disordered system into a new world order. Bahá'u'lláh provides the insight, the inspiration and the assurance toward its fulfilment. Shoghi Effendi has explained its relevance to the workings of the twofold process of disintegration and integration. A discussion of this theme will be the focus of the next chapter.

The prevailing world order, more aptly termed the present world disorder, stands on feet of clay. Its extreme turbulence and instabilities, qualifies it for the working of the butterfly effect, even though the world order relates to a social system, whereas the process of Chaos is explained and viewed primarily in the context of the natural sciences – biology, chemistry and physics. Ilya Prigogine and Isabelle Stengers draw attention to the relevance and implications of Chaos for systems other than the natural sciences. They propose that the process of Chaos and its butterfly effect can also be applied to social systems, pointing out that 'the application of this analogy to social phenomenon, even to history, is inescapable'. In systems that are far from equilibrium, a 'small fluctuation' may 'start an entirely new evolution that will drastically change the whole behaviour of the macroscopic system'.[22]

Erwin Laszlo – pointing to the features described by Prigogine and Stengers – also emphasizes the relevance of the science of Chaos and its butterfly effect to the social sciences. At the crucial tipping point in the evolution of a system, trends that have brought it to its present state break down. At this critical point – referred to by Laszlo as the 'chaos window' or the 'decision window', the system is exquisitely sensitive to a number of alternative small forces. The butterfly effect can take hold; any input, however small, can have enormous impact in changing existing trends and generating new trends and processes. A new trajectory is then irreversibly launched leading either to a breakdown or to a **breakthrough** of a new structure and a new mode of operation.[23]

Clearly, the prevailing world order is in state of disorder; it has the characteristics of the science of Chaos. We may be approaching the **critical point.** Fluctuations have set in making it prone to the workings of the butterfly effect. At such a critical point, the system chooses among a number of alternative factors which are presented to it; such a choice may or may not be totally random. One can wonder which one of a number of available alternatives might be favoured? The Bahá'í community may have little or no control over the operation of the butterfly effect nor over the choice made. However, the vision of Bahá'u'lláh for humanity imparts assurance that His Cause will prevail. Once the butterfly effect sets in, we may wonder, 'Might the path driven through the impetus of the Revelation of Bahá'u'lláh become the favoured choice?'

The Revelation of Bahá'u'lláh has introduced into creation **newly emerging entities** – forces and possibilities hitherto unknown. These forces are not of the phenomenal world; might such new entities possibly influence – at the critical point – the choice made by the system? Can these exert their impact in reshaping humanity through a 'universal fermentation', as expressed by Shoghi Effendi?[24] The theme of newly emerging entities will be discussed in the next chapter.

In this respect certain key questions warrant in-depth reflection. Can the Bahá'í community reap the benefits of the butterfly effect? Can the Bahá'í community stand *in readiness* to take advantage of the butterfly effect once it is set in operation? The answers given to these questions by the key protagonists in the growth of the Bahá'í Faith – the individual, the community and the institutions – must be an unequivocal 'yes'. Such questions lead to the essential features of the plans of the Bahá'í world. The directives of these plans provide strategies and core elements for the attainment of that state of readiness – well equipped and engaged in action. Thus, the Bahá'í community can stand prepared to benefit from such singular events in history.

In this regard, it is intriguing to consider the tremendous power that the Baháʾí community itself can wield. Though relatively small in size, but well prepared under the plans of the Baháʾí world, it can generate an enormous force which under opportune conditions, through its butterfly-like effect, can quicken 'whole groups and nations.'

Conditions which favour the outcome of the butterfly effect. In conclusion of this section, we may reflect on those factors that are fundamental to the successful outcome of the butterfly effect when applied to the growth of the Baháʾí Faith. At the core are those verities which can fulfil the needs of the human soul and induce the spiritual development and transformation of the individual and society. John McManners refers to the 'gold' in religions. He compares the success of Christianity, which had the 'gold', to the failure of Mithraism, which lacked it.[25] That gold, however, we must recognize, can in reality be none other than those **essential verities** at the heart of religions. The systematic plans of the Baháʾí world implement strategies for the infusion of those verities – which inspire and regenerate the individual – setting in motion a wave of collective transformation to fuel an ever-expanding process, an autocatalytic process.

An autocatalytic process. The butterfly effect is perceptive and illuminating. Once a choice is favoured by the system, an 'autocatalytic process' can set in.[26] As we have seen in Chapter 4, an autocatalytic process implies a continuous self-catalyzing process, that is, a process which becomes self-propelled. In that chapter we considered the implications of the autocatalytic process in the growth and crystallization of the Baháʾí community. In this chapter, the implication of the powerful autocatalytic process for the transformation of global society is highlighted, requiring further reflection.

When an autocatalytic process sets in, the wave of transformation spreads and continues to escalate. Once the unique features inherent in the Baháʾí Administrative Order become operational and manifest, they can empower a process which in turn can serve to propagate that wave of transformation. An essential requirement for this autocatalytic process to take hold is that the worldwide network of Baháʾí institutions and communities, as an organic whole, be intimately and indissolubly interconnected. Within the compass of the Baháʾí administrative system are institutions at the local, regional, national and global levels. Strong bonds and linkages bind these institutions to the community and to the individual at the grass roots – into a cohesive whole, as depicted in Chapter 1. Such a system is well positioned for the operation of an autocatalytic process; its anticipated outcome is significant acceleration of **a thousandfold** in the rate of growth and influence of the Bahá'í Faith. Such a process evokes once again the principle of coevolution discussed in Chapter 2.

Singular points

The workings of the butterfly effect in the course of human history relates to what James Clerk Maxwell called **singular points** in an essay of that title. Therein, he presented thought-provoking insights which apply in particular to our times. Maxwell derived this concept from his work on the simplest physical systems. He further extended this phenomenon to the course of history, proposing that at rare intervals in history there are moments which can be viewed as singular points. At these points a very small force, by its character and position in the whole constellation of events, can bring about a change of astonishing magnitude, as with a pebble starting an avalanche.[27] Maxwell believed that taking advantage of these points can produce great results:

> Every existence above a certain rank has its singular points: the higher the rank the more of them. At these points, influences whose physical magnitude is too small to be taken account of by a finite being, may produce results of the greatest importance. All great results produced by human endeavour depend on taking advantage of these singular states when they occur.[28]

Maxwell continued on to quote Shakespeare:

> There is a tide in the affairs of men
> Which, taken at the flood, leads on to fortune . . .[29]

Lewis Mumford proposes that, in reality, such a singular point may be at hand. Therefore, it is important to be prepared – like the early Christians – to take bold action.[30] He refers to Maxwell's insight that at such unique points in history an infinitesimal force can bring about significant change; this was an early expression of the butterfly effect.

Our particular point in time, with its attendant turbulence, instability, convergences and possibilities, has characteristics of a singular point in the course of human history. It is at such times that a relatively small force, when appropriately placed, can set in motion a landslide, an avalanche accelerating the course of history toward its ultimate destination, a world civilization. Nassim Taleb, in his widely acclaimed book *The Black Swan*[31] discusses the enormous impact of uncommon events. Such unexpected and rare events can under appropriate conditions have monumental outcomes, setting in motion the butterfly effect of the Chaos process.

Reference, once again, to the following statement of Shoghi Effendi underscores the suddenness of such a phenomenon and its revolutionizing effect:

> . . . will suddenly revolutionize the fortunes of the Faith, derange the equilibrium of the world, and reinforce a thousandfold the numerical strength as well as the material power and the spiritual authority of the Faith of Bahá'u'lláh.[32]

The course of history is moving toward its culmination, a global civilization. A new spiritual era is opening before us. It is in this light that the Bahá'í community sees the fulfilment of the mission of Bahá'u'lláh and the dynamic and significant role of the community of His followers in the process of acceleration of the course of history toward its culmination. Bahá'u'lláh proclaims: 'The whole earth is now in state of pregnancy. The day is approaching when it will have yielded its noblest fruits . . .'[33] These words hold the promise of that outcome.

Chain of events

Shoghi Effendi refers to a 'chain of events' prophesied by 'Abdu'l-Bahá – *sudden and revolutionizing events resulting in a thousandfold increase* in the growth and influence of the Bahá'í Faith. We can neither anticipate nor 'dimly visualize' the character, or the timing of the sequence of events which must precede 'mass conversion'. However, we know that such chain of events will be 'momentous and possibly catastrophic in nature' with an outcome that will 'revolutionize the fortunes of the Faith, derange the equilibrium of the world, and reinforce a thousandfold' its 'numerical strength'.[34]

On one hand, the prevailing worldwide crisis has permeated all dimensions of human society; this may impart an inkling of the world-shaking impact of such events on the temper of our times – on the hearts, minds and souls of the inhabitants of this planet. On the other hand, such a momentous chain of events in the course of history, together with developments in science and technology, must favour the accelerated advancement of the Bahá'í Faith.

Developments in science and technology favourable to growth

Developments in science, technology and innovations hold unforeseen possibilities. Space travel illustrates this point. Peter Russell, in his book *The Global Brain*, calls attention to this matter, citing an article published in 1948 in *Science Digest* predicting that 'landing and moving around the moon offers so many serious problems for human beings that it may take science another two hundred years to lick them'.[35] A later prediction suggested that landing on the moon would not be possible before the year 2000. The moon landing, however, became a reality in 1969, a mere 21 years from the prediction in *Science Digest*. What had not been taken into account was the monumental acceleration in scientific and technological developments and innovations. Similarly, unanticipated developments in science, technology and innovations hold unimagined possibilities for enhancing the growth of the Bahá'í Faith.

Such advances over a century and half since the birth of the Bahá'í Revelation have been astonishing. They have far surpassed the advances of previous centuries. These developments have continued, at a yet greater acceleration, during the past few decades. As we look back over this short span of time, we are impressed and in awe, astonished at that which may lie ahead – the prospect of a yet greater acceleration in the rate of development in all sciences and technologies. The Internet has generated unimagined possibilities for the spread of ideas and stimulation of discourse relating to all aspects of human society. In this global age, such developments are bound to exert an effect of astounding proportions on the spread of the transforming impact and the worldwide influence of Bahá'í ideals. Such an outcome will be sudden; the butterfly effect and the process of globalization may work in synergy to bring about a yet greater level of enhancement: *of a thousandfold, in the worldwide influence of the Bahá'í Faith.*

PART 2

6

THE TWOFOLD PROCESS AND GROWTH

> We stand on the threshold of an age whose convulsions proclaim alike the death-pangs of the old order and the birth-pangs of the new. Through the generating influence of the Faith announced by Bahá'u'lláh this New World Order may be said to have been conceived. We can, at the present moment, experience its stirrings in the womb of a travailing age – an age waiting for the appointed hour at which it can cast its burden and yield its fairest fruit
>
> *Shoghi Effendi* [1]

The worldwide expansion and development of the Bahá'í community under the plans of the Bahá'í world are remarkable for a Faith which had its beginning in the mid-nineteenth century. Nonetheless, the magnitude of the vision of Bahá'u'lláh for humanity – the creation of the 'nucleus of a glorious civilization'[2] – calls for a significant enhancement in its rate of growth and influence on society.

The previous chapter examined several unforeseen and unanticipated factors that wield the power to significantly accelerate the growth of the Bahá'í Faith. It was reasoned that once these factors – under opportune and favourable conditions – become operational, they can reinforce 'a thousandfold the numerical strength as well as the material power and the spiritual authority of the Faith of Bahá'u'lláh'.[3]

This chapter explores the impact on growth of a twofold process set in motion through the birth of the Revelation of Bahá'u'lláh. Within its compass, this process includes two intimately related forces: disintegration and integration, whose operation in history is inexorably bound to the growth and development of the Bahá'í Faith.

The phenomenon of 'newly emergent entities'

This chapter introduces the concept of newly emergent entities in the natural sciences and applies it to the advancement of the vision and principles of the Bahá'í Faith. Newly emergent entities hold the promise and power to bring into existence a new creativity hitherto unknown.

Newly emergent entities arise *de novo*[4] – that is, they start afresh. The operation of these forces is entirely new. A newly emergent entity introduces new possibilities and propensities into a system: that which was impossible becomes possible; that which was highly improbable becomes probable.

Two examples of newly emergent entities from the natural sciences are offered for the reader's reflection. These are the emergence of oxygen in atmosphere and the emergence of a new star in the physical universe.

Emergence of oxygen

Calling attention to the seminal work of Alexander Oparin and John Haldane,[5] Sir John Eccles, Nobel laureate in neuroscience, emphasizes the significance of newly emergent entities in the evolution of life on our planet.[6] Oparin and Haldane worked independently on prebiotic[7] conditions of life – a time when gaseous oxygen was rare or absent in the early earth atmosphere.

Oxygen, a newly emergent entity, appeared in the atmosphere as a significant product of the activity of photosynthetic molecules,[8] such as cyanobacteria, algae and plants. Cyanobacteria are credited with causing the Great Oxygen Event. Photosynthetic molecules capture the energy of the sun; together with carbon dioxide and water they produce carbohydrates and release oxygen. The emergence of oxygen in the atmosphere as O_2[9] – essential for respiration – was *de novo*. From then on oxygen became abundant, making animal life possible. Sentient beings evolved, capable of self-awareness and consciousness.[10] Humans – that unique creation – emerged with higher consciousness capable of analytical thinking and reasoning.

The emergence of oxygen – the essential stuff of life – is an apt metaphor for the emergence of the life-giving forces with their vivifying influence which have been introduced into existence through divine revelations.

Emergence of a new star

The birth of a new star in our physical universe is another powerful example of a newly emergent entity. The birth of a star generates around itself a new field of gravitational forces which had not been there before. Surely, these newly emergent forces did not arise from nothingness; their primeval origin had existed in the universe. Nonetheless, the gravitational forces which now surround the new star are *de novo* – introducing new possibilities that had not existed before. These forces pull, attract and create tension, generating conditions hitherto unimagined. That which was highly improbable becomes probable. That which was not possible becomes possible.

The birth of a star in our physical universe is a unique and insightful metaphor for the birth of a new Star in the spiritual universe. Though this new Star receives energy from a transcendent primordial source, its emergence in the spiritual firmament is *de novo*; it releases new forces and generates a new creativity formerly not known. The birth of the Star of the Revelations of the Twin Manifestations in the mid-nineteenth century inaugurated new Dispensations. It unleashed powerful gravitational forces – *onrushing forces* – into creation. Shoghi Effendi attributes the 'onrushing forces so miraculously released' to 'the agency of two independent and swiftly successive Manifestations'[11] – the Báb and Bahá'u'lláh.

Bahá'u'lláh affirms that through the Word of God the whole creation has been revolutionized, disclosing 'entities of a new creation':

> I testify that no sooner had the First Word proceeded, through the potency of Thy will and purpose . . . than the whole creation was revolutionized, and all that are in the heavens and all that are on earth were stirred to the depths. Through that Word the realities of all created things were shaken, were divided, separated, scattered, combined and reunited, disclosing, in both the contingent world and the heavenly kingdom, entities of a new creation . . .[12]

From this passage we understand that the Revelation of the Word has introduced commotion into the world system, shaking its very foundations. It has disclosed *entities of a new creation* and made 'the whole earth anew in this day'.[13]

On the power and influence of this new creativity, Bahá'u'lláh avows:

> In this day, the fertilizing winds of the grace of God have passed over all things. Every creature hath been endowed with all the potentialities it can carry . . . Every tree hath been endowed with the choicest fruits, every ocean enriched with the most luminous gems. Man, himself, hath been invested with the gifts of understanding and knowledge. The whole creation hath been made the recipient of the revelation of the All-Merciful, and the earth the repository of things inscrutable to all except God, the Truth, the Knower of things unseen.[14]

'Abdu'l-Bahá further proclaims that the Call of God – raised through the Revelation of Bahá'u'lláh – is the fountainhead for the monumental surge in creativity:

> The Call of God, when raised, breathed a new life into the body of mankind, and infused a new spirit into the whole creation. It is for this reason that the world hath been moved to its depths, and the hearts and consciences of men been quickened. Erelong the evidences of this regeneration will be revealed, and the fast asleep will be awakened.[15]

Thus, the birth in the spiritual firmament of the Star of the Twin Manifestations, the Báb and Bahá'u'lláh, has generated powerful forces; just as its analogue, the birth of a new star in the physical universe, generates new possibilities and new gravitational forces. These forces attract, pull and also create turbulence with consequent disequilibrium and chaos. Their tumultuous effect may be discerned from the following statement of Bahá'u'lláh:

> No sooner had that Revelation been unveiled to men's eyes than the signs of universal discord appeared among the peoples of the world, and commotion seized the dwellers of earth and heaven, and the foundations of all things were shaken. The forces of dissension were released . . .[16]

Numerous passages in the Bahá'í sacred texts, however, bear tidings of the *quickening, vivifying* and *regenerating* outcomes of that discord and dissension.

A twofold process of integration and disintegration

In *The World Order of Bahá'u'lláh*, Shoghi Effendi elucidates the origin, outcome and nature of these two forces.[17] These forces are integrative and disintegrative. The integrative or the constructive force 'stands associated with the nascent Faith of Bahá'u'lláh'.[18] It is advancing toward global consciousness, a global civilization and a new world order. The disintegrative force – its opposing tendency – is moving toward the disintegration of the prevailing world order. Each of these is 'tending, in its own way and with an accelerated momentum, to bring to a climax the forces that are transforming the face of our planet'.[19] Thus, the anticipated outcome of their interplay is clearly the transformation of our planet.

Shoghi Effendi illuminates the nature of this twofold process. The constructive force – the integrating force – is 'the harbinger of the New World Order that Faith must erelong establish';[20] it has 'instilled into humanity the capacity to attain the final stage in its organic and collective evolution'.[21] The disintegrating force is 'fundamentally disruptive'; it 'should be identified with a civilization that has refused to answer to the expectation of a new age, and is consequently falling into chaos and decline'.[22] It 'tends to tear down, with increasing violence, the antiquated barriers that seek to block humanity's progress towards its destined goal'.[23]

The dynamic interplay between these two tendencies compels reflection on their interrelationship and their eventual outcome.

Relationship between the two forces

Several insights may be gleaned from the statements of Shoghi Effendi. First, the dynamic process generated through the Revelation of Bahá'u'lláh is twofold; hence both the integrative and the disintegrative forces must be viewed as parts of the same process; however, as 'opposing tendencies' they are in opposition to one another. Second, a spiritual struggle prevails between them. Third, the disintegrative force is the consequence of a lack of response of civilization to 'the expectation of a new age'[24] – the new world order. Thus the disintegrative force may be characterized as a lack of response to the integrative; it is a deficit.

Shoghi Effendi calls attention to a spiritual struggle of 'titanic' magnitude between these two opposing tendencies:

> A titanic, a spiritual struggle, unparalleled in its magnitude yet unspeakably glorious in its ultimate consequences, is being waged as a result of these opposing tendencies, in this age of transition through which the organized community of the followers of Bahá'u'lláh and mankind as a whole are passing.[25]

Such titanic struggle creates tension, which exerts pressure on the world system as well as on the Bahá'í community. Pressure is an important factor in phase transitions. Increased pressure on a system accelerates its transition from one level to the next. Transition in phase – an enhancer of growth – was discussed in Chapter 2. We can apply this principle to transition in human civilization as well as in Bahá'í community. Increased pressure, the outcome of the titanic struggle between the two forces, can accelerate the transition of human civilization from one phase to the next higher phase – toward the oneness of the human race. Concomitant with this, increased pressure can accelerate the evolution and growth of the Bahá'í community, spurring its quantum leap from one level to the next. Overall the synergistic effect of the workings of the twofold process is bound to be salutary on the advancement of the Bahá'í Faith.

It should be noted that the disintegrative force, in reality a deficit, has no positive value. This important point relates to two fundamental principles of the Bahá'í Faith: first is the doctrine of good and evil, and second is the doctrine of the innate, original, nobility of the individual.

The Bahá'í doctrine of good and evil asserts that only the good has a positive value. Evil is the absence of good; just like its analogue, darkness, absence of light, evil does not have an absolute existence, an absolute value. This line of discussion leads to the question of the forces of light and darkness, to which refer numerous statements in the Bahá'í sacred scriptures. It is important, however, to be wary of assigning to the forces of darkness a separate existence. Hooper Dunbar, in his book *Forces of Our Time: The Dynamics of Light and Darkness*, also cautions the reader on this point.

The dark, the evil, 'the Evil One', all represent absences; they are deficits. Nonetheless, the absence of good can indeed have disastrous outcomes. Herein, a rhetorical question may be raised: Does it much matter whether the destructive process has an absolute value, or whether it is viewed as a deficiency – a lack of response to the integrative process? The answer to this question leads to the core Bahá'í belief on the force which guides the process of history. It relates to its fundamental conviction in the eventual outcome of the course of human history; that is, the fulfilment of God's purpose for humanity. Ultimately this line of discussion leads to reflection on the spiritual reality of man.

Original nobility, not original sin

The belief that man is *graven in the image of God* is fundamental to the great religions of the world.[26] In the Bahá'í Faith this belief is emphasized. Bahá'u'lláh affirms that man's creation is noble:

> O Son of Spirit! Noble have I created thee, yet thou hast abased thyself. Rise then unto that for which thou wast created.[27]

Thus, that inherent nobility must also extend *a priori* to the collective, to humankind. Bahá'u'lláh commands us to arise and fulfil that innate nobility; failure to arise results in abasement.

Belief in the nobility of man leads to reflection on the Christian doctrine of original sin. Once again, we may ask: Does it much matter whether we view the failure to arise to fulfil that innate nobility as a deficiency or whether we assign to it an absolute value – sin? This question goes to the very heart of the belief system of some religions and warrants an extensive theological and philosophical discourse. For the purpose of this writing, however, it should be emphasized once again that the Bahá'í doctrine of *original nobility* rather than original sin is fundamental to the transformation of the individual and the collective.

The old world order and the new world order

Bahá'u'lláh expounds on two world orders, the old and the new; these may be viewed as running parallel to the two forces of disintegration and integration. The force of disintegration (the destructive force) is associated with the old world order and the force of integration (the constructive force) is associated with the emerging new world order.

The disintegration of the old world order and the emergence of the new world order are accompanied with convulsions, described by Shoghi Effendi as the 'death-pangs of the old order and the birth-pangs of the new'.[28]

As discussed in the previous chapter, Bahá'u'lláh has foreshadowed the eventual ascendancy of the new world order through these words: 'Soon will the present-day order be rolled up, and a new one spread out in its stead.'[29] Thus assurance is given that a new order will supplant the present day order. Shoghi Effendi affirms that the emerging new world order holds a glorious promise.

The emergence of the new world order

Reflection on the emergence of the new world order amidst the convulsions of the old order evokes insights from the science of Chaos, a theme which was introduced and discussed in Chapter 5. Reference once again to the following words of Bahá'u'lláh illuminates this discussion:

> The world's equilibrium hath been upset through the vibrating influence of this most great, this new World Order. Mankind's ordered life hath been revolutionized through the agency of this unique, this wondrous System – the like of which mortal eyes have never witnessed.[30]

This statement conveys that the turbulence and the disequilibrium in the world system are the result of the influence of the new world order. The revolution in *mankind's ordered life* is the direct consequence of the new system introduced into creation through the birth of the Star of the Revelation of Bahá'u'lláh.

Furthermore, in the following passage Bahá'u'lláh states that the impending convulsions and chaos are the outcome of the prevailing defective world order:

> The signs of impending convulsions and chaos can now be discerned, inasmuch as the prevailing order appeareth to be lamentably defective.[31]

During our times, disorganization, disruption and chaos are readily discernible. The 'newly emerging entities', outcome of the birth of the Star of the Twin Manifestations, the Báb and Bahá'u'lláh, have generated new possibilities and created turbulence. The ever accelerating forces of globalization – like the analogy of that torrential flow of current in a riverbed,[32] 'the rapids of change', have caused instability and disequilibrium. The potentialities thus released have set in motion turbulence with its anticipated outcome – the emergence of a new world order. Though on the surface the world system appears disorganized, tumultuous and haphazard, nonetheless an underlying world order is emerging.

The prevailing world order is incapable of addressing the urgent needs of an increasingly interdependent world community – no matter how well intentioned that world order may be or how persistently and desperately it may attempt to improve conditions. Efforts in addressing the pressing demands of an emerging global culture with an old world mentality, outmoded methodologies and outworn institutions are bound to remain ineffective. Persistent efforts in accommodating global challenges, 'the imperative needs of a rapidly evolving age',[33] with strategies and methodologies centred on nationalism, partisanship and sectarianism, further exacerbate the turbulence and chaos.

Shoghi Effendi expounds on this theme:

> Is it not a fact that the fundamental cause of this world unrest is attributable, not so much to the consequences of what must sooner or later come to be regarded as a transitory dislocation in the affairs of a continually changing world, but rather to the failure of those into whose hands the immediate destinies of peoples and nations have been committed, to adjust their system of economic and political institutions to the imperative needs of a rapidly evolving age?[34]

Usage of the term 'world order'. In view of the prevailing world scene, 'world order' – an expression fundamental to the Bahá'í lexicon – may seem incongruent. To the overwhelming majority of the inhabitants of our planet, 'world disorder' is real and apparent. Puzzled by the assurance that Bahá'ís evince in a peaceful and auspicious world order, people often wonder with good reason: of which world order do the Bahá'ís speak?

Bahá'ís are given assurance that in this interplay between the two forces of disintegration and integration associated with the two world orders, the Revelation of Bahá'u'lláh is the driving force and will ultimately prevail in the construction of that new world order. They remain confident in the ultimate ascendancy of the order envisioned by Bahá'u'lláh. Their sacred writings impart a clear image, indelibly imprinted in their hearts and on their minds, making it possible for them to discern, *to see*. This enables a clear vision – the perception of two distinct but interrelated forces, the disruptive but also the constructive, that 'universal fermentation' which is reshaping humanity.

Shoghi Effendi writes in this regard:

> As we view the world around us, we are compelled to observe the manifold evidences of that universal fermentation which, in every continent of the globe and in every department of human life, be it religious, social, economic or political, is purging and reshaping humanity in anticipation of the Day when the wholeness of the human race will have been recognized and its unity established.[35]

Numerous evidences of the operation of the two processes are before us. These may not be readily discernible, due to the intimate interplay between the two forces and their consequent entanglements. To most observers the disruptive process predominates, overshadowing and obscuring the view of the constructive. However, the vision imparted through the writings of the Bahá'í Faith imbues one with a sharp perception: amidst the chaos and turbulence of our world, a constructive process – an emerging new world order – can be discerned.

The birth of a new world order amidst the death of the old. This chapter was launched with the following words of Shoghi Effendi:

> We stand on the threshold of an age whose convulsions proclaim alike the death-pangs of the old order and the birth-pangs of the new. Through the generating influence of the Faith announced by Bahá'u'lláh this New World Order may be said to have been conceived. We can, at the present moment, experience its stirrings in the womb of a travailing age – an age waiting for the appointed hour at which it can cast its burden and yield its fairest fruit.[36]

Shoghi Effendi evokes these words of Bahá'u'lláh:

> The whole earth is now in a state of pregnancy. The day is approaching when it will have yielded its noblest fruits, when from it will have sprung forth the loftiest trees, the most enchanting blossoms, the most heavenly blessings.[37]

The overwhelming majority of the inhabitants of our planet cannot readily discern that amidst the tumult of the world a *new birth* may be taking place; a constructive process is at work. Very few have expressed such awareness; among them are Alvin Toffler[38] and Carlos Fuentes,[39] who asks, 'Are we dying or are we being born?'

The metaphor of the hidden image. Metaphors and analogies are of special value in illustrating the importance of sharpening one's perception and viewpoint. The metaphor of a 'hidden image' is often employed by psychologists and some social scientists for this purpose. A picture is used which is a composite of two images. One image predominates; the other image is intertwined within and hidden from view. The predominating image is quite readily seen by most observers at first glance; the second image, however, is not as readily perceived.

Figure 1. The jungle

To demonstrate this point, we can try to visualize a picture such as **Figure 1**, composed of a predominating image of a jungle. Within it is another image, hidden from view. When this picture is first shown, most observers at first glance see only one image in the foreground, that of the predominating *jungle* around whose every corner may lurk unknown dangers. However, when next the hidden image is shown by itself, as in **Figure 2**, that of a *mansion*, one's perception sharpens. Upon viewing once again the composite picture, as in **Figure 3**, a remarkable thing happens! Now the observer can immediately see the hidden image crystal clear and magnificent, *the mansion within the jungle*! What is significant here is that with prior explanation and instruction the perception has sharpened. The viewer can now see the hidden image of the mansion, a refuge crystal clear, magnificent and inviting. In fact, the perception has become so sharp that many observers now see the hidden image – the mansion, the refuge – predominating and in the foreground; no longer in the background!

Figure 2. The mansion

We can apply this metaphor to our world scene. What predominates in the foreground is extensive disintegration of all aspects of human life at both individual and collective levels. This image obstructs the view of the underlying hidden picture – a constructive process, an emerging new world order. What is significant here, is the remarkable sharpening

Figure 3. The mansion within the jungle

of perception that takes place once the image of the constructive process – the emerging *new world order* – has been explained and shown. One can discern it with clarity once its features and anticipated outcomes are articulated and integrated into one's psyche, and once this image becomes etched on one's mind. The effect is a significant expansion in perception, such that upon observing the world scene one may readily discern – see – the constructive process of the emerging *new world order*: the mansion, the refuge within the jungle. Of special significance is that now that mansion is no longer seen in the background; rather, it *predominates in the foreground* – inviting, beckoning, and a *refuge*. It is the integration into the psyche of the vision of that refuge that brings about such level of transformation in worldview, in perception.

With the vision of the new world order deeply etched on their minds, in their hearts and souls, Bahá'ís are dedicated to the construction of that magnificent edifice. Many others see only the disruption and the chaos obscuring the view of that refuge. They regard the assurance Bahá'ís evince in the outcome of the course of history as naïve, simplistic and incredulous. They do not recognize that the vision articulated by Bahá'u'lláh is the reason for that unshakable assurance. With such a crystal clear vision before them, Bahá'ís strive to play their role in the process of history – toward a more advanced civilization, the vision of Bahá'u'lláh for humanity. They know deep in their souls and minds that within the jungle, hidden from view, lies that refuge, that sanctuary – the World Order of Bahá'u'lláh. This perception empowers them to labour toward the construction of the nucleus of that glorious civilization – to stay the course and look beyond the present, in line with the injunction of 'Abdu'l-Bahá: 'Look ye not upon the present, fix your gaze upon the times to come.'[40]

A metaphor from the physiology of vision. The physiology of the visual system provides another valuable metaphor for the sharpening of perception. This metaphor illustrates why one does not readily perceive a process that is in its early phase of emergence.

Our vision can discern objects which have distinct edges – objects with well-defined lines – but has difficulty constructing an image from isolated points or dots, especially if the points are widely spaced and widely separated from one another. This phenomenon can be readily demonstrated by viewing images whose edges are composed of dots and thus lack well-defined edges. The more widely spaced the dots are from one another, the more difficult it is to connect the dots into a sharp line. This becomes especially challenging if the dots are embedded in yet other pictures. The more closely spaced the dots are the clearer the perception becomes. The image becomes crystal clear only when the dots are so closely spaced that sharp edges – lines – can form.

This feature of our physical vision has its analogue in the world scene – the visualization of an emerging constructive process. One can readily perceive processes that are sharply defined, such as the disruption and disintegration of the current world order. But one has difficulty perceiving the widely spaced emerging dots of the constructive process. At first, these dots appear as isolated points. It is only when the process is well advanced that the emerging dots become more closely spaced, enabling one to see. Thus the connection of these dots into distinct edges and lines facilitates and enables visualization and perception of the constructive process which is progressing toward a new world order and a global civilization. In our times, among the few who are able to discern those emerging dots, evidence that things are getting better, is the popular cognitive scientist Steven Pinker, who refers to the 'better angels of our nature'.[41]

Globalization

At this point in time, as we witness the convulsions surrounding the death of an old order and the birth of the new, it is of paramount importance to gain an appreciation of the interactions between the disintegrating and the integrating processes, the courses they are bound to follow, and the prospect of a glorious culmination. The acceleration of both these 'two fundamental forces of the historical process' is the consequence of the onrushing course of globalization that is sweeping across our planet.

Globalization is inescapable; it is intimately tied to the evolution of human society.[42] On one hand, it can benefit all spheres of human existence. It brings together nations and cultures whose problems can no longer be addressed and solved in isolation from one another. Yet, on the other hand, globalization is associated also with pitfalls; among these are unbridled materialism, disparities in distribution of wealth and opportunities, and deterioration of moral rectitude. The trend toward globalization has been built into the very process of human history; its course is unalterable. Its outcome may depend on us – whether or not we choose to strive for a moral and righteous global society wherein unity and justice can prevail for all.

A brief history

The conception of the world as one globe for long remained beyond reach. The map of the world has changed significantly over the centuries, from that of one continent and one ocean to many continents and oceans. The Roman statesman Seneca as early as in the first century AD anticipated that: 'An age will come after many years when the ocean will lose the chain of things, and a huge land lie revealed.'[43]

The travelogue of Marco Polo in about 1300 AD and his description of the Mongol empire and the Grand Khan (Kublai Khan) is said to have inspired and persuaded Christopher Columbus to find a 'maritime equivalent' to these journeys by sailing the Atlantic Ocean. Although significant discoveries had been made by other explorers, notably the Vikings several centuries earlier, some mark the beginning of the process of globalization to 1492 when Columbus set sail and was quickly followed by other European explorers, who rejoiced and exulted in 'finding' new continents.[44] By 1537, the Portuguese mathematician Pedro Nunes delighted in 'new islands, new lands, new seas, new peoples and what is more, a new sky and new stars.'[45]

The trend toward globalization set by these voyages of discovery can be viewed as the 'seaming together' of Eurasia and the Americas which had split 250 million years earlier from one land mass known as Pangaea. The phenomenon known as the Columbian Exchange[46] had a slow but a significant beginning. Globalization at this time had an important biological component as countless species of animals and plants (as well as disease-causing organisms) were introduced to the newly discovered lands and continents.

In the next half-millennium the forces of globalization rapidly accelerated with the 'discoveries' and colonization of Australasia and the African continent and voyages of exploration to the Arctic and Antarctic regions.

Then, with the advent of the Twin Manifestations – the Báb and Bahá'u'lláh – this process became infused with an expanded meaning. The dynamic vision and force of the Revelation for this day inspires, guides and channels its course toward a viable global civilization – the vision of Bahá'u'lláh for humanity.

The accelerating trend toward global consciousness is a significant feature of modern times. The concept attained definition on 23 May 1844, when the very first communication was transmitted by wire over a distance of forty miles, from Baltimore to Washington. That historic telegraph used Morse Code to communicate a few significant words from the Old Testament: 'What hath God wrought',[47] fortuitously signalizing at once two momentous events: the birth of the Bahá'í Era through the Declaration of the Báb on that same day in the city of Shiraz, Iran, heralding (although unrecognized at the time) a global civilization, and the beginning of an era of rapid communication. Since that epic date our world has come a long way, to the age of Internet and now beyond.

The quest for a global civilization. A global age had been anticipated for centuries. From the very beginning of human life on this planet, the unification of people and nations and the advent of an age of brotherhood and peace have been a cherished hope of humankind, expressed through the songs of poets,[48] the vision of visionaries, and the prophecies of the prophets.[49] Some level of unification of the world inspired and shaped the passion and the aim of conquerors throughout history, such as Genghis Khan, Alexander the Great and Napoleon, who set out to accomplish this through invasion and conquest.[50] All to no avail.

The concept of a global world is only recent. Shoghi Effendi writes in this regard:

> It would be stimulating to follow the history of the growth and development of this lofty conception which must increasingly engage the attention of the responsible custodians of the destinies of peoples and nations. To the states and principalities just emerging from the welter of the great Napoleonic upheaval, whose chief preoccupation was either to recover their rights to an independent existence or to achieve their national unity, the conception of world solidarity seemed not only remote but inconceivable.[51]

Referring to the proclamation by Bahá'u'lláh of the oneness of mankind, Shoghi Effendi further expounds on this theme:

> Upon the consummation of this colossal, this unspeakably glorious enterprise – an enterprise that baffled the resources of Roman statesmanship and which Napoleon's desperate efforts failed to achieve – will depend the ultimate realization of that millennium of which poets of all ages have sung and seers have long dreamed. Upon it will depend the fulfillment of the prophecies uttered by the Prophets of old when swords shall be beaten into ploughshares and the lion and the lamb lie down together. It alone can usher in the Kingdom of the Heavenly Father as anticipated by the Faith of Jesus Christ. It alone can lay the foundation for the New World Order visualized by Bahá'u'lláh . . .[52]

It is only in our times that the vision of world solidarity can become a reality. The Kingdom of the Heavenly Father was foretold, but the much longed-for attainment of that quest remains unfulfilled. It is only in our times that it is possible to envision the realization of that vision. It is in our times that we have at long last viewed planet Earth as one globe, with that magnificent Earthrise above the lunar landscape. The foundation of a global civilization was set in the 20th century, the 'century of light'.⁵³ The unification of this planet was the hope and dream of bygone generations, but it was not possible then, for the concept of the world as one entity had no reality.

Ever since the Declaration of the Báb, the forces of globalization have been rapidly accelerating toward a climax – their culmination. Those dots of the constructive process are progressively emerging. Some of these dots are in science, technology and innovations; some are in political unions, some in the fields of transportation and communications. Over time these dots will increase in number, becoming ever more closely spaced; they will align to form those sharply defined edges enabling a clear perception of that unique entity, a global civilization. Such a world civilization, that 'priceless jewel', is enshrined in the 'shell of the World Order of Bahá'u'lláh'; the Bahá'í Faith itself is its 'sole begetter'.⁵⁴

Globalization is a challenge to be met. The accelerating forces of globalization bring increasingly to the forefront the pressing needs of a global age. The long-sought-after world culture and civilization must be an entity which can effectively address these urgent needs.

In this respect questions are often raised. How can a global civilization address global needs? What are the prerequisites of a viable and sustainable world civilization? How can such a civilization be constructed?

The scale and duration of the process of building 'the nucleus of the glorious civilization' are expressed through these words of the Universal House of Justice as 'an enterprise of infinite complexity and scale, one that will demand centuries of exertion by humanity to bring to fruition', and requiring contributions from numerous like-minded organizations and agencies in addition to those of the Bahá'í community.⁵⁵

Though a variety of contemporary organizations and scholars have made contributions to this field, the structure and sustainability of such a global entity remain yet unexplored. The nature and essential character of a world culture and civilization based on moral and spiritual principles can be gleaned from the writings of Bahá'u'lláh. The principles of collective security which He proclaimed to the kings and rulers of His time provide guidance toward the attainment of that objective.⁵⁶ The beliefs and aspirations of the Bahá'í Faith on this fascinating theme invite examination, study and reflection.⁵⁷

The rapidly accelerating forces of globalization are pushing the world system to the brink; like their analogue, the rapids of flow,[58] these rapids of change have generated turbulence. At such times there is a desperate need for a *breakthrough*. During such periods of instability, ideals and principles that contain the seed of collective transformation can catch on like wildfire. The forces of globalization now sweeping across our planet are bound to significantly enhance the rate of growth and expansion of the Bahá'í Faith toward actualization of a world culture and civilization based on ethical and spiritual foundations.

Our times: A turning point

Our times are singular and portentous; they foreshadow a turning point of utmost magnitude. This juncture in the course of history is associated with extreme turmoil as the world moves toward a glorious culmination – the crystallization of the forces of globalization into a viable, vital and sustainable global civilization through the World Order of Bahá'u'lláh.

Turning points bring about major change, altering the course of history. Turning points mark convergences, a coming together of elements and forces; they define a new direction, generating new possibilities, new consciousness and a new state of mind.

Among turning points that shaped the course of history in the then known world were these few: the two-hundred-year Crusades between 1096 and 1270 AD, the invention of movable type making possible a vast expansion in learning due to the printing revolution,[59] the Renaissance and the rise of humanism, and the Columbian Exchange. Among turning points in more recent times are: the moon landing and the exploration of outer space; the discovery of the molecular structure of DNA and the mapping of the human genome[60] (see the Glossary); genetic engineering; the Internet and the digital revolution, to name just a few.

During our particular times, the discoveries of science and technology have opened new vistas, new frontiers. We have gone to the moon and beyond. Our worldview has expanded from local to global with all its implications – from the mentality of an old world order to that of a new world order.

As an outcome of the forces of globalization, our societies have become multicultural, with increasing diversity – inclusive of multitudes of nationalities, races, ethnicities and religions. At the same time, these forces have introduced increased turbulence into the world system. Amidst this turbulence we can discern the workings of the twofold process of disintegration and integration bound to bear their impact on the worldwide advancement of the Baháʼí Faith. It can be claimed that, in its depth as well as in its breadth, we are at the threshold of an expansive overarching turning point in the history of humankind. Its breadth spans the entire planet; its depth reaches all dimensions of human life at individual and collective levels. Its culmination will be the coming together of the human race in a world civilization – in fulfilment of the vision of the Baháʼí Faith.

The temper and tenor of our times mark it as a **singular point** in the course of human history. The twofold process of disintegration and integration, with its associated tension and revolutionizing effect, is accelerating toward its climax – a major **turning point** in the course of human history.

The vision of the World Order of Baháʼu'lláh – the refuge

The vision of the World Order of Baháʼu'lláh invigorates Baháʼís, inspiring them to work toward its fulfilment. This vision beckons; its features have been articulated, explained and defined.

Its cornerstone is the consciousness of the oneness of mankind – 'the pivot round which all the teachings of Baháʼu'lláh revolve'. This is not merely an ideal, 'but stands inseparably associated with an institution adequate to embody its truth, demonstrate its validity, and perpetuate its influence'. Such a vision 'implies an organic change in the structure of present day society, a change such as the world has not yet experienced'.[61]

Such is the grand vision of the final stage in the evolution of human society:

> The principle of the Oneness of Mankind, as proclaimed by Baháʼu'lláh, carries with it no more and no less than a solemn assertion that attainment to this final stage in this stupendous evolution is not only necessary but inevitable, that its realization is fast approaching, and that nothing short of a power that is born of God can succeed in establishing it.[62]

The distinguishing features of this refuge, the World Order of Bahá'u'lláh, are described in these words of Shoghi Effendi:

> The unity of the human race, as envisaged by Bahá'u'lláh, implies the establishment of a world commonwealth in which all nations, races, creeds and classes are closely and permanently united, and in which the autonomy of its state members and the personal freedom and initiative of the individuals that compose them are definitely and completely safeguarded. This commonwealth must, as far as we can visualize it, consist of a world legislature, whose members will, as the trustees of the whole of mankind, ultimately control the entire resources of all the component nations, and will enact such laws as shall be required to regulate the life, satisfy the needs and adjust the relationships of all races and peoples. A world executive, backed by an international Force, will carry out the decisions arrived at, and apply the laws enacted by, this world legislature, and will safeguard the organic unity of the whole commonwealth. A world tribunal will adjudicate and deliver its compulsory and final verdict in all and any disputes that may arise between the various elements constituting this universal system. A mechanism of world inter-communication will be devised, embracing the whole planet, freed from national hindrances and restrictions, and functioning with marvellous swiftness and perfect regularity . . . A world language will either be invented or chosen from among the existing languages and will be taught in the schools of all the federated nations as an auxiliary to their mother tongue . . .[63]

Shoghi Effendi continues on to describe an astounding vision:

> In such a world society, science and religion, the two most potent forces in human life, will be reconciled, will cooperate, and will harmoniously develop . . . The economic resources of the world will be organized, its sources of raw materials will be tapped and fully utilized, its markets will be coordinated and developed, and the distribution of its products will be equitably regulated.[64]

The Bahá'í world community remains assured that the twofold process set in motion through the birth of the Star of the Twin Manifestations, the Báb and Bahá'u'lláh, will culminate in the construction of the World Order of Bahá'u'lláh. It remains confident in the fulfilment of the promise of victory given in the Lawḥ-i-Sayyáḥ, when on His arrival as a prisoner in the penal colony of Akka in 1868, Bahá'u'lláh proclaimed: 'Upon Our arrival We were welcomed with banners of light, whereupon the Voice of the Spirit cried out saying: "Soon will all that dwell on earth be enlisted under these banners".'[65]

Our times are opportune for a transformation that is sweeping across the face of our planet. Concomitant with this must be the advancement of the Bahá'í community – that *fermenting* agent – *toward its own turning point, a significant acceleration in its growth and influence.*

7

THE FLOW OF HISTORY AND GROWTH

Some sparks of history flare briefly and then extinguish. Some have important effects but leave underlying problems unresolved, others ignite epic conflagrations. Such sparks serve as catalysts; the society begins the process of regeneracy leading to a climax of death of the old order and birth of a new order.

William Strauss and Neil Howe[1]

The growth of the Bahá'í community and its worldwide expansion are tied inexorably to the course of human history and the temper and tenor of our times. Questions are frequently raised that require thoughtful reflection. Does history hold a bright prospect? Is it moving toward a culmination, 'the omega point', as envisioned by Teilhard de Chardin? Do our times presage the collective transformation of humankind, as anticipated by Lewis Mumford? Do we stand at the threshold of a new era, as suggested by Alvin Toffler? Do our times foreshadow a major transition in history? Does such a transition portend a shift to a higher level of equilibrium – to an era of relative stability – as proposed by Robert Wright? Does our particular time, with its characteristic features of turbulence, instabilities, convergences as well as divergences, qualify as a 'singular point' in the history of humankind, as suggested by James Clerk Maxwell? Are we indeed on the verge of a global civilization?[2]

Teilhard de Chardin had a keen awareness of the significance of these particular times in course of history. He observed, 'A great many internal and external portents – political and social upheavals, moral and religious unease – have caused us all to feel, more or less confusedly that something tremendous is at the present taking place in the world.' He then asks, 'but what is it?'[3] Lewis Mumford maintains, 'In short, the moment for another great historic transformation has come.'[4] More recently, Robert Wright draws attention to the significance of our times.[5]

Is it possible that such a collective transformation foreshadows a revival of incalculable magnitude – tantamount to a spiritual renaissance of humankind? Can we envision the uniqueness of our role, as accelerators of the course of history toward its consummation in a global civilization? Such weighty questions compel earnest consideration.

At the threshold of a new civilization

Future generations, looking back, will view our times as a *singular point* and a major *turning point* in the course of history. Such a turning point is bound to be expansive, its ramifications extending to all dimensions of human life at the individual and collective levels. Our times may serve as a prelude to a *new awakening*. We may be at the threshold of a new era leading to a global civilization. Such bold assertions compel thoughtful reflection on the significance of our role in this process. Overwhelmed by the task at hand, we may wonder if it could be possible that seemingly insignificant humans can play such a privileged role in advancing history toward its culmination? If so, must we not seize this opportunity – the uniqueness of our times – to take appropriate and focused action?

Such ponderings prompt consideration of the breadth of morality and spirituality that must underlie the very foundation of a viable civilization. These in turn compel contemplation on the essential role of the major religions of the world in the process of history and advance of civilization. The religious worldview is thus evoked, leading in turn to reflection on the philosophy of history. Herein, of particular relevance are insights provided by the Bahá'í Faith.

Civilization: Material and spiritual dimensions

Civilization has been defined as 'the largest cultural grouping of people below that of the human race'.[6] It represents a society in an advanced state of organization and social development. A viable civilization must include two essential dimensions – the material and the spiritual. In this regard, statements from 'Abdu'l-Bahá abound:

> [A]lthough material civilization is one of the means for the progress of the world of mankind, yet until it becomes combined with Divine

civilization, the desired result, which is the felicity of mankind, will not be attained.⁷

For material civilization is not adequate for the needs of mankind and cannot be the cause of its happiness. Material civilization is like the body and spiritual civilization is like the soul. Body without soul cannot live.⁸

For results which would win the good pleasure of God and secure the peace and well-being of man, could never be fully achieved in a merely external civilization.⁹

In another statement, 'Abdu'l-Bahá likens material civilization to a lamp and divine civilization to the light, emphasizing that 'the glass without the light is dark' and that 'material civilization is like the body'; without divine civilization, it is dead.¹⁰ He calls attention to 'two calls to success and prosperity' for the 'happiness of mankind'; one call is 'progress of material world', the other is 'the soul-stirring call of God':

> The one is the call of civilization, of the progress of the material world. This pertaineth to the world of phenomena, promoteth the principles of material achievement, and is the trainer for the physical accomplishments of mankind . . . through the efforts of the wise and cultured in past and subsequent ages. The propagator and executive power of this call is just government.
> The other is the soul-stirring call of God, Whose spiritual teachings are safeguards of the everlasting glory, the eternal happiness and illumination of the world of humanity, and cause attributes of mercy to be revealed in the human world and the life beyond.¹¹

'Abdu'l-Bahá, quoting the Qur'án, writes that a 'superficial culture, unsupported by a cultivated morality, is as "a confused medley of dreams", and external lustre without inner perfection is "like a vapour in the desert which the thirsty dreameth to be water".'¹²

The essential oneness of the human race

Oneness of the human race is fundamental to the mission of the Bahá'í Faith – the establishment of a global civilization. Shoghi Effendi affirms that the Cause of Bahá'u'lláh

> stands identified with, and revolves around, the principle of the organic unity of mankind as representing the consummation of the whole process of human evolution. This final stage in this stupendous evolution . . . is not only necessary but inevitable, . . . is gradually approaching, and . . . nothing short of the celestial potency with which a divinely ordained Message can claim to be endowed can succeed in establishing it.[13]

The organic unity of humankind is the culmination, the pinnacle, of history.

The course of history

A meaningful discourse on the process of history leads invariably to the discipline of the philosophy of history, first conceived by Voltaire and concerned with the purpose and outcome of the course of human history. Some few among notable 20th-century scholars who made significant contribution to this field were the German philosophers and historians Georg Hegel and Oswald Spengler, and the English philosophers and historians R. G. Collingwood and Arnold J. Toynbee.[14]

Over centuries, questions germane to the philosophy of history[15] have intrigued historians. Among these are the following:

- Does the course of history show discernible patterns?

- Does the trajectory of history follow an orderly course?

- Is the course of history progressive?

- Is destiny enfolded in the course of history?

- Is there a supra-historical element which guides the course of history?

- Is there a universal history of humankind?

- Is history moving in the direction of the unified history of humankind with its culmination in a one world civilization?

It is important to note that all these themes fall within the compass of an overarching question: Is there a meaning to history? There is a spectrum of positions on this point that ranges from those who see no meaning to history whatsoever, to those who do not know whether there is a meaning or not, to those who see meaning, purpose and a culmination to history.[16] This latter view envisions a glorious outcome fulfilled in an age of brotherhood and peace. Such is the position of the great religions of the world. This view acquires its significance in the Bahá'í perspective on history; its anticipated culmination finds fulfilment in a unified history of humankind.

Pattern, order and progression to the course of history

The eminent historian Arnold J. Toynbee explores, analyses and sheds light on the question: Does the process of history exhibit a discernible pattern, order or progression? The insights he provides serve as a springboard for the discussion that follows.

Two alternative fundamental views of history

Toynbee explains and analyses two alternative fundamental views of history, identifying them as Indo-Hellenic and Judeo-Zoroastrian.[17] He characterizes the Indo-Hellenic view, prevalent in the Greco-Roman as well as in the Indian world, as the cyclic view of history. The Judeo-Zoroastrian view, which also includes Christianity and Islam, he characterizes as the linear view of history.

These two views may be illustrated through two figures respectively, **Figure 1** and **Figure 2**. Both of these diagrammatic representations are by the author of this writing and are based on Toynbee's analysis.

THE DYNAMICS OF GROWTH

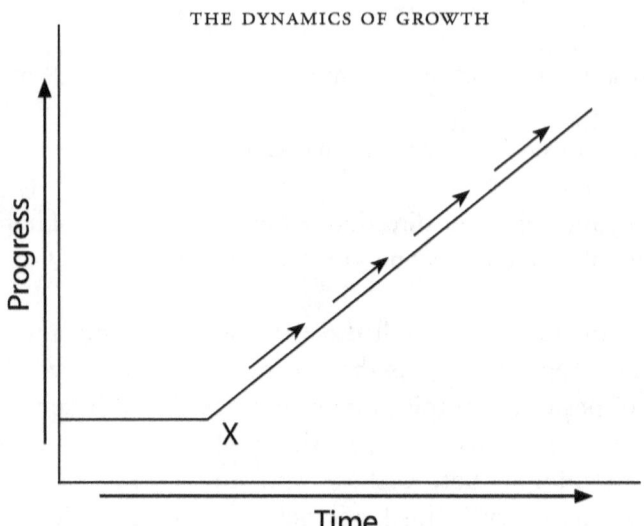

Figure 1. Course of history: Linear view

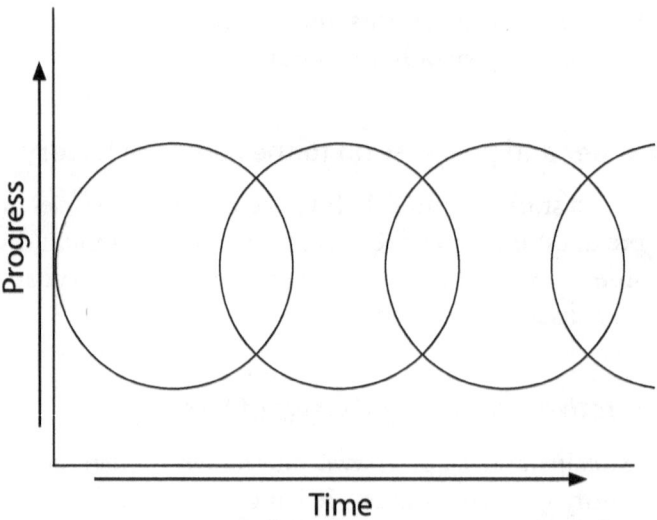

Figure 2. Course of history: Cyclic view

Figure 1 represents the linear view of history. An epic event, the advent of the respective Prophet-Founder (in Christian faith Jesus Christ), marks the starting point (x) to spur progress in history and advance in civilization. Thereafter, the trajectory of history takes an upward course. Figure 2 represents the cyclic view of history. This view follows a pattern which may be represented by recurrent cycles repeated over time. This view does not account for a unique epic event nor for progress in the course of history.

Strengths and shortcomings of the linear and cyclic views of history.
Toynbee sees strengths as well as shortcomings and inadequacies with both these views – the linear and the cyclic.

The linear view has strength inasmuch as it accounts for progress in the course of history. This view, however, has a major shortcoming. It instils self-centredness; it recognizes only one single epic event in history, restricted to a specific time and place. Such a unique and non-recurrent event is considered the motive force for progress in history propelling its upward course. Specifically, according to prevailing belief among many Christians, the advent of Jesus Christ over two thousand years ago was that one and only event which impelled progress in the course of history.

Self-centredness, however, is a major flaw inherent in this exclusive and restrictive view of history. Toynbee emphasizes that self-centredness is 'one of the intrinsic limitations and imperfections, not merely of human life but of all life on the face of the Earth' and that 'Self-centredness is an intellectual error, because no living creature is in truth the centre of the universe.'[18]

The linear view of history, as discussed by Toynbee, is held by a significant number of the followers of the Christian and Muslim religions who adhere tenaciously to belief in exclusivity of salvation or 'finality' of God's revelation through their respective religion. It is essential to recognize, however, that such assertions find no justification in their sacred texts. The Hindu, Buddhist, Zoroastrian, Jewish, Christian and Muslim holy scriptures allude to, prophesy and emphasize continuation of revelation and progression in divine truth through a much-anticipated advent promised to occur at some future time.

The following verse from the New Testament attests to the Christian expectation of the continuation of revelation through the advent of the Spirit of Truth.

> I have yet many things to say unto you, but ye cannot bear them now. Howbeit when he, the Spirit of truth, is come, he will guide you into all truth: for he shall not speak of himself; but whatsoever he shall hear, that shall he speak: and he will shew you things to come.[19]

Nonetheless, views on the finality of revelation and exclusivity of salvation prevail among large numbers of the followers of religions. Insistence on such claims – specifically during this age of global consciousness – presents major impediments to the oneness of the human race and advance of civilization. These two faults promoted by followers of religions will be discussed further in Chapter 8.

According to Toynbee, the **cyclic view** of history – which he characterizes as the Greco-Indian view – has the advantage of being free from self-centredness. This view recognizes that such epical events recur over time. Toynbee, nevertheless, states that this view has a major shortcoming in not accounting for progress in the course of history. Cycles rise, fall and decline – repeating themselves over time with no consequent advancement or progress.

Toynbee argues that neither of these fundamental alternative views of history – the **linear** or the **cyclic** – warrant adoption as we have 'observed the sinister side of each'.[20]

Strauss and Howe also discuss the linear and cyclic views of history, pointing out the strengths as well as the shortcomings of the linear. However, in addition to Toynbee's linear and cyclic, they propose a third view – one that is haphazard, lacking any order or path.[21] This view of history is not compatible with a religious worldview. Nonetheless, during our times – of distress, disillusionment and confusion – such an outlook undoubtedly has numerous proponents.

The Bahá'í view of history

The foregoing discussion provides a backdrop for reflection on the Bahá'í view of history, as conveyed explicitly through numerous passages from the Bahá'í sacred writings. This view is central to the vision and mission of Bahá'u'lláh for humanity.

The ascending spiral view of history. The Bahá'í view may be represented by a diagram of an *ascending spiral*, as shown in **Figure 3**. It is important to note that this diagram is based on the understanding of the present author; all such representations may fall short in capturing principles and doctrines that are spiritual and multi-dimensional in essence. Nonetheless, it is offered for the reader's consideration in the hope that it may inspire reflection and promote discourse.

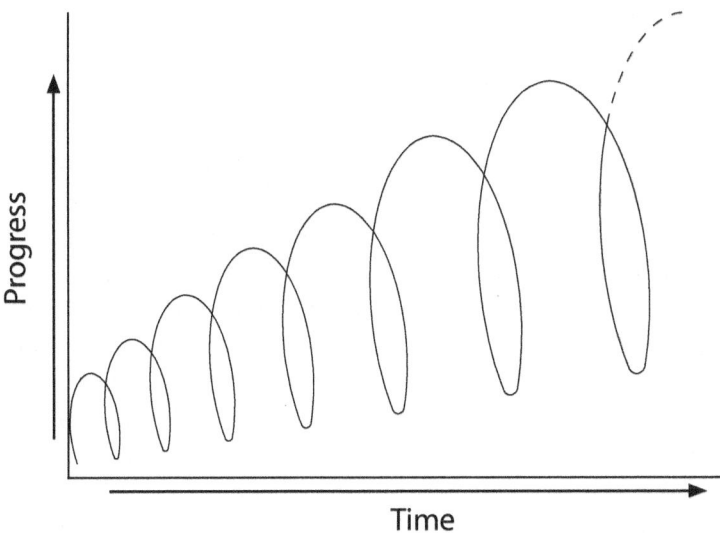

Figure 3. Course of history: Ascending spiral view

At each turn of the spiral, or gyre, each successive cycle becomes larger; that is, civilizations continue to progress and advance over time. Each cycle is grander than that which preceded it; each succeeding civilization is more advanced.

Strengths of the ascending spiral view. The ascending spiral view, like the linear view, accounts for progress in history. The Baháʼí view of history has features of both the linear and the cyclic views, with the strengths of both but the shortcomings of neither. It addresses the question of progress, which confers significance on human history. Epic events associated with the advent of the Prophet-Founder of a world religion impel continuing progression to the course of history. Unlike the linear view, however, the ascending spiral view is free from the sin of self-centredness, described by Toynbee as 'the sin of hybris' [hubris], as it accounts for the recurrence over time of such events. The major shortcoming of the linear view is the question of exclusivity: that only one event in history such as the advent of a Prophet-Founder was the one for all time, never to be repeated – for example, the advent of Jesus Christ, as mentioned earlier. In reality, the sacred texts and prophecies of all major religions emphasize and foretell *continuation* in revelation of divine truth but not *finality* of revelation.

The Jewish prophets anticipate the promised advent of the 'Glory of the Lord', the 'Everlasting Father', the 'Prince of Peace', the 'Wonderful', the 'Counsellor', the 'Rod come forth out of the stem of Jesse' and the 'Branch grown out of His roots'. Christians await the 'Comforter' and the 'Spirit of Truth'. Muslims expect the 'Great Announcement'; Shi'ah Islam the return of the Imam Husayn and Sunni Islam the descent of the 'Spirit of God'. Zoroastrians anticipate the promised world saviour, the advent of Saoshyant. Hindus await the reincarnation of Lord Krishna as the 'Most Great Spirit', the 'Tenth Avatar', the 'Immaculate Manifestation of Krishna'. Buddhists expect the advent of a Buddha named Maitreye, the Buddha of universal fellowship.[22] Such anticipations abound in all sacred scriptures. All these prophetic references, Bahá'ís believe, find fulfilment in Bahá'u'lláh's Revelation. Shoghi Effendi emphasizes that 'to attempt an exhaustive survey of the prophetic references to Bahá'u'lláh's Revelation would indeed be an impossible task'.[23]

Bahá'u'lláh Himself bears witness to this:

> All the Divine Books and Scriptures have predicted and announced unto men the advent of the Most Great Revelation. None can adequately recount the verses recorded in the Books of former ages which forecast this supreme Bounty, this most mighty Bestowal.[24]

The Bahá'í view of history neither tolerates nor accommodates notions of exclusivity. Each succeeding epical event bears a mission of a yet greater intensity; this view imparts progression to the course of human history and impetus to the advance of civilizations. Increasing levels of societal order are measures of that advance. Each higher level represents attainment of unity at a yet larger scale – from the unity of family to unity of tribe, to unity of city-state, to unity of a nation and now toward unity of humankind. The oneness of the human race fulfilled in a global civilization is the anticipated promise.

At this point, the attention of the reader is specially drawn to a doctrine of the Bahá'í Faith that is fundamental to its view of history. This doctrine is based on the premise that the great religions of the world are all divine in origin and are interconnected and progressive in their mission.[25] Religion is pivotal to the advance of civilizations; thus progress is the hallmark of the ascending spiral view of history. The Bahá'í principle of the oneness and unity of religions will be discussed more extensively in Chapters 8 and 9.

In this particular cycle, we are at the beginning of a new *gyre*, a world culture, an advanced level of civilization. The Irish poet William Butler Yeats in his poem 'The Second Coming' employs the image 'turning and turning in a widening gyre'. He perceived his time as the last phase of a great Christian cycle. Yeats had a glimpse of the near approach of a great event expressed through these words: 'Surely some revelation is at hand, Surely the Second Coming is at hand.'[26]

This poem of Yeats, in addition to foreshadowing a propitious event, the Second Coming, also portends that 'mere anarchy is loosed upon the world'. In line with the science of Chaos, an event as awe-inspiring as the Second Coming of Christ must of necessity be attended by turbulence and anarchy. The eschatology of all major religions anticipates that wonderful day of fulfilment – wonderful yet at the same time awesome, heralding the 'Day of Judgement'. The associated anarchy and turbulence set the stage for the advance of civilization to its next level, just as anticipated from the science of Chaos. The process set in motion in 1844 signalizes the beginning of that new gyre.

Destiny enfolded in the course of history

That history may be directed toward an inevitable destination was intimated in 1944 by the British historian Herbert Butterfield, who also wrote, 'there is something in the nature of historical events which twists the course of history in a direction which no man ever intended'.[27]

Several theorists have expressed the belief that the purpose and destiny of history has been immanent and enfolded within itself from the beginning of human life on this planet; they thus propose that the course of history is merely an unfoldment of that destiny. In support of this view a few scholars expound on this verse from the New Testament: 'In the beginning was the Word [Logos], and the Word was with God . . .'[28]

'Logos'[29] has several depths of meaning, encompassing 'Word', 'reason' and 'purpose'. The term has been discussed variously over time: about two thousand years ago Philo of Alexandria[30] believed that Logos signifies a 'divine logos', immanent in the world. Some scholars propose that the direction and culmination of history were enfolded within the process of history from the very beginning of time; thus Logos is the driving force which guides the direction and unfoldment of history.[31] It should be noted, in particular, that the idea of history as an unfoldment of divine purpose is fundamental to the major religions of the world[32] including the Bahá'í Faith.

The premise of religions on the destiny of history: Emergence of order

That history has some kind of a glorious culmination, an emerging order, is central to the theology and the eschatology[33] of the major religions of the world – the Hindu, Buddhist, Zoroastrian, Jewish, Christian, Muslim, Bábi and Bahá'í.

The eschatology of religions addresses the 'last things', that is, the 'end of the world' and the consequent ultimate destiny of humankind. The metaphorical terms 'Day of Judgement', 'end of the world' and 'Day of Resurrection' imply an end point, a culmination to the course of human history at which time an anticipated event will take place, an overarching order will emerge. The great religions of the world believe that the 'last things' signify the beginning of a whole new phase, leading to the advent of an era of peace and brotherhood. That end point for the Jews is the time when:

> they shall beat their swords into plowshares, and their spears into pruning hooks; nation shall not lift up sword against nation, neither shall they learn war any more . . .[34]

> . . . and the wolf shall dwell with the lamb, and the leopard shall lie down with the kid; and the calf and the young lion and the fatling together . . .[35]

For the Christians, that end point is the advent of the Kingdom of God on Earth. For the Muslims, it is the Day of Resurrection. For the Buddhists, it is the time of Universal Brotherhood. For the Bahá'ís, it is the attainment of the oneness of humankind in the Golden Age. Clearly, all religions share the belief that the course of history is directed toward a destiny – a wonderful outcome, some mode of coming together when peace and brotherhood will prevail. The vision of Bahá'u'lláh illuminates that glorious outcome at the end point – which is in reality a *beginning point*, as it ushers in a new era signalized by attainment of the oneness of the human race and its fulfilment in a global civilization under a new world order. Progress in the course of history is implicit in the religious worldview. The ultimate purpose of history on planet Earth is the fulfilment of God's promise through the coming together of humankind.

That the tumultuous flow of history might give birth to an emerging order is exhilarating and intriguing. It evokes once again the science of Chaos, discussed earlier in Chapter 5.

Does the course of history follow the science of Chaos?

Reflection on the insightful analogy of the flow of water in a river bed, as discussed in Chapter 5, serves to illustrate the workings of the process of Chaos in history. The accelerated rate of change since the mid-nineteenth century in science, technology and innovations has escalated the flow, the *rapids of change,* to a torrential level; thus, it has introduced turbulence, instability and commotion into the course of the history of our times. Out of such turbulent flow, order is emerging.

The process of Chaos is ubiquitous; as we have seen in Chapter 5, it extends beyond the natural sciences to social sciences – to the history of humankind, an important focus of these pages. In the context of history, two fundamental questions face us: 'Is the course of history moving in the direction of total disintegration?' Or alternatively, as anticipated by the science of Chaos: 'Is the course of history following a pattern of apparent disorganization, albeit with an emerging order?' How can one distinguish between these two possibilities?

Reflection on these questions evokes a fundamental law of physics, the second law of thermodynamics.[36] According to this law, human society from the very beginning of human life on this planet, if left to itself, should have moved toward increasing levels of disorder and disintegration. However, a retrospective look at the trajectory of history shows the contrary – society has progressed, over time, through increasing levels of order. We may rightly ask: Does an inherent order underlie the process of history?

Furthermore, might the course of the history of humankind display the property of *fractal,* a mathematical feature of the science of Chaos, as discussed in Chapter 5? Specifically, does the trajectory of history exhibit a pattern which is repeated over time at grander and grander levels? Is it possible to discern escalating levels of collective unity, repeated at larger and larger scales, similar to the property of fractal of the process of Chaos?

An overview of the course of history, from the very beginning of the emergence of human society to the present time, displays increasing levels of collective unity at each level of society, from the smallest unit in the scale of human organization – the family – to tribe, then to city-state, and then to nationhood. At this time, when we are clearly on the verge of a global society, can we look to prospects for global unity? Might this feature of self-similarity at all levels of expansion of society qualify the system of history as a true Chaotic process with fractal dimensions? [37]

The trajectory of history suggests that its course might indeed be following the process of true Chaos. That our turbulent and chaotic times hold the promise of an emerging order is in line with the Bahá'í worldview on the ultimate destiny of humankind. Shoghi Effendi refers to the attainment of these progressive levels of unity in human organization:

> This will indeed be the fitting climax of that process of integration which, starting with the family, the smallest unit in the scale of human organization, must, after having called successively into being the tribe, the city-state, and the nation, continue to operate until it culminates in the unification of the whole world, the final object and the crowning glory of human evolution on this planet.[38]

The prospect for attainment of 'the crowning glory of human evolution on this planet' is exhilarating. However, the path to this glorious outcome is tumultuous. It is essential to bring to mind and appreciate that turbulence and instability precede attainment of a higher level order; they set the stage for the forging of strong cohesive ties and bonds – in this case toward the oneness of the human race. The forces that have been generated in our world are sweeping humankind toward global consciousness and the inescapable need for a global world order. That which is taking place in our very midst is a precursor to what Shoghi Effendi views as a 'fitting climax of that process of integration' – unification of the whole world and transformation of human civilization, 'the final object and the crowning glory of human evolution on this planet'.[39]

Shoghi Effendi continues with this sweeping statement:

It is this stage which humanity, willingly or unwillingly, is resistlessly approaching. It is for this stage that this vast, this fiery ordeal which humanity is experiencing is mysteriously paving the way. It is with this stage that the fortunes and the purpose of the Faith of Bahá'u'lláh are indissolubly linked.[40]

Turbulence holds enormous energy for the formation of higher-level bonds

As discussed in Chapter 5, turbulence is a key feature of the process of Chaos. It captures and holds a force sufficiently powerful for the creation of a higher-level order. That Chaos precedes strong bond formation was shown in chemical systems by Ilya Prigogine, who provided evidence that self-maintaining systems, even at a chemical level, can recreate new order when they reach chaotic states.[41] Thus Chaos precedes the formation of strong bonds and their transformation into higher order bonds. The application of this principle to the formation of higher levels of collective unity in the course of history should be readily apparent.

Many express scepticism about the view that history may be headed toward higher levels of unity. In support of their contention, they often provide as evidence a world system which has become progressively more disunified. At first glance such arguments may seem convincing. It is essential to note, however, that the attainment of each level of societal unity has been preceded by significant tumult and turmoil. Reflection on the formation of city-states, nation building, or even the development of European integration supports this point.[42] Furthermore, such turbulence may continue to pose challenges to a system, as we now witness in Europe, until it is further solidified. Turbulence precedes the formation of each level of unity; in line with the science of Chaos, it sets the stage for the formation of higher level bonds.

Shoghi Effendi calls attention to the example of the American Civil War that welded the states of the American Republic into a nation:

> Could anything less than the fire of a civil war with all its violence and vicissitudes – a war that nearly rent the great American Republic – have welded the states, not only into a Union of independent units, but into a Nation, in spite of all the ethnic differences that characterized its component parts . . . We have but to turn our gaze

to humanity's blood-stained history to realize that nothing short of intense mental as well as physical agony has been able to precipitate those epoch-making changes that constitute the greatest landmarks in the history of human civilization.[43]

The foregoing discussion on the course of history has been centred on the premise that its unfoldment displays attributes and characteristics of the science of Chaos. Its features of turbulence, instability and disequilibrium mask a higher level order in the process of emergence. Prigogine and Stengers have encouraged the extension of the science of Chaos to the process of history.[44] Such extension imparts fascinating insights into the tumultuous events of our times and their outcome in the unification of humankind. This understanding is implicit in the Bahá'í view of the course and outcome of history and is fundamental to the grand vision which Bahá'u'lláh offers to humanity.

A supra-historical element

That a transcendent force is guiding the course of history toward its destiny is implicit in the theology of all the great religions of the world and explicit in the Bahá'í sacred writings. The mission of the Bahá'í Faith is centred on the conviction that the destiny of humankind is immanent in history and that a supra-historical element guides its course toward that culmination. Shoghi Effendi in several of his writings refers to the 'guiding Hand that has released forces' and to the 'Hand that directs' and controls their destiny[45] toward the fulfilment of the divine purpose for humanity – the glorious advent anticipated by the great religions of the world. That the plan of God is at work is affirmed by Bahá'u'lláh. The Universal House of Justice reiterates this fundamental belief: 'The Major Plan of God is at work and the forces it generates impel humanity towards its destiny.'[46]

A unified history of humankind

Is history directed toward its culmination in a unified history of humankind? This question has intrigued historians over centuries. That history may be headed toward the unification of the entire human race in one global civilization is an auspicious prospect, thrilling and exhilarating.

It is exhilarating in that it is that 'one thing' which can shed light on the tumult and chaos of the course of history. It is that 'one thing' which can impart understanding of and insight into the events of our times.

Far back in 1896, Lord Acton, a distinguished historian, articulated the idea of a universal history of humankind:

> By Universal History I understand that which is distinct from the combined history of all countries, which is not a rope of sand, but a continuous development, and is not a burden on the memory, but an illumination of the soul. It moves in a succession to which the nations are subsidiary. Their story will be told, not for their own sake, but in reference and subordination to a higher series, according to the time and the degree in which they contribute to the common fortunes of mankind . . .[47]

In more recent times, several notable scholars have expressed their conviction that history is destined to culminate in a global society. Robert Wright writes: 'Globalization, it seems to me, has been in the cards not just since the invention of the telegraph or the steamship, or even the written word or the wheel, but since the invention of life.'[48] Jeremy Rifkin, in *The Empathic Civilization,* presents an overview of the history of humankind; he expresses optimism about the empathetic nature of man and argues that such empathy can serve as the 'social glue' binding people to one another. Rifkin discusses the emergence of world and biosphere consciousness in a world in crisis, emphasizing urgency in averting a planetary collapse.[49]

The vision of the Bahá'í Faith is based on the doctrine of the nobility of man as an individual and consequently as the collective. The mission of the Faith is centred on forging cohesive bonds among members of the human race, fundamental to the establishment of a global civilization. The focal point of the mission of Bahá'u'lláh for humanity is the premise that history is directed toward its culmination in the *unified history of humankind.* Such a culmination will be, to reiterate the words of Shoghi Effendi, the 'crowning glory of human evolution on this planet'.[50]

One world civilization: Fruit of the unified history of humankind

The attainment of a unified history of humankind is fraught with challenges, barriers and obstacles. In 1996 Samuel Huntington, in *The Clash of Civilizations and the Remaking of World Order,* expressed the view that the struggle and clashes divided across the lines of religion, ethnicity, culture and civilization are now the major challenges that face humanity. The events of our particular times draw focused attention to the urgent need to overcome these critical challenges. On one hand, unprecedented mass migration – a characteristic feature of our times – exacerbates this clash. On the other hand, it provides opportunities for forging more extensive bonds of unity among varied populations from diverse civilizations, religions, cultures and ethnicities. Consistent with the science of Chaos, overcoming the attendant turbulence and tumult is bound to escalate our collective society over time to a higher level of order.

Religion: Impetus to the advancement of civilizations

'Major religions emerge as the primary driving forces of the civilizing process,' writes the Universal House of Justice.[51] The Logos, the Word of God, is endowed with such power as to bring about the collective regeneration and transformation of human culture and civilization. Divine truth revealed through the great religions of the world is the motive force for the advancement of civilizations. 'Abdu'l-Bahá asserts:

> The purpose of these references is to establish the fact that the religions of God are the true source of the spiritual and material perfections of man, and the fountainhead for all mankind of enlightenment and beneficial knowledge. If one observes the matter justly it will be found that all the laws of politics are contained in these few and holy words.[52]

Evidence from history supports the premise that the great religions in the past – the Zoroastrian, Hindu, Buddhist, Jewish, Christian and Muslim – have served as powerful forces toward the generation of the world's great civilizations. For example, progress in European civilization can be attributed to a great extent to the influence of Christianity and Islam.

Arnold Toynbee argues convincingly that the 'higher religions' play a major role in the regeneration and advance of civilizations; he views the impetus for the advancement of civilizations as a spiritual one, provided by religions. Such a premise has very few proponents in our times, which may explain why the recognition and appreciation of this eminent historian is incommensurate with his remarkable erudition.

Toynbee's assertion is based on his extensive study of the world's religions and their role in the development of great civilizations. His treatise on the rise and fall of civilizations is covered in an impressive 12-volume work, *A Study of History*. This historian provides insightful analysis on the significant role of the great religions of the world toward the advancement of civilizations.

An emerging world religion – a chrysalis for a more advanced civilization

Toynbee observes that civilizations rise, reach a climax and then decline, and that higher religions play a pivotal role in their regeneration. He further proposes that religions provide the environment within whose matrix civilizations develop.[53] At the time a civilization is in decline there appears, usually from the outside, a universal religion.[54] This universal religion continues to develop as civilization continues to decline; it serves as a ***chrysalis*** – a protective and nurturing milieu within whose sheltered environment the next higher level of civilization takes shape.[55]

A chrysalis is an apt metaphor for an emerging world religion that develops alongside the decline of civilization. Several questions come up that urge reflection. Is there in existence at the present time a universal religion that is developing alongside the disintegration of our present-day civilization? Does the Bahá'í Faith fulfil the conditions of that sheltered environment – the chrysalis – in whose matrix a more advanced civilization is taking shape, destined to emerge in time as that dazzling butterfly?

Reflection on these questions leads to several salient points. The Bahá'í Faith is that universal religion which is developing alongside the deterioration of our present-day civilization. It is the chrysalis for the nurturing and development of the next level of civilization envisioned by Toynbee. Shoghi Effendi refers to the World Order of Bahá'u'lláh in these words: 'that promised World Order, the shell ordained to enshrine that priceless jewel the world civilization, of which the Faith itself is the sole begetter'.[56]

Insights imparted by the chrysalis metaphor

The poetic metaphor of the chrysalis holds rich and profound insights. It prompts reflection on the role of the Baháʼí Faith as the 'sole begetter' of an advanced world civilization. It inspires contemplation on the grand vision of Baháʼuʼlláh for the transformation of human society. It bestows significance on the role of the individual in such a process; it instils nobility.

The first insight to be gleaned from this elegant metaphor is that the environment of the chrysalis – the universal religion – is *essential* for the development and nurturing of the butterfly– the world civilization.

The second insight is that the chrysalis serves a necessary *protective* function throughout the entire process of metamorphosis of the caterpillar into a butterfly until the time the butterfly – the world civilization – is ready to emerge. It is only when the process is complete and the butterfly has gained viability and vitality that it is able to emerge; *not before that time*. The chrysalis, the Baháʼí Faith, and the World Order of Baháʼuʼlláh, surround, nurture, protect and *enshrine* that priceless jewel, while it is developing and taking shape.

The third insight is that as metamorphosis into the butterfly is taking place, the process remains *invisible*. Similarly, as the world civilization is morphing within the chrysalis of the Baháʼí Faith, it remains imperceptible and invisible to those surrounding it – until that butterfly, its wings well developed and strong, emerges out of its chrysalis *ready to soar*.

At this present time, as that world civilization is developing within the sheltered environment of the World Order of Baháʼuʼlláh, it remains invisible to the world at large. Precious few are those who are able to perceive that amidst the confusion, disorganization and disintegration of our society, such an exquisite event is taking place; that a world civilization is morphing. There are fewer yet who can sufficiently appreciate the momentous role they are privileged to play in such a historic process.

Toward a spiritual renaissance

That which is taking place within the chrysalis of the Bahá'í Faith is a major transformation – a *spiritual renaissance*. We must bear in mind that while such a momentous event is happening in our very midst, of necessity it remains *invisible*.

A careful look at past world history shows that as major transformations were taking place, they remained characteristically invisible and imperceptible to those surrounding and even to those experiencing them. The Renaissance of the 14th to 17th centuries AD, which marked the transition from the medieval to the modern world, was not apparent as it was happening.[57] Recorded expressions of the time did not bear any indication that something exceptional was taking place; it was only years later that it was recognized that a major cultural and spiritual transformation had occurred and its impact was felt and appreciated.

Similarly, the vast majority of humankind is unaware of the wave of transformation that is sweeping across our planet at this very time. The magnitude of the spiritual renaissance which is taking place in our midst remains yet unrecognized and unappreciated. Such a renaissance will mark a major transition, from an *old world order* to a *new world order*, from national civilization to global civilization. The significance and magnitude of the emerging world civilization staggers the imagination; its scope, grandeur, and splendour will be recognized when that dazzling butterfly emerges from its chrysalis at the *ordained time*.

A more advanced civilization

Such a transformation is in reality a transmutation, a transubstantiation at the very core of humanity, at both individual and collective levels. Such a transubstantiation calls attention to the substance of man – the true reality of man – a change from material reality to spiritual reality. Transmutation generates a *new race of being* – a new race of men and women. Such a momentous transformation must inevitably exert its influence on the affairs of the entire human race. The Universal House of Justice pronounces:

> Our work is intended not only to increase the size and consolidate the foundations of our community, but more particularly to exert a

positive influence on the affairs of the entire human race.[58]

The Universal House of Justice writes that the Bahá'í Faith can channel the forces of a world civilization through its institutions: 'Bahá'u'lláh has given to the world institutions to operate in an Order designed to canalize the forces of a new civilization.'[59]

Lewis Mumford emphasizes that self-transformation must be at the very foundation of the oneness of mankind and that institutions which promote it may already be present among us. He points to the importance of seminal ideas with their unifying images and designs in this process of self-transformation.

> The political unification of mankind cannot be realistically conceived except as part of this effort at self-transformation . . . Fortunately this transformation is not a sudden desperate move. So deeply it is bound up with the whole broad movement of culture that it has long been taken as the goal of history by many prophetic minds . . . many institutions favoring this transformation are already in existence: indeed many social agents that now work to the undoing of man, like science itself, will actually contribute powerfully to this transformation, once the seminal ideas, with their unifying images and designs, have become clarified.[60]

Herein we are faced with key questions. Does the Bahá'í Faith supply the seminal ideas, the unifying images, as well as the design, for the transformation of human society? Can the Bahá'í Faith supply the dynamic power capable of giving birth to a world civilization?

'Abdu'l-Bahá states that the fulfilment of the promise of oneness and unity of the world of humanity requires a dynamic power:

> Today on this earth there are many souls who are promoters of peace and reconciliation and are longing for the realization of the oneness and unity of the world of humanity; but this intention needeth a dynamic power, so that it may become manifest in the world of being.[61]

Bahá'u'lláh affirms that the object of every Revelation is to effect transformation.

[I]s not the object of every Revelation to effect a transformation in the whole character of mankind, a transformation that shall manifest itself both outwardly and inwardly, that shall affect both its inner life and external conditions? [62]

The mission of the Revelation of Bahá'u'lláh is to bring about a vital and viable global civilization. Dedicated to this end, the Bahá'í community is building its capacity through the global plans of the Bahá'í world.

[T]he capacity created in the Bahá'í community over successive global Plans renders it increasingly able to lend assistance in the manifold and diverse dimensions of civilization building, opening to it new frontiers of learning.[63]

It must be noted, however, that the Bahá'í Faith does not claim to design and construct a world civilization in isolation from other agencies and institutions who may be better suited for this task. Such a civilization will be attained together with the contributions and expertise of like-minded individuals, groups and institutions. The Universal House of Justice draws attention to this point:

[T]he civilization that beckons humanity will not be attained through the efforts of the Bahá'í community alone. Numerous groups and organizations, animated by the spirit of world solidarity that is an indirect manifestation of Bahá'u'lláh's conception of the principle of the oneness of humankind, will contribute to the civilization destined to emerge out of the welter and chaos of present-day society.[64]

Belief in the indispensable role of the Bahá'í Faith in the process of civilization building does not diminish the importance nor the significance of the efforts exerted by others.[65] As the Bahá'ís endeavour 'to create the nucleus of the glorious civilization enshrined' in the teachings of Bahá'u'lláh, it will be important to remember that such a glorious objective will take time; its building 'is an enterprise of infinite complexity and scale, one that will demand centuries of exertion by humanity to bring to fruition'.[66]

The words of Lewis Mumford quoted in this section express hope and anticipation for the self-transformation of mankind – the goal of history. This hope can be realized through the transformation of the individual and culture. The Bahá'í Faith provides those 'seminal ideas, with their unifying images and designs'. Its vision and mission are centred on individual and collective transformation through the dynamic force made readily accessible for the pressing needs of our times by the Revelation of Bahá'u'lláh, the wellspring of the civilizing process.

Our times

For Robert Wright, the current era has the 'aura of a threshold' in which history evolves by leaping from one level of equilibrium to a higher level. He foreshadows a leap, a major 'shift', in our times and foresees that the current turbulence will eventually yield to an era of relative stability.[67] Our times are significant, whether we view them as the 'threshold' of Wright or the 'singular point' of Clerk Maxwell, or convergence of forces toward the 'omega point' of Teilhard de Chardin when the consciousness of all of humanity crystallizes.[68] All these signify a turning point in the course of history and the fortunes of humankind.

In this regard, Toynbee writes: 'A time may come when the local heritage of the different historic nations, civilizations and religions will have coalesced into a common human heritage of the whole human family.'[69] Whether we accept or reject the notion that history is progressive, we can nonetheless discern the signs of globalization in all dimensions of human life, at both individual and collective levels. History is accelerating toward its culmination in a unified history of humankind.

Globalization is inescapable. The type of outcome it produces depends very much on the forces that motivate and propel it. Viable globalization must be based on global consciousness – a supremely exalted state of the collective conscience. The attainment of such global consciousness requires a motive force of great magnitude and potency not of this phenomenal world. Bahá'u'lláh has likened the magnitude of the transforming and transmuting influence of such a force, the Word of God, to that of an exquisite metaphor, the elixir – a legendary substance in alchemy which can transform base metal into gold. He attests to the power of the divine Elixir – the Word of God – and asserts that its potency 'transcendeth the potency of the Elixir',[70] for it can transform the base metal of human character into purest gold.

Several theorists have proposed that history in reality may be heading toward 'the realization of divinity'.[71] This resonates with the Bahá'í view of history – that is, the infusion of the sense of the sacred into human affairs, and the immanence of divine destiny in history. Bahá'u'lláh's breathtaking vision of the emerging new world order and the prospect of its crystallization into a one world culture are the overarching inspiration for this age. Our times are opportune for transformation.

Science, technology and innovations have annihilated distance. Rapid transportation has brought diverse people into close proximity. The ever-expanding scope of information is made accessible worldwide through the Internet; with amazing flow and rapidity it traverses geographical boundaries. These facilitate intellectual interaction and discourse, the coming together of minds and the shaping of collective consciousness. However, this material civilization, this body, needs to be infused with spiritual civilization; otherwise, globalization would only generate greater discord and would hardly be worth the effort it requires.

Our times are unique, their events monumental, with implications that lie beyond comprehension. The advent of the Bahá'í Faith is that epic event at this point in the course of human history; it is the catalyst for the transformation of civilization, the 'spark of history'. The words of Strauss and Howe which launched this chapter continue to resonate:

> Some sparks of history flare briefly and then extinguish. Some have important effects but leave underlying problems unresolved, others ignite epic conflagrations. Such sparks serve as catalysts; the society begins the process of regeneracy leading to a climax of death of the old order and birth of a new order.[72]

The Bahá'í Faith is that *spark of history that can ignite epic conflagrations; the Elixir that can transmute the dross of this world into gold.*

8

THE PARADIGM OF ONENESS OF RELIGION AND GROWTH[1]

> Without the sense of infinite significance, and infinite possibility that the axial religions have kept alive, the passage to world culture would hardly be worth the effort it demands; for the limited goals of peace, order, power, security, wealth, knowledge, would be only disheartening mirages that leave the thirsty soul dry, if they were regarded as life's ultimate consummations . . . On the premises that each of the world religions has hitherto held, none of them can hope to embrace within its fold the entire body of humanity.
>
> *Lewis Mumford*[2]

Passage to world culture demands transformation in the collective character and conscience – of such magnitude as to transmute human substance into a new race of being. The Word of God is that divine Elixir which alone can spark such a level of transformation – as from base metal to gold – as to forge a world culture and mold it into a global civilization.

The Logos – the divine Word revealed through religion – is the propeller of history; it can enkindle that 'sense of infinite significance, and infinite possibility'. Herein, one is faced with an inescapable question: Which of the world's existing religions can bring about the collective transformation of society and its fruition in a global civilization? This enigma resounds through the assertion of Lewis Mumford: 'On the premises that each of the world religions has hitherto held, none of them can hope to embrace within its fold the entire body of humanity.'[3] Mumford recognizes the transcendent influence of higher religions on culture and civilization; he is nonetheless faced with a quandary in envisioning that any of the existing world religions known to him qualifies as that dynamic force that can guide and channel world culture into a world civilization. He bases this dilemma on the premises these religions have hitherto held. Their two fundamental shortcomings are: first, insistence on the finality of divine revelation in their respective Faith; and second, their claim to exclusivity of salvation through their Prophet-Founder. These two major pitfalls are anathema to the oneness and unity of humankind.[4]

Reflection on these two shortcomings leads to a key question: Is there any religion in existence at this time whose followers are free from the faults of insistence on finality of revelation and exclusivity of salvation? The Bahá'í Faith, free from such limitations, offers a cogent response centred on its doctrine of the oneness of religion. It includes within its embrace a diversity of cultures, ethnicities and creeds. This most recent world Faith which originated in the mid-19th century remains unknown and unrecognized by the overwhelming majority of the inhabitants of this planet, including Lewis Mumford. The Revelation of Bahá'u'lláh is that 'spark of history'[5] that can weld diverse religions, nationalities, races and ethnicities into a global civilization.

The great religions of the world have served, throughout history, to inspire and regenerate individuals and to spur societal change. The Bahá'í Faith, the expression of the divine Word for our times, falls within the compass of 'religion', though the prevailing concepts of religion fall short of capturing its fundamental nature: 'The Bahá'í Cause is a phenomenon unlike anything else the world has seen.'[6]

The term 'religion' employed in this writing refers to the pure conception of those great religions of the world – channels for the divine Word – that throughout time have spurred progress in human civilization and culture. Those religions of which history bears record include the Hindu, Buddhist, Zoroastrian, Jewish, Christian, Muslim, Bábí and Bahá'í Faiths.

The central mission of these is to connect the individual to the higher Reality, the source of Good; they thus inspire the fulfilment of that inherent nobility of man – that engraven 'image of God' – fundamental to them all.[7] Religion is a powerful force for bringing about transformation in the character of the individual and the collective – humankind. Religion is other than theology. It is other than dogmas and creeds. It is concerned with human existence – material and spiritual, individual and collective.

Voices of distress over religious discord are increasingly raised in all corners of the world. Such discord is the major challenge of our times, in particular as struggles and clashes that face our world are along the lines of religion, ethnicity, culture and civilization.[8] Humanity struggles to make sense of the diversity of the world's religions. Which one of these holds the truth? How can one explain and justify the differences in their theologies and traditions? Such questions have introduced puzzles begging a resolution that can gratify the mind and satisfy the soul. As over the years solutions were not available, the very best one could have hoped for was mere tolerance.

The Bahá'í principle of the oneness of religion transcends tolerance. It provides the spiritual paradigm and the rationale essential to understanding religious diversity.

The essential role of religion

Is there a need for religion?

History provides ample evidence that lack of appreciation and respect for 'other' convictions have been major factors in harbouring animosity, discord, wars and acts of violence. These have led to the prevailing notion that religion is a disunifying force. Numerous examples are offered in support of this view, among them: the infamous Crusades between Christians and Muslims, discord and conflict between Hindus and Muslims, wars between Catholics and Protestants, and currently acts of violence of radical Muslims against the Islamic and non-Islamic world as well as the horrific acts of terrorism evident in our times. Fanaticism and rising religious extremism continue to incite discord and contention.

With an increasing sense of urgency, a perennial question is raised once again, concerned with the peace and security of our world. If religion is the cause of warfare and strife, are we not better off without it? Bahá'u'lláh admonishes: 'The purpose of religion as revealed from the heaven of God's holy Will is to establish unity and concord amongst the peoples of the world; make it not the cause of dissension and strife.'[9]

'Abdu'l-Bahá advises: 'If religion proves to be the source of hatred, enmity and contention, if it becomes the cause of warfare and strife and influences men to kill each other, its absence is preferable.'[10]

Bahá'u'lláh affirms that the fundamental reality of religions is one. In the words of 'Abdu'l-Bahá:

Bahá'u'lláh promulgated the fundamental oneness of religion. He taught that reality is one and not multiple, that it underlies all divine precepts and that the foundations of the religions are, therefore, the same. Certain forms and imitations have gradually arisen. As these vary, they cause differences among religionists. If we set aside these imitations and seek the fundamental reality underlying our beliefs, we reach a basis of agreement because it is one and not multiple.[11]

'Abdu'l-Bahá cautions that religion can be diverted to wrong ends:

> Our purpose is to show how true religion promotes the civilization and honor, the prosperity and prestige, the learning and advancement of a people once abject, enslaved and ignorant, and how, when it falls into the hands of religious leaders who are foolish and fanatical, it is diverted to the wrong ends, until this greatest of splendors turns into blackest night.[12]

He warns that the followers of religions are holding to imitation and 'counterfeit' rather than to 'the sacred reality of religion'.

> That which was meant to be conducive to life has become the cause of death; that which should have been an evidence of knowledge is now a proof of ignorance; that which was a factor in the sublimity of human nature has proved to be its degradation. Therefore, the realm of the religionist has gradually narrowed and darkened, and the sphere of the materialist has widened and advanced; for the religionist has held to imitation and counterfeit, neglecting and discarding holiness and the sacred reality of religion.[13]

He further emphasizes the underlying inconsistency between 'true religion' and 'counterfeit and imitation':

> True religion is the source of love and agreement amongst men, the cause of the development of praiseworthy qualities, but the people are holding to the counterfeit and imitation, negligent of the reality which unifies, so they are bereft and deprived of the radiance of religion.[14]

Religions must rid themselves of their accretions

The noted historian Arnold J. Toynbee recognizes the presence of two types of elements in higher religions: the non-essential and the essential counsels and truths. It is imperative, he argues, to disengage the essence of mankind's religious heritage from the non-essential 'accretions' which have been added over time due to the transition of higher religions through time and space. Various influences on higher religions have resulted in accretions to such an extent that these religions have become alien to their essential truths. It is important to remove such spurious additions in order to catch sight of the essence within. Toynbee emphasizes that it is essential to 'winnow the chaff away from the grain', but warns that this task must be undertaken with caution and ever so much care and delicacy.

Herein, Toynbee presents an insightful discussion, comparing a religion to a masterpiece painting which has acquired, over time, overlying layers of varnish and paint. Stripping away such accumulations is necessary, while at the same time remaining mindful that the underlying masterpiece escapes undamaged.[15] At times, such additions can include other paintings added on top; once these are removed the full beauty of the original masterpiece can be revealed. He cautions that this delicate task must be carried out ever so carefully, such that the canvas underneath remains intact. This analogy is thought-provoking; the insights therein have significant relevance to the present state of the great religions of the world. Over time, religion, like that masterpiece, has acquired additional spurious layers which overlie and obscure the reality and beauty of its pure essence. It is essential to remove such accumulations in order to unveil the magnificence of the unadulterated Truth beneath the 'counterfeit'.

'Abdu'l-Bahá advises detachment 'from the external forms and practices of religion' in order to find 'the truth at the core' and to investigate the 'original intention' of religions.

> We should, therefore, detach ourselves from the external forms and practices of religion. We must realize that these forms and practices, however beautiful, are but garments clothing the warm heart and the living limbs of Divine truth. We must abandon the prejudices of tradition if we would succeed in finding the truth at the core of all religions.[16]

When the overlying accretions – the 'external forms and practices of religion' as well as the 'prejudices of tradition' – are removed, the Divine truth at the core is revealed. When the masterpiece is thus exposed, it will be possible to verify that the essence at the heart of all religions is one and the same. The Bahá'í principle of the oneness of religion – progressive revelation – speaks to this point.

In quest of a viable global civilization, a question is frequently raised: Is there a need for religion? On one hand, as we have seen, history provides evidence that religions have been the cause of disunity and wars. Discord, contention and misunderstanding among them have posed major barriers to the oneness of the human race. Yet on the other hand, throughout the course of human history religions have served as the civilizing force[17] spurring the advancement of society. It can be argued convincingly that religions have served as a major impetus to individual and collective transformation and moral readjustment. A viable civilization must include spiritual as well as material attributes. The spiritual is inspired by religion and the material by scientific knowledge. A vital and sustainable world civilization may be achieved through the potency of the Word of God, the Logos.

Fundamental to the oneness of the human race is resolution of differences among the great religions of the world and their coming together in the spirit of acceptance, respect and reverence. The oneness of the human race can be actualized only through the adoption of a worldview which recognizes and reveres the divine essence of the great religions of the world and appreciates their essential oneness.

Religion and civilization. Toynbee acknowledges the essential role of the higher religions:

> The higher religions have had a longer hold on a greater number of minds and hearts than any other institution known to us up to date; and this hold has been due to the light that they have thrown for man upon his relation to a spiritual presence in the mysterious Universe in which man finds himself.[18]

Toynbee anticipates the oneness of the whole human race and the possible role religions may play at that time.

A time may come when the local heritages of the different historic nations, civilizations and religions will have coalesced into a common heritage of the whole human family. If that time does come, an effective judgment between the different religions may then at last begin to be possible. We are perhaps within sight of this possibility, but we are certainly not within the reach of it yet.[19]

We are indeed within the reach of this possibility, if we address those major limitations that prevail among the followers of the great religions of the world which have hitherto kept them apart. The Bahá'í principle of the oneness of religion should be considered in this light.

The Bahá'í principle of the oneness of religion

The Bahá'í doctrine of progressive revelation is an antidote to the misconstrued perceptions held by followers of world religions; these have posed barriers to the oneness of humankind. Doctrines which insist on exclusive hold of the truth and the path to salvation continue to generate animosity, contention, wars and bloodshed. Such beliefs promote the sense of 'otherness'. The Bahá'í doctrine of the oneness of religion overcomes *otherness*, transcending it to achieve '*togetherness*'. As the latest divine revelation, the Bahá'í worldview has the power to fuse cohesive bonds among the followers of the world's religions. Its transforming power is demonstrated by the Bahá'í model, within whose embrace diverse religions come together in mutual respect and harmony.

The Bahá'í principle of progressive revelation is fundamental to appreciation of religious diversity. This principle may be viewed as a model, the 'paradigm' of the dynamic relationship among the great religions of the world.

The terminologies used in this writing: 'oneness of religion', 'progressive revelation', and 'paradigm' of the oneness of religion all bear similar meaning and express the Bahá'í principle (doctrine or premise) of religion. The principles of the oneness of religion and progressive revelation are conventional usages in Bahá'í texts. The principle of progressive revelation will be discussed further in Chapter 9. The paradigm of the oneness of religion relates to the concept of paradigm as discussed by Thomas Kühn; this is of special relevance and serves as an important backdrop to the discussion that follows.

Oneness of religion: An expanded paradigm

The prevailing paradigm among followers of the major religions of the world has the two afore-mentioned limitations: belief that exclusivity of truth and exclusivity of the path to salvation are restricted to their respective religion. The Bahá'í Faith addresses these two major shortcomings. It expands the *paradigm of exclusivity* to *a paradigm of inclusivity*.

The Bahá'í worldview may be regarded as 'post-Copernican' in reference to the tumultuous Copernican revolution in the 16th century which precipitated the overthrow of the geocentric model of universe with the Earth at the centre and replaced it with the heliocentric model with the Sun at the centre. 'Abdu'l-Bahá alludes to the ancient view of the cosmos and its relevance to the knowledge in our times. He asks:

> Would the announcements and theories of ancient astronomers explain our present knowledge of the suns and planetary systems? Would the mask of obscurity which beclouded medieval centuries meet the demand for clear-eyed vision and understanding which characterizes the world today? [20]

The Bahá'í premise of religion imparts a new understanding to the spiritual cosmos, the counterpart of the physical cosmos. In the spiritual cosmos, the Sun of Truth – the Divine Reality – is at the very centre; all the great religions revolve around it. This concept of religion is incompatible with notions of exclusivity of truth and salvation and is central to the thesis of this chapter.

The Bahá'í doctrine of oneness of religion requires acceptance of the validity of the great religions of the world, as well as recognition of their divine origin and their essential interconnectedness. Such an all-inclusive and all-embracing principle is firmly rooted in the essential oneness of the human race and is fundamental to the construction of a viable global civilization. In particular, at this juncture in history a sincere and uncompromising acceptance of this principle is an imperative if humanity is to achieve its successful passage to a world culture and a world civilization. Integration of this principle into collective consciousness is bound to bring significant enhancement in the growth of the Bahá'í Faith as multitudes from diverse religions find resolution to the prevailing misconstrued and discordant views.

Paradigm, a word derived from the Greek 'paradigmia', was introduced by Thomas Kühn in his seminal work *The Structure of Scientific Revolution* to signify one's worldview; how one believes knowledge or systems work.[21] The term is described as a pattern or model, an exemplar.[22] Though this expression has often been misused and overused, nevertheless it holds insightful implications which may be applied to the Bahá'í premise of the oneness of religion.

Kühn's exposition of the paradigm shift which took place through the Copernican revolution is of particular relevance to the following discussion on the Bahá'í paradigm of religion. He discusses several stages entailed in a paradigm shift; these include:

a. challenge to the prevailing paradigm through new findings and data;
b. accumulation of puzzles and inconsistencies;
c. the need for paradigm expansion;
d. resistance to the new paradigm;
e. opposition to and rejection of the new paradigm;
f. acceptance and adoption of the new paradigm; and finally
g. assimilation of the new paradigm.

Kühn explores these stages in the context of the Copernican revolution, which forced a paradigm shift from the established geocentric model (paradigm) of the cosmos, with Earth at the centre of universe, to a heliocentric model (paradigm) with the Sun at the centre. His study provides valuable insights germane to the discussion that follows. Similarities can be drawn and insights gleaned by applying Kühn's cogent analysis to the stages entailed in adoption of the Bahá'í paradigm of religion – the paradigm of truth limited to one religion expanded to a paradigm wherein truth is at the core of all religions.

In the discussion that follows, the stages entailed in the Copernican revolution will be discussed according to Kühn's analysis and will be correlated with the stages involved in expansion of the prevailing paradigm of religions to the Bahá'í paradigm of the oneness of religion.

The Copernican revolution

The urge to account for the mystery of creation in a comprehensible manner (in accordance with the state of knowledge of the time) has been a longstanding quest since the emergence of human consciousness. Explanation of the creation of the universe was fundamental to the Greeks and Romans as well as to religions. The Judeo-Christian view promoted the notion that the universe had a distinct beginning in a not very distant time in the past: according to statements in the Old Testament, the creation of the universe took place in seven days. St Augustine[23] basing his understanding on verses in the Book of Genesis, accepted 5000 BC as the approximate date.

The geocentric paradigm of the universe. Aristotle[24] in 340 BC argued the sphericity of Earth; he believed that the Earth was stationary and that the Sun, moon and stars orbited around it in circles. This view was further elaborated by the astronomer Ptolemy[25] in 140 AD into a complete cosmological model. Ptolemy formulated the geocentric model, a paradigm of Earth at the centre of universe. The circular course of the orbits around Earth was based on Plato's[26] view that the perfect form of motion is a circular one. Planet Earth was thus placed at the very centre, surrounded by eight spheres that carried the moon, the Sun, and the five known planets. The outermost sphere carried the fixed stars. What lay beyond was irrelevant as it was not viewed as part of the observable universe.

Ptolemy's model was supported, adopted and promoted by the early Christian Church as a picture of the universe that was in accord with scripture. It confirmed the literal understanding of the Bible.[27] Hence, the early Church found the cosmology of Aristotle and Ptolemy convenient; there was no conflict as the language of science supported its beliefs. The Ptolemic model reinforced religious sentiments and was compatible with the Christian doctrine of salvation through Jesus Christ. Planet Earth maintained its unique distinction – its position of centrality in the entire cosmos. Around it revolved all other heavenly bodies including the Sun itself. The Ptolemic paradigm of the universe also provided a model wherein a place could be designated as heaven. At one time, the moon was considered the residence of the souls of those who had passed away. Dante's *Divine Comedy*, which has influenced centuries of Western thought, literature and art,[28] was in turn influenced by the Ptolemic model of the universe.

Stages entailed in a paradigm shift

a. Challenge to the prevailing paradigm through new findings and data

The geocentric model of the universe. In time, the Ptolemic paradigm of the universe ceased to make sense. It was based on a pattern of thinking which had created dilemmas and inconsistencies; the literal understanding of certain Biblical verses on creation and the Christian doctrine of salvation posed barriers that seemed impenetrable. Furthermore, emerging new data did not fit into the old model of the universe.

The prevailing paradigm of religious truth. Similarly, a paradigm of religious truth based on *exclusivity of truth and salvation* was justified at a time when peoples, cultures and religions were geographically isolated. Under such conditions, this paradigm was effective and relevant to its particular time; it inspired its followers, encouraged their undeviated focus and motivated action. Such a view, however, is no longer tenable.

With the passage of time, our world has emerged out of isolation. Increasing interactions among peoples, cultures and religions have given rise to puzzles, conflicts and inconsistencies which cannot be resolved by the prevailing paradigm – the exclusive hold on truth and salvation by any one religion. The realities and possibilities of our global age raise inescapable questions which can no longer find satisfaction in a perspective which is limited – incapable of accommodating the needs, challenges and dilemmas humankind is facing. A restrictive and exclusive paradigm cannot inspire global consciousness, nor can it channel the accelerating forces of globalization toward a viable one world civilization.

New patterns of interaction characterize our times. As a consequence of rapid transportation, communication and mass migrations, peoples of diverse ethnicities, cultures and religious backgrounds are brought together into close proximity, making significant interreligious exposure a reality of our age. Opportunities abound for close association and

THE PARADIGM OF ONENESS OF RELIGION AND GROWTH

ties of friendship with followers of other religious traditions such as the Hindu, Buddhist, Zoroastrian, Jewish, Christian, Muslim and Bahá'í; these create heightened awareness of the truths and nobility inherent in the teachings of all these religions and the transformation in character they instill in their followers.

Insistence on exclusivity of truth and attainment of salvation through any one religion creates anomalies, paradoxes and puzzles. How can the truth and mystical sentiments of the sacred scriptures of those other religions be reconciled?

b. Accumulation of puzzles and inconsistencies

The geocentric model of the universe was faced with new observations and mounting data that did not fit into the prevailing model; these posed puzzles challenging the Earth-centred model of universe.

The prevailing paradigm of religion. The Bahá'í Faith recognizes and reveres the station of the Revealers of God's truth such as Jesus Christ, bearer of God's Truth, and a path to salvation. However, divine truth was revealed before Christ and continued after Him; on this theme, the Bahá'í writings abound. We face the enigma of exclusivity should we reflect on the question: What about those who lived before the advent of Christ, for whom salvation (according to the Christian doctrine of exclusivity) was unattainable, out of reach? The solution to this puzzle was attempted by Dante in his *Divine Comedy*. What of those countless other beings – possibly intelligent living forms on other planets, in other solar systems, in other galaxies – in this immense universe? Knowledge of the vastness of our universe was not available during Dante's lifetime; thus he was spared from having to address the question: 'What of other beings in this vast universe?'

The current knowledge of our universe, with its awe-inspiring vastness, staggers the imagination. The Bahá'í Faith maintains that God's creation is incalculable. Thus it is likely that in the immensity of the universe there are planets in other solar systems in other galaxies whose conditions are favourable for harbouring life. Though we cannot state with certainty that there are other intelligent beings in the universe, it is nevertheless highly probable. In response to the question, 'concerning the nature of the celestial spheres', Bahá'u'lláh affirms: 'Know thou that every fixed star hath its own planets, and every planet its own creatures, whose number no man can compute.'[29]

The question, remains whether these creatures are similar to us. Shoghi Effendi, writing in 1937, addressed this matter:

> Regarding the passage on p. 163 of the 'Gleanings'; the creatures which Bahá'u'lláh states to be found in every planet cannot be considered to be necessarily similar or different from human beings on this earth. Bahá'u'lláh does not specifically state whether such creatures are like or unlike us. He simply refers to the fact that there are creatures in every planet. It remains for science to discover one day the exact nature of these creatures.[30]

Knowledge of the universe has significantly increased in our times. The question stands whether such countless creatures – albeit dissimilar to us in physical shape, physiology and molecular constituents due to adaptations to their particular environments – are endowed with intelligence and hence *engraven with the image of God*, capable of knowing and worshipping God? This is a fascinating possibility; a definitive answer, however, must come eventually from science. In the light of this discussion, it may be well to reflect on these words of 'Abdu'l-Bahá:

> Then wilt thou observe that the universe is a scroll that discloseth His hidden secrets, which are preserved in the well-guarded Tablet. And not an atom of all the atoms in existence, not a creature from amongst the creatures but speaketh His praise and telleth of His attributes and names, revealeth the glory of His might and guideth to His oneness and His mercy: and none will gainsay this who hath ears to hear, eyes to see, and a mind that is sound.[31]

The observable universe alone includes countless super-clusters of galaxies, each with immeasurable numbers of galaxies, each galaxy in turn with numerous solar systems, each with orbiting planets. The essential question remains: Are there other planets capable of harbouring intelligent life in our universe, in our super-cluster of galaxies, in our Milky Way galaxy? Are such intelligent beings also *engraven* with the image of God? Is salvation also available to them? Or are they denied the knowledge of God's truth and guidance on the path to salvation? Is such a notion compatible with belief in a just Creator? In response to these questions, some may continue to assert that planet Earth is unique, the one and only planet with conditions favourable for nurturing and sustaining intelligent life, the 'chosen' planet among all in this vast universe. The immediate reaction to this assertion must be, 'What a waste of God's immense creation.'

Such were the probing questions raised in a session of the Second Parliament of World Religions in 1993.[32] These questions challenge the doctrine of exclusivity of salvation as promoted by the followers of many religions. Any religious worldview that confines God's grace to a restricted place and time in history is faced with inherent contradictions. A tenacious hold on belief in exclusivity of truth and salvation introduces major problems and inconsistencies, to the extent of travesty and irreverence toward a Creator we believe is loving and benevolent.

c. The need for paradigm expansion

The geocentric model of universe. Kühn explains that increasing puzzles lead to a situation which *forces* expansion of one's worldview, one's paradigm. When faced with new observations and data, attempts are nonetheless made to somehow accommodate such inconsistencies within the structure of the old paradigm. These efforts, however, create yet greater contradictions.

Thus advancement in the knowledge of our planetary system based on accumulated data instigated a *coup d'état* – the overthrow of the rule of the Ptolemic geocentric model of the universe (with Earth at the centre and the Sun and moon revolving around it) and its replacement with the Copernican (a heliocentric model with the Sun at the centre). History provides ample evidence that the transition and replacement of the geocentric with the heliocentric model was akin to a *revolution*, a *coup d'état* (a term also used by Kühn); it was met with much reaction, resistance and opposition.

The prevailing paradigm of religion. Similarly, there is a need for an expansion of the paradigm of religions. How can our experience, knowledge and observations be accommodated by a paradigm which may have worked well when cultures and religions were geographically isolated and knowledge of the universe was limited? How can we address the challenges of our times arising from the ever-increasing exposure to clashing civilizations, cultures and religions?

The Bahá'í paradigm of religion provides a viable solution to such emerging puzzles and conundrums. In order to flourish spiritually, intellectually and materially in a multi-religious world community, it is essential to expand the prevailing paradigm of exclusivity and to revitalize it to one of *inclusivity*. With such expansion, one's worldview is transformed.

d. Resistance to the new paradigm

The heliocentric model of the universe. Resistance to the heliocentric model came from those who were committed to and invested in the old paradigm. There were desperate efforts – in view of accumulating data – to hold on to the established paradigm of the cosmos by attempting to modify and articulate it differently. In the face of the new findings, ludicrous attempts were made to retain, at all costs, the prevailing geocentric model. Epicircles[33] were introduced in order to accommodate the new data on the orbit around the Sun. Such modifications only introduced greater absurdities. Attempts that tamper with truth are bound to destroy the structure and the very fabric of an outdated paradigm as well as any belief in its veracity.

The Bahá'í premise of the oneness of religion. It is intriguing to draw a parallel between the underlying factors which contributed to resistance and vehement opposition to the new paradigm in the two systems: the physical cosmos and the spiritual cosmos of religions; that is, on one hand the heliocentric model of the cosmos, and on the other hand the Bahá'í premise of the oneness of religion.

The implications of these two sets of paradigm expansions bear striking similarities. Both confronted barriers posed by a literal understanding of the respective authoritative texts. Both encountered resistance from those entrenched in the old paradigm. Much of the resistance to the Bahá'í paradigm of religion has been led by those invested in the old paradigm – the authorities in the field of religion.

Both sets of paradigm expansions were faced with challenges: the need for reeducation, adoption of new language and methodologies and the need to acquire a whole new state of mind.

e. Opposition to and rejection of the new paradigm

Opposition to and rejection of the heliocentric model of universe lasted for over a century. New findings and data presented by scientists such as Giordano Bruno,[34] Tycho Brahe,[35] Johannes Kepler,[36] Galileo[37] and others accumulated. The story of Genesis no longer seemed to make sense. However, opposition to new findings was fierce, to such an extent that when – with the invention of the telescope – Galileo gathered evidence in support of the new model of the universe, he was denounced by his university and was forced by the Inquisition to 'abjure, curse and detest' his views of the heliocentric model of the solar system. Giordano Bruno was burned at the stake.

Opposition to and rejection of the Bahá'í paradigm of the oneness of religion continue, particularly in the country of its birth. Vehement opposition led to the persecution, imprisonments and exiles of Bahá'u'lláh, the Prophet-Founder of the Bahá'í Faith, Who proclaimed the principle of the oneness of religion in the mid-19th century. Persecution, imprisonment and execution of the proponents of the Bahá'í paradigm have been intense. During its early history, over 20,000 who adopted and defended this paradigm were put to death. Persecutions continue and persist to this day, including denial of the right to higher education to Bahá'ís and imprisonment of those who seek to provide it.

There is as yet little knowledge or familiarity with the Bahá'í premise of the oneness of religion among the inhabitants of this globe; thus it can hardly be inferred that this paradigm has been resisted or even opposed by large numbers worldwide. Nonetheless, observations based on the relatively small percentage of the world's population who have knowledge of this principle show that on one hand, there are those who have embraced and defended it sacrificially, while on the other hand, there are also those who have opposed it. It can be surmised that when the Bahá'í premise of religion is more widely known there will be those who will rise to resist and reject it; on the other hand vast numbers will also arise to embrace it.

f. Acceptance and adoption of the new paradigm

Acceptance and adoption of both paradigms – the heliocentric model of the universe and the Bahá'í doctrine of the oneness of religion – require overcoming barriers and acquiring a new vision, a new mindset – tantamount to an expansion in consciousness.

The American social scientist Howard Margolis considers well-entrenched 'habits of the mind' barriers to a new paradigm.[38] Such deeply ingrained habits include religious dogmas promoted over centuries based on a literal understanding of a respective scripture. In adopting the new paradigm, the major challenge is to acquire a new state of mind.

In this context, it is important to bear in mind that resistance and opposition to the expansion of the paradigm of the universe from geocentric to heliocentric persisted over a century. However, once accepted, research in the science of the universe advanced significantly.

Similarly, it is anticipated that once the initial resistance to the Bahá'í paradigm of the oneness of religion is overcome – once those essential tools, language and modes of expression are employed – the process of its acceptance will accelerate.

g. Assimilation of the new paradigm

Once the expanded paradigm is adopted it must become integrated into one's belief system – into one's psyche, into one's way of life.

When the heliocentric model of the universe was recognized and accepted, the outcome was a major transformation – through transcending those 'habits of the mind'. Since, significant advancements have been made in knowledge of the wider universe. The rate of increase in knowledge of the cosmos has increased by leaps and bounds. Discoveries have extended past our solar system to galaxies and superclusters of galaxies. Reaching beyond the Earth to the moon and farther out to other planets are exciting realities.

The assimilation of the Bahá'í paradigm is vital for the needs of this global age, as it has power to spark a major transformation in the culture and history of our times and the fortunes of humankind; it can enhance exploration and understanding of the spiritual cosmos.

When the expanded paradigm of the oneness of religions is integrated into one's consciousness, then it will be possible to overcome the barriers of the religious dogmas of exclusivity of truth and salvation. It is then that at long last puzzles and enigmas will find their resolution. Assimilation of such an expanded paradigm is tantamount to opening new vistas to unimagined possibilities.

The Bahá'í paradigm of the oneness of religion, progressive revelation, is now recognized and adopted by a relatively small but significant percentage of the inhabitants of our planet; its transformative power has been set in motion. When this paradigm is adopted, assimilated and integrated into consciousness of a critical mass of the inhabitants of this planet, it is then that a fuller measure of its transformative power will become evident; the growth and worldwide advancement of the Bahá'í Faith will significantly accelerate. It is then that the Bahá'í Faith can look to the prospect of embracing within its fold a sizeable body of humanity.

With the assimilation of a new paradigm, all things acquire new meaning. When a new paradigm is integrated into one's consciousness transformation ensues; one sees with new eyes, all things take on new meaning.

With the adoption and assimilation of the heliocentric model of the universe, the earth and the sun took on their rightful meaning and their proper place in the universe. The Earth was no longer at the centre, with the moon and the known planets as well as the Sun itself revolving around it; rather, the Earth was just one planet revolving around the Sun. The significance of the Sun and the Earth changed radically. Such a change had profound implications; it introduced a quantum leap in comprehension. It changed and transformed consciousness from Earth-centredness to Sun-centredness.

Similarly, the assimilation of the Bahá'í premise of the oneness of religion can bring about a major transformation in worldview, from exclusivity to inclusivity of truth. Religions find their proper placement – as planets revolving in their orbits around the divine reality, the Sun of truth. The transition of worldview from *dogma-centredness* to *God-centredness* brings about a profound transformation. The assimilation of the Bahá'í paradigm confers on each religion its rightful place; not at the centre, but rather as a planet revolving around the Sun – the divine truth – and receiving illumination from that Source.

An in-depth reflection on the Bahá'í premise of the oneness of religion is compelling. It imbues one with a new worldview, a new eye, a new mind. Once integrated into one's consciousness, all of a sudden beliefs and doctrines take on expanded meaning. Bahá'u'lláh affirms that all things are made new:

> The time of former things is past and a new time has become manifest, and all things are made new by the desire of God. But only a new eye can perceive and a new mind can comprehend this station.[39]

All things are infused with new meaning! This is tantamount to a transformation of great magnitude, reminiscent of the transformation which takes place in visual gestalt.[40] With the assimilation of the expanded paradigm, old data can be explained, albeit with fresh understanding. In the context of the new paradigm, the fundamental facts remain unchanged. The facts about the universe were not altered with expansion in the view of the universe. The essential truths underlying religions are not altered. Rather, within the framework of the Bahá'í paradigm of the oneness of religion, they regain their *original intention*.

9
PROGRESSIVE REVELATION AND GROWTH

> The foundation of all the divine religions is one. All are based upon reality. Reality does not admit plurality, yet amongst mankind there have arisen differences concerning the Manifestations of God. Some have been Zoroastrians, some are Buddhists, some Jews, Christians, Muslims and so on. This has become a source of divergence, whereas the teachings of the holy Souls Who founded the divine religions are one in essence and reality. All these have served the world of humanity. All have summoned souls to peace and accord. All have proclaimed the virtues of humanity. All have guided souls to the attainment of perfections.
>
> 'Abdu'l-Bahá[1]

Having in the last chapter correlated Kühn's stages with the Bahá'í paradigm of the oneness of religion, we will now explore the specific features of the Bahá'í premise of progressive revelation – as articulated by Bahá'u'lláh, and expounded by 'Abdu'l-Bahá and subsequently by Shoghi Effendi. Within it, inconsistencies are resolved; each religion finds its anticipated fulfilment and its rightful place. It provides a dynamic framework for the attainment of interreligious understanding essential to the construction of a viable world civilization based on spiritual principles. In the realm of matter, the quest of science for that elusive unified theory of everything remains yet unfulfilled. In the spiritual realm, the quest for that *unified premise* of religions finds its fulfilment at long last in the Bahá'í principle of progressive revelation.

The Bahá'í worldview on interrelationship among religions is represented by the principle of continuing progressive revelation. This view honours and embraces them all. Within this overarching principle the seemingly discordant doctrines find their resolution. The Bahá'í worldview is an expanded paradigm which requires a major shift – an expansion in one's perception – from one which confines divine truth to one religion to one that places it at the centre of all religions, to be disclosed progressively over time.

Essential features of the Bahá'í premise of progressive revelation

The Bahá'í doctrine of progressive revelation includes several fundamental convictions. It asserts that divine truth is absolute and that its revelation through the divine Educators is progressive over time. It affirms that revelation of divine knowledge has been continuous throughout history, through Krishna, Buddha, Zoroaster, Moses, Jesus, Muhammad, the Báb and Bahá'u'lláh, the Prophet-Founders of whom history bears record. These Educators are from the same divine source; their mission is to effect the regeneration of the individual and society and to provide solutions to the urgent needs of their specific age. At this point in the course of history, when our planet has become an interdependent unit, the great religions of the world can, at long last, come together in harmony and oneness. The concept of continuing progressive revelation is implicit in the sacred scriptures of all the great religions of the world – in the Hebrew Bible (the Jewish Biblical canon), the Christian New Testament and the Muslim Qur'án[2] as well as in the Hindu, Buddhist and Zoroastrian sacred texts. The Bahá'í principle of oneness of religion is one common faith[3] that acknowledges the validity of all the great religions of the world. Its specific mission is to transform human society, and to provide guidance for its transition to a viable global civilization based on spiritual principles.

Revelation is progressive and continuing

Following are a few excerpts from Bahá'í sacred writings on the doctrine of the oneness of religion. These selections proclaim that divine revelation is progressive and continuing, that religious truth is not absolute but relative and that the Revelation of Bahá'u'lláh is the latest link in the chain of ever-continuing revelations. 'Abdu'l-Bahá writes:

> Religion is the outer expression of the divine reality. Therefore it must be living, vitalized, moving and progressive. If it be without motion and non-progressive it is without the divine life; it is dead. The divine institutes are continuously active and evolutionary; therefore the revelation of them must be progressive and continuous.[4]

Shoghi Effendi explains:

> The fundamental principle enunciated by Bahá'u'lláh is that religious truth is not absolute but relative, that Divine Revelation is a continuous and progressive process, that all the great religions of the world are divine in origin, that their basic principles are in complete harmony, that their aims and purposes are one and the same, that their teachings are but facets of one truth, that their functions are complementary, that they differ only in the nonessential aspects of their doctrines, and that their missions represent successive stages in the spiritual evolution of human society . . .[5]

> . . . the Revelation identified with Bahá'u'lláh . . . unhesitatingly acknowledges itself to be but one link in the chain of continually progressive revelations, supplements their teachings with such laws and ordinances as conform to the imperative needs, and are dictated by the growing receptivity, of a fast evolving and constantly changing society, and proclaims its readiness and ability to fuse and incorporate the contending sects and factions into which they have fallen into a universal Fellowship, functioning within the framework, and in accordance with the precepts, of a divinely conceived, a world-unifying, a world-redeeming Order.[6]

Two diagrams are used to explain the Bahá'í doctrine of the oneness of religions and the interrelationship among them. **Figure 1** is a diagrammatic representation of the Bahá'í principle of progressive revelation. The disclosure of Truth through the divine Educators is progressive and continuous over time. The circles (seen at this angle as ovals) represent divine Revelations – those of which history bears record – through successive dispensations brought by the divine Educators: Krishna, Buddha, Zoroaster, Moses, Jesus, Muhammad, and the Twin Manifestations, the Báb and Bahá'u'lláh (for 'Manifestation' see the Glossary) These Educators, in response to the requirements of time and place, disclose progressively ampler measures of divine guidance to humanity. They all are centred on the same divine core, whose scope is infinite (represented by the infinity symbol ∞). This core includes those essential eternal verities; among these are belief in ultimate Reality – God –, the human soul, and the innate spiritual reality of man. These core truths are also imparted to

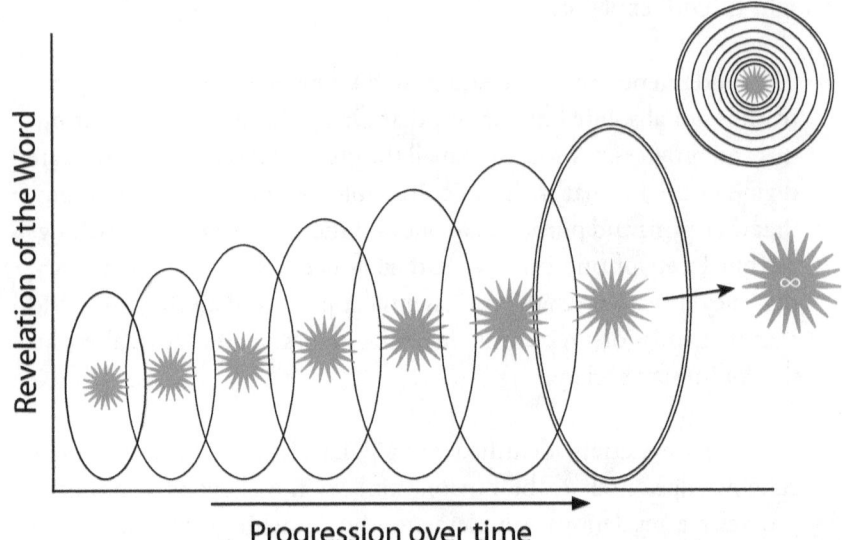

Figure 1. Continuing revelation through religions

man incrementally over time, in greater and greater abundance than that which had been conveyed through previous revelations.

Figure 1 draws attention to the importance of perspective – that is, the need to acquire a refined *point of view* – when looking at religions. In this figure, we note that a head-on view through the common axis connecting their core may be represented by the **inset figure** in the upper right corner; this inset represents religions as concentric circles surrounding the same ***common core.*** This view calls attention to common features shared by all religions.

Reflection on this image may enhance one's appreciation of the essential connection and relationship among religions. All these great religions of the world, in essence, have that common core. They are all from the same divine source and they revolve around the same Reality.

Figure 2 is an enlargement of the inset in Figure 1. This diagram similarly highlights the common features shared by all religions, in several respects. As discussed, the concentric circles all encompass the same radiant ***common core***, the eternal verities (represented by the star). These are surrounded in turn by common areas shared by consecutive religions, such as the golden rule, justice, rectitude of character, and other ethical and spiritual principles.

Furthermore, there is also an ***additional area*** in each successive religion. These represent the guidance each provides in response to the specific requirements of the time, 'the imperative needs of a fast evolving and constantly changing society'. The fundamental mission of a religion – in addition to the regeneration of the individual and society – is to provide solutions to the challenges and urgent needs of its time.

These diagrams draw attention to the two aspects of religion: the fundamental: those eternal verities which remain changeless; and the teachings which evolve over time in response to the requirements of time, place and conditions of life. 'Abdu'l-Bahá elucidates these two distinct aspects of religion:

> [T]he divine law has two distinct aspects or functions: one the essential or fundamental, the other the material or accidental. The first aspect of the revealed religion of God is that which concerns the ethical development and spiritual progress of mankind, the awakening of potential human susceptibilities and the descent of divine

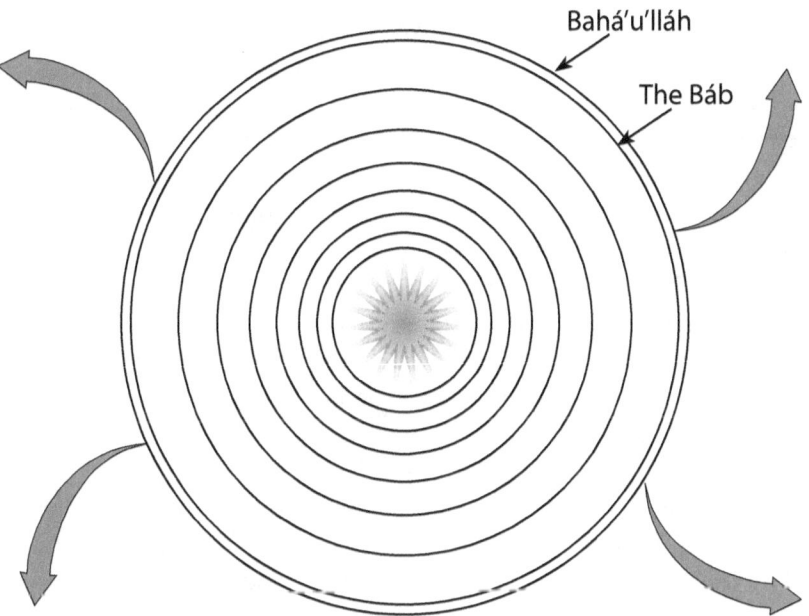

Figure 2. Unified paradigm of religions: Progressive revelation

bestowals. These ordinances are changeless, essential, eternal. The second function of the divine religion deals with material conditions, the laws of human intercourse and social regulation. These are subject to change and transformation in accordance with the time, place and conditions.'[7]

He further explains:

> [T]he foundation of the religion of God remains permanent and unchanging. It is that fixed foundation which ensures the progress and stability of the body politic and the illumination of humanity. It has ever been the cause of love and justice amongst men. It works for the true fellowship and unification of all mankind, for it never changes and is not subject to supersedure. The accidental, or nonessential, laws which regulate the transactions of the social body and everyday affairs of life are changeable and subject to abrogation.[8]

In the history of religions, there are numerous examples of such nonessential laws which were subject to change. Among them, in the Jewish religion, is the law on plurality of wives and laws and ordinances on theft and murder. 'Abdu'l-Bahá explains that such laws were in keeping with the conditions of the times, but not compatible with conditions of the present day: 'His Holiness Moses lived in the wilderness and desert of Sinai; therefore His ordinances and commandments were in conformity with those conditions.'[9] Our particular time requires divine guidance that can speak to the needs of a global age.

The Bahá'í paradigm of the oneness of religion makes sense of religious diversity. It imparts an expansive worldview that emphasizes the evolutionary and progressive features of religions. Figure 2 shows the circles, representing religions, as progressively larger over time. The outermost circle, representing the Dispensation of Bahá'u'lláh, is the largest; here a word of caution is needed. The largest circle represents an 'ampler measure' of revealed truth disclosed to humanity through its revelation by Bahá'u'lláh. This does not signify 'superior merit' but rather its direct relevance to the specific conditions and the evolving needs of humanity – an 'age infinitely more advanced', as Shoghi Effendi expounds:

If the Light that is now streaming forth upon an increasingly responsive humanity with a radiance that bids fair to eclipse the splendor of such triumphs as the forces of religion have achieved in days past; if the signs and tokens which proclaimed its advent have been, in many respects, unique in the annals of past Revelations; if its votaries have evinced traits and qualities unexampled in the spiritual history of mankind; these should be attributed not to a superior merit which the Faith of Bahá'u'lláh, as a Revelation isolated and alien from any previous Dispensation, might possess, but rather should be viewed and explained as the inevitable outcome of the forces that have made of this present age an age infinitely more advanced, more receptive, and more insistent to receive an ampler measure of Divine Guidance than has hitherto been vouchsafed to mankind.[10]

Divine revelation continues into the future

Figure 2 also calls attention to the **continuation of divine revelation into the future.** The outward directed arrows in this figure emphasize that revelation through the divine Educators will continue into the future, beyond the Dispensation of Bahá'u'lláh. The principle of the oneness of religion proclaimed by Bahá'u'lláh precludes any claim to finality in revelation. God's truth is infinite; thus it can never be disclosed in totality. Furthermore, the needs and challenges of an ever developing and changing world require continuation of divine guidance into the future; thus one of the major barriers – religious exclusivity – is removed for all time.

Shoghi Effendi cautions categorically against any notion of *finality* in revelation; such a claim is an inexcusable departure from the fundamental principle of progressive revelation:

> It should also be borne in mind that, great as is the power manifested by this Revelation and however vast the range of the Dispensation its Author has inaugurated, it emphatically repudiates the claim to be regarded as the final revelation of God's will and purpose for mankind. To hold such a conception of its character and functions would be tantamount to a betrayal of its cause and a denial of its truth. It must necessarily conflict with the fundamental principle which constitutes the bedrock of Bahá'í belief, the principle that

religious truth is not absolute but relative, that Divine Revelation is orderly, continuous and progressive and not spasmodic or final. Indeed, the categorical rejection by the followers of the Faith of Bahá'u'lláh of the claim to finality which any religious system inaugurated by the Prophets of the past may advance is as clear and emphatic as their own refusal to claim that same finality for the Revelation with which they stand identified.[11]

Quoting the words of Bahá'u'lláh, Shoghi Effendi continues:

To believe that all revelation is ended, that the portals of Divine mercy are closed, that from the daysprings of eternal holiness no sun shall rise again, that the ocean of everlasting bounty is forever stilled, and that out of the tabernacle of ancient glory the Messengers of God have ceased to be made manifest must constitute in the eyes of every follower of the Faith a grave, an inexcusable departure from one of its most cherished and fundamental principles.[12]

And elsewhere he reiterates:

Nor does Bahá'u'lláh claim finality for His own Revelation, but rather stipulates that a fuller measure of the truth He has been commissioned by the Almighty to vouchsafe to humanity, at so critical a juncture in its fortunes, must needs be disclosed at future stages in the constant and limitless evolution of mankind.[13]

The culmination of the Adamic Cycle

The Revelation of the Báb marks the termination of the 'Adamic Cycle', the cycle of religious revelations which started with Adam. The Revelation of Bahá'u'lláh marks the inauguration of the Bahá'í Cycle. Bahá'u'lláh extols the chain of successive revelations in the Adamic Cycle:

Contemplate with thine inward eye the chain of successive Revelations that hath linked the Manifestation of Adam with that of the Báb. I testify before God that each one of these Manifestations hath been sent down through the operation of the Divine Will and Purpose, that each hath been the bearer of a specific Message, that each hath been entrusted with a divinely-revealed Book and been commissioned to unravel the mysteries of a mighty Tablet. The measure of the Revelation with which every one of them hath been identified had been definitely fore-ordained. This, verily, is a token of Our favor unto them, if ye be of those that comprehend this truth . . .[14]

The Adamic cycle includes the Hindu, Buddhist, Zoroastrian, Jewish, Christian and Islamic revelations, ending with the Báb. Shoghi Effendi refers to the culmination of this cycle:

> The Faith of Bahá'u'lláh should indeed be regarded, if we wish to be faithful to the tremendous implications of its message, as the culmination of a cycle, the final stage in a series of successive, of preliminary and progressive revelations. These, beginning with Adam and ending with the Báb, have paved the way and anticipated with an ever-increasing emphasis the advent of that Day of Days in which He Who is the Promise of All Ages should be made manifest.[15]

Divine truth in the Adamic Cycle was disclosed progressively over the dimensions of time and space. The Hindu and Buddhist Faiths appeared in a part of the world which was geographically isolated from that which was the origin of the Zoroastrian, Jewish, Christian, Muslim, Bábí and Bahá'í Faiths. It should also be noted at this point that in addition to these known divine Educators of whom history bears record, there were other Manifestations; divine guidance has always been made available to humankind. This point is emphasized through a letter written on behalf of Shoghi Effendi:

> the only reason there is not more mention of the Asiatic Prophets is because Their names seem to be lost in the mists of ancient history . . . We are taught there always have been Manifestations of God, but we do not have any record of Their names.[16]

At this particular point in the history of humankind, advances in science and technology have annihilated distance. Our globe has become one entity. All religions can now come together in one common Faith; thus the anticipations of both lines of religions can find their fulfilment.

The Hindu and Buddhist religions, whose origin is India attain the fulfilment of their prophecies in the Bahá'í Faith – the advent anticipated in their sacred scriptures. The Zoroastrian, Jewish, Christian, and Islamic religions, whose origin is the Middle East, also attain their fulfilment in the Bahá'í Faith. In this global age the designations 'Eastern' and 'Western', commonly used in reference to the two respective lines of religion, are no longer applicable, nor are they meaningful. All of these great religions are within the compass of the Adamic Cycle – with Muhammad, the 'Seal', the end of that cycle, linked to the Manifestation of the Báb.

Shoghi Effendi explains the pivotal position of the advent of the Báb in the Adamic Cycle:

> He Who was, in the words of 'Abdu'l-Bahá, the 'Morn of Truth' and 'Harbinger of the Most Great Light,' Whose advent at once signalized the termination of the 'Prophetic Cycle' and the inception of the 'Cycle of Fulfilment' . . .[17]

And the Bahá'í writer Adib Taherzadeh describes the unique placement of the advent of the Báb in the course of religious history:

> He stood in between two religious cycles. With His advent He closed, on the one hand, the 'Prophetic Cycle', which began with Adam as the first Manifestation of God in recorded history and ended with the Dispensation of Islam and, on the other, He opened the 'Cycle of Fulfilment' whose duration, according to the Writings of Bahá'u'lláh and 'Abdu'l-Bahá, will be at least five thousand centuries.[18]

Bahá'u'lláh has initiated the Bahá'í Cycle – the 'Cycle of Fulfilment'. The specific mission of the Bahá'í Faith is to address the urgent needs of this age – a time when geographical isolation no longer poses barriers in a global age.

The temperament of a respective time

The temperament of the culture of a respective time to which Prophet-Founders brought divine revelation is essential to an appreciation of the progressive character of their mission. These Educators disclosed only a set portion of divine truth to tribes and cultures which were at differing levels of development and receptivity. Muhammad came to dissenting tribes of idol-worshippers, while Jesus Christ came to the monotheistic Jewish people. The magnitude of divine revelation through Muhammad in isolated Arabia amidst the peoples and tribes of His time should be readily apparent. Through the transforming influence of His message, the idolaters became monotheists. The revelation of Muhammad induced in these people a significant level of advancement – as a quantum leap.

Toward the attainment of human destiny

Progress in science and technology since the mid-19th century has introduced significant changes in all dimensions of human life, requiring the adoption of an expansive worldview which can be responsive to the temper and tenor of our times. The Bahá'í doctrine of the oneness of religion and progressive revelation is fundamental to such a worldview.

Among those who have embraced this paradigm, many have dedicated their lives and resources to its promotion. Yet, on the other hand, it has met with opposition and rejection by those dedicated to the doctrine of finality of truth and exclusivity of salvation in their respective religion. As we have before seen, rejection and opposition to a new paradigm often precede its acceptance, adoption and assimilation.[19]

Increasing religious fanaticism has given rise to a grave situation in our world; this is especially critical in our times as the forces of globalization are on the move and are rapidly accelerating. The realities of our age pose significant challenges to misconceived and misconstrued doctrines of exclusivity promoted by many followers of the major religions of the world. On one hand, globalization has resulted in more tenacious adherence to those literal beliefs, thus intensifying fundamentalism, militancy and aggressiveness. On the other hand, its challenges have raised questions and inspired interest in the significance and diversity of religions. There is a notable increase in interfaith activities and organizations vested with the noble mission of improving dialogue, understanding and fellowship among religions, and finding resolution to the interreligious conflicts that prevail in our global society.

All such endeavours draw concentrated attention to the urgent need for an all-encompassing worldview that can explain and address religious multiplicity and diversity. There is a dire need for a belief system that can unify all religions. Leo Tolstoy, the eminent Russian writer and philosopher of the early 20th century, had an intense desire to address this desperate need, to such an extent that he considered devising a universal religion that would include all religions.[20] However, the enormity of this task is such that only the Word of God, the *Divine Elixir,* has the dynamic power to bring into reality such a monumental mission.

The time for adoption and integration of the Bahá'í principle of the oneness of religion is now. It was not relevant before. Shoghi Effendi writes that the revelation brought by Jesus Christ

> focused attention primarily on the redemption of the individual and the molding of his conduct, and stressed, as its central theme, the necessity of inculcating a high standard of morality and discipline into man, as the fundamental unit in human society. Nowhere in the Gospels do we find any reference to the unity of nations or the unification of mankind as a whole. When Jesus spoke to those around Him, He addressed them primarily as individuals rather than as component parts of one universal, indivisible entity.[21]

Shoghi Effendi emphasizes this point:

> What other interpretation can be given to these words, addressed specifically by Bahá'u'lláh to the followers of the Gospel, in which the fundamental distinction between the Mission of Jesus Christ, concerning primarily the individual, and His own Message, directed more particularly to mankind as a whole, has been definitely established: 'Verily, He [Jesus] said: "Come ye after Me, and I will make you to become fishers of men." In this day, however, We say: "Come ye after Me, that We may make you to become the quickeners of mankind."'[22]

The knowledge of our planet Earth was limited; the concept of one globe and one human race did not exist before. Our knowledge of the geography of our world has significantly expanded ever since the mariners sailed the oceans on their voyages of discoveries.[23]

The forces of globalization have rapidly accelerated since 1844 with the advent of the Dispensations of the Báb and Bahá'u'lláh. The image of our earth as one entity is a recent view, seen for the first time in 1969 when astronauts first landed on the moon. Our times demand the adoption of an all-encompassing worldview inclusive of all religions and all people. Any view that is exclusive – limiting truth to one religion – will be incapable of bringing together the diverse sectors of humanity. The principle of the Bahá'í Faith on the oneness of religion provides that longed-for doctrine.

It is anticipated that once this principle is widely known and integrated into the consciousness of the inhabitants of this planet, significant acceleration in the growth of the Bahá'í Faith will ensue. As religion is a potent force in civilization, it possesses such dynamism as to 'quicken mankind' – to transform human society and culture.

The Bahá'í principle of continuing progressive revelation has momentous implications; it can revolutionize mindsets, marking a turning point in the fortunes of humankind. There are numerous examples of revolutionary breakthroughs. In the domain of biology, the discovery of the structure of DNA as shown through the data of Watson, Crick, Wilkins and Franklin,[24] transformed the field. This new model of DNA provided the framework for major advances, leading to prospects for the betterment and refinement of human life. In the domain of religion, the Bahá'í principle of the oneness of religion sets the high point. It has significant implications for inspiring individuals to arise and fulfil their inherent nobility. *It can transform and transmute mindsets and civilizations. It can quicken the human race toward the attainment of its destiny.*

PART 3

10
THE WORLDWIDE BAHÁ'Í COMMUNITY AND THE UNIFICATION OF WORLD SOCIETY

> ... the reconstruction of mankind, as the result of the universal recognition of its oneness and wholeness, will bring in its wake the spiritualization of the masses, consequent to the recognition of the character, and the acknowledgment of the claims, of the Faith of Bahá'u'lláh – the essential condition to that ultimate fusion of all races, creeds, classes, and nations which must signalize the emergence of His New World Order.
>
> *Shoghi Effendi*[1]

The growth and expansion of the Bahá'í community has been the central focus of this book. Increase in the worldwide influence of the Bahá'í Faith is an imperative if its principles are to be integrated into human consciousness and character; thus the transformative power of the Revelation of Bahá'u'lláh can spiritualize the masses – toward the construction of a long-anticipated global civilization under a new world order, its fruition in a new race of men and women.

Millions of Bahá'ís across the face of this planet add their compelling voices to those of other organizations, groups and individuals who are also dedicated to this noble calling – a quest which for centuries has stirred deep longings in humankind.

Creating the nucleus of a global civilization is an enterprise of great magnitude requiring a profound change at the level of the individual and the structure of society. At its very foundation, such a change must be based on a measure of transformation that can extend beyond the individual to the collective such that it may bring forth societal change and advance in civilization. The Bahá'í Faith supplies the motive force for regeneration in the character of society, tantamount to a *spiritual renaissance*. Such magnitude of transformation is a requisite for the emergence of a new world order and a vital and sustainable world culture within whose nurturing environment a new race of men and women can flourish and all classes, nations and religions can find their fulfilment.

Inexorably tied to this lofty objective is the worldwide advancement of the Bahá'í community itself – such that the message of Bahá'u'lláh can *penetrate*, *suffuse*[2] and transform the consciousness of vast numbers of the inhabitants of this planet.

As emphasized throughout this writing, such level of growth must include two essential and inseparable dimensions: quantitative growth – that is, growth in the number of those who become connected to the mission of Bahá'u'lláh; and qualitative growth – that is, transformation, the outcome of integration and assimilation of the spirit and principles of the Bahá'í Faith into one's consciousness. This concept of growth remains fundamental to the creation of that vital and sustainable world civilization envisioned by Bahá'u'lláh, illumined by 'Abdu'l-Bahá, expounded by Shoghi Effendi and addressed through the systematic plans of the supreme head of the Bahá'í Faith today, the Universal House of Justice.

The World Order ushered in by Bahá'u'lláh

Shoghi Effendi provides an insightful analogy, likening the 'embryonic World Order of Bahá'u'lláh'[3] to the development of an embryo in the womb – a theme introduced in Chapter 6.[4]

The present-day order is defective and at risk of collapse

Bahá'u'lláh 'solemnly asserts' that 'the day is approaching when We will have rolled up the world and all that is therein, and spread out a new Order in its stead. He, verily, is powerful over all things.' Bahá'u'lláh draws attention to the failure of the current world order: 'The signs of impending convulsions and chaos can now be discerned, inasmuch as the prevailing Order appeareth to be lamentably defective.'[5]

In the Tablet of the World (Lawḥ-i-Dunyá) Bahá'u'lláh emphasizes the instability of the present order; its *hardened clay* can crumble with a *mere touch of moisture*:

> Wherefore fear ye, O My well-beloved ones? Who is it that can dismay you? A touch of moisture sufficeth to dissolve the hardened clay out of which this perverse generation is moulded.[6]

The image of 'feet of clay' is an insightful and powerful metaphor from the Book of Daniel in the Old Testament describing the dream of King Nebuchadnezzar.[7] The king saw a great image; its head was of gold, its breast and arms of silver, its belly and thighs of brass, its legs of iron; but its feet were part iron and part clay. In his dream, the whole image broke; the pieces were carried away in the wind. Daniel offered his interpretation, relating the king's dream to the rise and fall of worldly powers. A series of weaker kingdoms would follow after Nebuchadnezzar; these would finally break up, like the great image with feet of clay. Next, these would be replaced with the kingdom of God.

Such is indeed the present order of the world – it rests on *feet of clay*; though seemingly majestic, its instability is extreme.

The collapse of powerful empires and civilizations

Shelley's celebrated poem 'Ozymandias' (the mighty Egyptian Pharaoh Ramses II) encapsulates the evanescence of powerful empires:

> And on the pedestal those words appear:
> My name is Ozymandias, king of kings:
> Look on my words, ye Mighty, and despair! . . .
>
> . . . Nothing beside remains. Round the decay
> Of that colossal wreck, boundless and bare
> The lone and level sands stretch far away.[8]

The collapse of civilizations is a timely and widely discussed concern. Jared Diamond, in his book *Collapse: How Societies Choose to Fail or Succeed*, attributes the collapse of a variety of civilizations to several fundamental causes – among them, inappropriate use and abuse of the environment, and failure to foresee impending disasters in order to take prompt and appropriate action. At the foundation of some of the causes that could have been averted was the desecration of the sacred. The restoration of the sense of the sacred is fundamental to the preservation of civilization and the reconstruction of human society.

The seemingly mighty superstructure of the present world system is at risk of collapse. Its vulnerability to breakage is apparent. Its cracks are widening; its feet of clay are crumbling. One may ask: Can its downfall be averted? Might that unstable structure be replaced by one which rests on solid foundations – on secure and stable feet? Might the edifice, Bahá'u'lláh's World Order, provide that impervious structure, solid and resistant to crumbling? Could the establishment of His World Order inaugurate an era unparalleled in human history? Is such an Order emerging out of the welter and confusion of present-day Chaos?

Evoking the process of Chaos of the science of Chaos from Chapter 5, we may wonder: Might the present-day convulsions, turbulence and disorder in human affairs serve as a precursor to the formation of higher-level bonds of unity among the peoples of the world and the advancement of civilization to its next level – a global civilization? [9]

In the passage from the Tablet of the World, wherein Bahá'u'lláh emphasizes the instability of a structure molded of clay, He assures His followers that there is no cause for dismay: 'Who is it that can dismay you?' [10]

Numerous statements of Bahá'u'lláh and Shoghi Effendi support the conviction that out of the present-day Chaos a new world order is emerging. In 1936 Shoghi Effendi referred to the 'catastrophic fall of mighty kingdoms and empires destined to precede the establishment of the World Order of Bahá'u'lláh'.[11] In this pivotal document, he identified the outbreak of the First World War as the opening of the 'Age of Frustration' destined to precede the establishment of that World Order. In 1944 in *God Passes By,* he pointed out that the First World War had been 'the first stage in the titanic convulsion long predicted by Bahá'u'lláh'.[12] In 1957 in *Citadel of Faith* he marked the Second World War as 'the second stage in the global havoc'.[13] 'Alí Nakhjavání in *Shoghi Effendi: Author of Teaching Plans* offers his explanation that the concept of 'frustration' is the awareness that humanity failed to achieve its aims, hopes and aspirations for happiness and welfare.[14] Fundamentally, the frustration was brought about by failure of humanity to heed the counsel of Bahá'u'lláh. During the years of His exile in Adrianople and in the fortress town of 'Akká (1868–1892), Bahá'u'lláh, issued summons to the kings and rulers of the world; therein He pronounced warnings and offered solutions which could have averted the impending havoc of two world wars and the ever continuing global turmoil. Alas, that window of opportunity was not seized.

As the Age of Frustration is destined to precede the establishment of the World Order of Bahá'u'lláh,[15] we are presently in the throes of that Age but can without 'dismay', rather with anticipation, look to the realization of the vision of Bahá'u'lláh for humanity. The Age of Frustration and the World Order of Bahá'u'lláh find their meaning and significance in the light of the two-fold process of disintegration and integration discussed in Chapter 6.

Shoghi Effendi draws a comparison to the collapse of Roman civilization during the first centuries of the Christian Era which preceded the emergence of the Christian civilization:

> Must humanity, tormented as she now is, be afflicted with still severer tribulations ere their purifying influence can prepare her to enter the heavenly Kingdom destined to be established upon earth? Must the inauguration of so vast, so unique, so illumined an era in human history be ushered in by so great a catastrophe in human affairs as to recall, nay surpass, the appalling collapse of Roman civilization in the first centuries of the Christian Era? Must a series of profound convulsions stir and rock the human race ere Bahá'u'lláh can be enthroned in the hearts and consciences of the masses, ere His undisputed ascendancy is universally recognized, and the noble edifice of His World Order is reared and established?[16]

Shoghi Effendi affirms that the new World Order is destined to arise upon the ruins of a tottering civilization: 'the attendant tribulations and commotions which a travailing age must necessarily experience, as a prelude to the birth of the new World Order, destined to rise upon the ruins of a tottering civilization . . .'[17]

Lest we become excessively distressed over the downfall of the present world order, we need to take heart from Bahá'u'lláh's loving assurance that there is no need for fear and dismay: 'Wherefore fear ye, O My well-beloved ones? Who is it that can dismay you?'[18]

Shoghi Effendi foresees an auspicious outcome: 'the World Order which, lying enshrined in His teachings, is slowly and imperceptibly rising amid the welter and chaos of present-day civilization'.[19]

With the dawn of the World Order of Bahá'u'lláh beckoning, we are heartened by the words of the Universal House of Justice in a significant statement in 1985 addressed to the peoples of the world:

> For the first time in history the dream of peace on earth is within the reach of the nations. Indeed peace is the next stage in the evolution of this planet. Humanity has the choice of reaching peace after unimaginable catastrophes or achieving it by an act of will.[20]

This statement brings to mind the words of Bahá'u'lláh, 'All men have been created to carry forward an ever-advancing civilization.'[21]

The need for guidance of Divine Manifestations

Using the analogy of the natural flow of water in a river, Bahá'u'lláh refers to grave disruption introduced in its flow. Such disorder and its outcome, in an elegant metaphor explained in Chapter 5, supports the discussion in that chapter on the process of Chaos. It alludes to a 'subtle mystery' – the need for the divine guidance of the 'Unique Hidden One' and the 'Eternal Essence' for the resumption of order in the flow of that River:

> Similarly, ponder upon the mysteries of divine decree and destiny. Whatever hath appeared or will appear is like this river. Each thing moveth or reposeth in its proper place. But if something contrary to this natural flow of events is manifested, the order of the world becometh gravely disrupted. Couldst thou but grasp this subtle mystery, which is more hidden than any other mystery, thou wouldst find thyself independent of all this and all other questions. It is for this reason that, in every age and century, as He desireth, the Unique Hidden One and the Eternal Essence manifesteth that true River and real Sea and causeth it to flow, adorning it with a new temple and a new vesture.[22]

The Revelation of Bahá'u'lláh – source of worldwide regeneration

The Revelation of Bahá'u'lláh has instilled into 'every human frame' and all created things a worldwide regeneration:

Through the movement of Our Pen of glory We have, at the bidding of the omnipotent Ordainer, breathed a new life into every human frame, and instilled into every word a fresh potency. All created things proclaim the evidences of this world-wide regeneration. This is the most great, the most joyful tidings imparted by the Pen of this Wronged One to mankind.[23]

A new race of being

Bahá'u'lláh affirms:

> Is not the object of every Revelation to effect a transformation in the whole character of mankind, a transformation that shall manifest itself, both outwardly and inwardly, that shall affect both its inner life and external conditions? For if the character of mankind be not changed, the futility of God's universal Manifestations would be apparent.[24]

At the very heart of a vital, viable, and sustainable world civilization is the transformation of that unique phenomenon – man. Human beings, Bahá'u'lláh asserts, are endowed with innate nobility.[25] That innate nobility yearns for transcendence, its fulfilment in a new race of being.

In 1992 Francis Fukuyama published a widely discussed book, *The End of History and the Last Man*. Fukuyama's thesis is that the struggle of man for recognition is the force that drives the course of human history toward its culmination. He considers the achievement of liberal democracies to be the end of man's struggle, thus 'the end of history'. Fukuyama leaves the reader with several fundamental and inescapable questions: What then? What more is there to be achieved once the struggle is fulfilled? What faces humankind at the culmination of history; will it be a void? What is the purpose of it all – the end of it all?

The Bahá'í Faith views the end of history as 'the coming of age of the entire human race'. Shoghi Effendi asserts that the Revelation of Bahá'u'lláh's 'supreme mission is none other but the achievement of this organic and spiritual unity of the whole body of nations'. He pronounces that this coming of age, by its very nature, should be regarded, 'as far as this planetary life is concerned, as the furthermost limits in the organization of human society' – the farthest limit of man's collective life on this planet. That culmination, 'that highest stage in the stupendous evolution of man's collective life on this planet' will not be an end, but only a beginning. When this highest stage in organization of human society has been attained, it will then serve as the environment for the nurturing and continuing progress of man: 'man, as an individual will, nay must indeed as a result of such a consummation, continue indefinitely to progress and develop'.[26]

Further reflection on the premise of Fukuyama leads once again to the nature of man – the true reality of man. The phrase 'Last Man' in the title of his book is at first glance intriguing; it may imply that the culmination of history – the end of man's striving for recognition – will be the very end of man. This, in turn, leads to the question: What then becomes of man? What is the destiny of man? Will he be bored or fulfilled by liberal democracy? Will he be annihilated or will he flourish? Will this be the very end of man? Or will the 'last man' be the end of man as we know it? Will such an end represent a transition into a new man – the emergence of the *first man* symbolizing a new entity, a new race of men and women, a new being? We may indeed draw such inference from Fukuyama's thesis.

When that longing for self-recognition is achieved, a new race of men and women come into being to carry forward progress in the course of history toward the founding of a world civilization and culture. With such a consummation to humankind's collective life on this planet, man will continue to develop indefinitely.[27]

Such a beginning, the *first man* – the new race of men and women – will mark in reality the commencement of 'humanhood', that is, women and men arising to that for which they were created. This will signify the fulfilment of that innate nobility in this plane of existence and continuing beyond.

Man's longing for self-transcendence

The struggle for recognition is at the core of Fukuyama's thesis. It reflects man's longing for self-transcendence, a key driving force throughout history. This belief is central to the theology of the great religions of the world and fundamental to advance in civilization.

The transformation and emergence of a new race of women and

men as anticipated by Bahá'u'lláh is the distinguishing function of His Revelation. In the words of Shoghi Effendi:

> Otherwise, the supreme and distinguishing function of His Revelation, which is none other than the calling into being of a new race of men, will remain wholly unrecognized and completely obscured.[28]

The Universal House of Justice envisions a 'glimpse of that race of being, consecrated and courageous, pure and sanctified, destined to evolve over generations under the influence of Bahá'u'lláh's Revelation'.[29] The plans of the Bahá'í world for growth are centred on the raising and nurturing of such a new race of being.

The Bahá'í Faith emphasizes the centrality of the individual to the advancement of civilization; this role is of such significance that Bahá'u'lláh considers it the underlying purpose for the creation of man. With these words He asserts that: 'All men have been created to carry forward an ever-advancing civilization.'[30]

Transformation to a new self

The individual is charged with the task and the privilege of carrying civilization forward to higher levels. Fundamental to this is self-transformation – the creation of a *new self*. Lewis Mumford writes:

> Man's principal task today is to create a new self; this self will necessarily take as its province the entire world, known and knowable and will seek not to impose a mechanical uniformity, but to bring about an organic unity, based upon the fullest utilization of all the varied resources that both nature and history have revealed to modern man. Such a culture must be nourished, not only by a new vision of the whole but a new vision of a self capable of understanding and cooperating with the whole . . . In short the moment for another great historic transformation has come.[31]

Such self-transformation is fundamental to the transformation of world society and the unification of humankind. What is needed is transformation from self-centredness to self-transcendence and the acquisition of a new vision of self inseparable from the vision of the whole, dedicated to the organic unity of humankind. Such a transformation is taking place in our very midst in numerous individuals in countless communities across the face of our globe under the influence of the Revelation of Bahá'u'lláh. Such *global entities hold the hope and promise for the unification and transformation of humankind.*

The Bahá'í worldwide community and the oneness of the human race

Data from studies cited earlier in this book show the extent of the worldwide spread of the Bahá'í Faith. Such a global spread characterizes the Bahá'í community as a world community that is not limited to one patch of earth but permeates the entire globe. Arnold J. Toynbee identifies such worldwide communities as 'diasporas' and includes the Bahá'í community among them.[32]

Some may contend the suitability of the term 'diaspora' applied to the Bahá'í community. In the past, diasporas were the outcome of trade, war and persecution – as matters of necessity rather than choice. Whichever definition of diaspora we choose to adopt has little bearing on the argument presented herein. The worldwide spread of the Bahá'í Faith has resulted from its followers scattering far and wide throughout the world.

They set out with dedication, 'light as the spirit', 'pure as air', 'blazing as fire', 'unrestrained as the wind'[33] – to proclaim the Faith of Bahá'u'lláh; their sacrifice was for the sole reason of making His transforming message accessible to humankind, toward the spiritualization of the masses and the reconstruction of society.

Shoghi Effendi pays tribute to those dedicated individuals:

> Bracing the fearful cold of the Arctic regions and the enervating heat of the torrid zone; heedless of the hazards, the loneliness and the austerity of the deserts, the far-away islands and mountains wherein they will be called upon to dwell; undeterred by the clamor which the exponents of religious orthodoxy are sure to raise, or by the restrictive measures which political leaders may impose; undismayed by the smallness of their numbers and the multitude of their potential adversaries; armed with the efficacious weapons their own hands have slowly and laboriously forged in anticipation of this glorious

and inevitable encounter with the organized forces of superstition, of corruption and of unbelief . . .[34]

Elsewhere too he praises such stalwart heroes and heroines:

> Conscious of their high calling, confident in the society-building power which their Faith possesses, they press forward, undeterred and undismayed, in their efforts.[35]

In our particular times, the Universal House of Justice, on the eve of the centenary in 2016 of the Tablets of the Divine Plan – the charter for the growth of the Bahá'í Faith – pays tribute to those dedicated Bahá'ís all over the world who have acted 'under the Mandate of 'Abdu'l-Bahá':

> We pay homage to the humblest ministrations and ceaseless endeavours of the Faith's devoted rank and file, as well as to the extraordinary accomplishments of its heroes, knights, and martyrs. On vast continents and scattered islands, from arctic regions to desert climes, atop mountain plateaus and across lowland plains, in crowded urban quarters and villages along rivers and jungle paths, you and your spiritual forebears brought the message of the Blessed Beauty to peoples and nations.[36]

The role of worldwide communities in the unification of world society

With utmost dedication and self-sacrifice, these valiant followers of Bahá'u'lláh succeeded in establishing across the face of this planet the underlying structure of a vital Bahá'í community. The heart of such a global community pulsates – to diffuse the vivifying and transforming lifeblood, the message of the Bahá'í Faith.

This reality evokes Toynbee's cogent and compelling arguments regarding the significance of worldwide communities he calls 'diasporas'. Toynbee points out that such communities have distinct identity and are not limited to one patch of earth but are spread across the face of this planet. Though a minority in any one place, nevertheless their *conscience is worldwide*. Such worldwide diasporas have vitality, viability and efficacy; they hold the promise for the unification of world society.[37]

The Bahá'í worldwide community qualifies elegantly as a diaspora, with a distinct identity which is not limited to one patch of earth but is worldwide. Although at this time it is a minority in any one place, its conscience is global in every place.

The Bahá'í community can be distinguished from the worldwide communities of minorities to which Toynbee refers. In contrast to all others, the Bahá'í community by its nature and character is the one best suited to bring about the unification of the human race.

Distinctive characteristics of the Bahá'í worldwide community. Such a bold assertion is based on several distinctive characteristics of the Bahá'í community. **First,** it is a community dedicated to the mission of building a world society; thus it can contribute to the creation of a viable world civilization. **Second,** inasmuch as the Bahá'í community embraces within its fold a diversity of religions, races, cultures, tribes, nationalities and ethnicities, it constitutes a microcosm of humanity, a veritable model of unity. **Third,** its doctrine of oneness of religions inculcates respect and acceptance of the divine truth of the world's religions and their essential interconnectedness – indispensable to the oneness of humankind. This important doctrine was the focus of Chapters 8 and 9 in this book. **Fourth,** its vision of a world civilization is centred on spiritual and moral revival. **Fifth,** in contrast to other worldwide communities – described as diasporas by Toynbee – the primary concern of the Bahá'í community is not self-preservation; rather, it is dedicated sacrificially to the mission of the oneness of the human race. It consecrates its life and resources to the fulfilment of the vision of Bahá'u'lláh for humanity.

The worldwide Bahá'í community is dedicated to infusing the body of material civilization with the transforming spirit brought for our age through the Revelation of Bahá'u'lláh. Its role is that of a catalyst forging bonds of unity toward the construction of a global civilization.

The Bahá'í community and advancement of the plans of the Bahá'í world

We can envision only dimly the impact of the teachings of Bahá'u'lláh on the course of human history and future civilizations. The principles of His Faith are bound to flourish and transform individuals and society. The Bahá'í world community, through the guidance of its strategic and systematic plans, is committed to bringing to the attention and consciousness of the generality of humanity the solutions which this Faith offers to the dilemmas of society.

All the plans of the Bahá'í world for growth are successive stages in the unfoldment of the Divine Plan of 'Abdu'l-Bahá; they derive their inspiration and guidance from this Charter and are aimed at making available the transformative message of Bahá'u'lláh to vast numbers of the inhabitants of this planet, as discussed in Chapter 3. Selfless dedication and a high level of commitment in execution of the plans of the Bahá'í world have characterized the action of the Bahá'í community, assuring success in its growth and worldwide advancement.[38]

Recognition of the claims of the Faith of Bahá'u'lláh

The 'recognition of the character, and the acknowledgment of the claims, of the Faith of Bahá'u'lláh' are the 'essential condition' for the 'spiritualization of the masses' and the 'reconstruction of mankind',[39] wherein the oneness of world society can find its fulfilment through fusion of all races, creeds, classes and nations in 'an Order that shall come to be regarded as the fairest fruit of a slowly maturing age'.[40]

At this point in time, Bahá'u'lláh remains yet unrecognized by large numbers of the inhabitants of this planet. The personage of Bahá'u'lláh and His life are historical realities. Government records, documents and edicts bear accounts of Him. Two centuries after Jesus Christ, there were scant few who had any awareness of the historical existence of Jesus or even an inkling of the significance of His mission; nor could anyone have vaguely imagined that His cause would, in time, inspire and create the great Christian civilization. His early followers and contemporaries could not have envisioned the magnitude of His message. Those who surrounded the person of Jesus could not *see* – perceive – the halo which was later painted in by Christian artists. Most likely, Jesus Christ was physically indistinguishable from others, as He had to be identified through Judas's kiss of betrayal.[41] Yet Christianity has proven to be an irresistible force in history inspiring countless individuals and civilizations.

To illustrate the point that Jesus Christ was unrecognized by the vast majority of His contemporaries, the historian John McManners refers to a story published by Anatole France on Christmas Day 1891 in an anticlerical newspaper. The story imagines Pontius Pilate in retirement, talking about the old days in Jerusalem; the name of a crucified miracle worker, Jesus of Nazareth, comes up. The name of Jesus Christ eludes him! – 'Jesus, Jesus of Nazareth, I can't remember him.'[42]

Empires have formed and empires and kingdoms have collapsed and perished. The Roman Empire itself fell; yet the Christian Faith survived, flourished and spurred a transformation of immeasurable magnitude in individuals and society.

In less than two centuries the Bahá'í community has spread well beyond the land of its birth and intense persecutions to distant continents and remotest islands, as foreshadowed by Bahá'u'lláh:

> Should they attempt to conceal its light on the continent it will assuredly rear its head in the midmost heart of the ocean and, raising its voice, proclaim: 'I am the life-giver of the world!'[43]

The Bahá'í community is forging ahead under the unfolding stages of the Divine Plan so that the redemptive message of Bahá'u'lláh can *penetrate and suffuse* collective consciousness. The Universal House of Justice discloses a glorious and promising vision:

> a grassroots stirring, an organic flowering, a resistless movement that has grown imperceptibly at times and at others in great surges to eventually embrace the entire world.[44]

It points to the challenging requirements of the present hour:

> requirements both urgent and sacred, which, when sacrificially and persistently addressed, may hasten 'the advent of that Golden Age which must witness the proclamation of the Most Great Peace and the unfoldment of that world civilization which is the offspring and primary purpose of that Peace'.[45]

And that:

> [T]he Divine Plan continues at the present time with the intensive effort to establish a pattern of community life that can embrace

thousands upon thousands in clusters that cover the face of the planet.[46]

The Universal House of Justice expresses admiration for the valiant executors of the Divine Plan and calls this and future generations of Bahá'ís to action:

> You have written the story of the unfoldment of the Divine Plan on the scroll of its first century. Before you, beloved friends, lies stretched out the blank scroll of the future on which you and your spiritual descendants will inscribe fresh and lasting deeds of renunciation and heroism for the betterment of the world.[47]

The betterment of the world, fostered and advanced by that new race of men and women under the influence of the revelation for this day, remains the fervent aspiration of that vital worldwide Bahá'í community. Its fulfilment is bound to bring about the *spiritualization of the masses toward reconstruction of human society and the emergence of His New World Order.*

GLOSSARY

Active medium. A medium capable of becoming activated, used in this book in the context of the generation of the laser beam as an analogue for the human soul. In contrast to other life forms, the human soul can become activated and transformed.

Adamic Cycle. Historical period that includes revelations through divine educators starting from Adam to the present time, consisting of those of whom history bears record in the Hindu, Buddhist, Zoroastrian, Jewish, Christian and Islamic revelations. The end of the Adamic Cycle is linked to the Manifestation of the Báb.

Alchemy. Humanity's long quest for a method to convert base metals into precious gold came to be thought of as the 'science' of alchemy. Bahá'u'lláh applies the metaphor of 'elixir' from alchemy to the Divine Elixir, the Word of God, which has power to transform the human soul.

Alexander the Great. 356–323 BC. Alexander III, King of Macedonia and conqueror of the Persian Empire, is considered one of the greatest military geniuses of all times. He died at the age of 33 without designating a successor to the Macedonian Empire. His reign and conquests were replete with brutality.

Analogy. Analogies show a resemblance in properties between two things or concepts that have similar features. 'Abdu'l-Bahá often uses analogies from nature, such as the cultivation of plants, the development of the seed and leaves in plants, the development of a plant from a seed, the development of embryos, as well as numerous other examples.

Aristotle. 384–322 BC. Born in Greece, he was one of Plato's most famed students. He made important contributions to diverse disciplines including mathematics, biology, ethics and logic.

Ascending spiral view of history. This represents the Bahá'í view of history. At each turn of this spiral or gyre, the cycle becomes larger; that is, civilizations, over time, continue to advance. The ascending spiral view has some of the features of the linear as well as the cyclic views of history (q.v.) As in the linear view, revelation through a respective Prophet-Founder imparts progression to the course of history. However, as in the cyclical view, it is devoid of the 'sin of hubris' as it acknowledges the recurrence of such epical events. See Chapter 7 for a discussion.

Augustine of Hippo. 354–430 AD. Bishop of Hippo. Also known as Saint Augustine, he was a philosopher and theologian who lived in the Roman Africa Province. In his early years he was heavily influenced by Manichaeism but later converted to Christianity and was baptized in 387. He developed his own approach and perspective to philosophy and theology. The writings of Augustine were influential in the development of Western Christianity.

Autocatalytic process. In an autocatalytic process the reaction product serves also as a reactant. An autocatalytic process is a self-catalyzing process whereby catalysis progresses continuously, gathering speed over time. As an analogy in the context of this writing, when an autocatalytic process sets in, the wave of transformation propagates and escalates.

Axial. Term used by the philosopher Karl Jasper to describe the profound change of a religious and moral nature which took place within the span of the 6th century BC. Lewis Mumford also uses the term 'axial religions'. Axial has to do with values. Early major religions such as the Buddhist and Zoroastrian came forth, while those that appeared later continued the transformation begun then. 'With this a new kind of person and a new kind of community took form' (see Mumford, *The Transformations of Man*, 1978). The term 'axial', as used by Mumford, marks a significant turning point in human history.

Bahá'í Cycle. The Báb in 1844 opened the Bahá'í Cycle – the 'Cycle of Fulfilment' whose duration, according to the Writings of Bahá'u'lláh and 'Abdu'l-Bahá, will be at least five thousand centuries. See passages in Chapter 9.

Boundary conditions. Conditions which prevail at the boundary between two levels. These conditions signify great resistance to transition from one level to the next. In this book, boundary conditions signify resistance to change at an interface between two levels. However, once the resistance is overcome, a remarkable transformation in state can take place, tantamount to a *quantum leap*. See Chapter 2.

Brahe, Tycho. 1546-1601 AD. Danish astronomer. His work on astronomical instrumentation, designing and building instruments, calibrating them and periodically checking their accuracy were significant in making key contributions to the Copernican Revolution.

Bruno, Giordano. 1548-1600 AD. Italian philosopher, mathematician and astronomer. He was burned at the stake in 1600 by the civil authorities because of his 'heretical' theories of the cosmos.

Butterfly effect. Term first used in 1972, by Edward Lorenz, to show that the small current generated by the flapping of the wings of a butterfly in one part of the world, under appropriate conditions, can escalate to a magnitude with tornado-like impact in a distant part of the world. The butterfly effect was first shown in the field of meteorology. See Chapter 5 for a discussion.

Catalyst. In chemistry, defined as a substance, usually used in small amounts, which enables a chemical reaction to proceed at a faster rate or under different conditions than otherwise possible. A catalyst facilitates a chemical reaction without undergoing change itself. Enzymes serve as catalysts in chemical reactions.

Cell cycle. When a single cell divides in two, it goes through a cycle called the *cell cycle,* also known as the *cell division cycle.* The cycle is of varying time duration, depending on the type of cell, and includes events that occur from the time the cell initiates the process leading to its actual division into two cells. For a discussion of the cell cycle, its phases and their implications for the process of growth of the Bahá'í community, see Chapter 1.

Central Figures. There are three Central Figures of the Bahá'í Faith. The Báb (1819-1850), Forerunner to Bahá'u'lláh, and Bahá'u'lláh (1817-1892), the Inaugurator of the Bahá'í Dispensation, are **Manifestations of God** (q.v.). 'Abdu'l-Bahá (1844-1921), appointed by Bahá'u'lláh as His Successor and the Centre of His Covenant, is the third Central Figure of the Bahá'í Faith. The twin successors to 'Abdu'l-Bahá were Shoghi Effendi (see **Guardian**) and the Universal House of Justice, the supreme governing body of the Bahá'í Faith, elected for the first time in 1963.

Chaos. In common usage the term is applied to systems that are disorderly and tumultuous. However, the science which is now described as 'Chaos' is not disorderly; though it may appear so, it nevertheless has an emerging order. It is important to distinguish between two types of chaos: (1) disorderly with no emerging order; and (2) a process which only appears disorderly but is not, through which order emerges. It can be claimed that the term 'chaos' as applied to the second type is a misnomer. Nevertheless, similar to a number of misnomers which have crept into science, we are compelled to retain the term for the second type at this time. For the purpose of the discussions in these pages the term 'Chaos' (with a capital 'C') is used for type (2): that is, the process which appears disorderly and tumultuous but camouflages an emerging order. This type of Chaos follows the science of Chaos; it has scientific parameters. This conception of Chaos is implied through the statement of Bahá'u'lláh, 'The world's equilibrium hath been upset.' For further discussion see Chapter 5.

Chrysalis. Also known as cocoon; a protective covering within which a moth is encased while it is undergoing its development – its metamorphosis into a butterfly. For a discussion of the relevance of chrysalis to the theme of this book see Chapter 7.

Civilization. A society in an advanced state of organization and social development; also defined as 'the largest cultural grouping of people below that of the human race'.

Cluster. Term used to define geographical units of the Bahá'í community for a focus on growth. Cluster units were introduced by the Universal House of Justice in the series of plans beginning in 1994.

Co-evolution. The mutual evolutionary impact of species that are intimately linked and dependent on one another. Co-evolution is the dynamic process that brings about reciprocal evolutionary changes in such species. Thus, through the process of co-evolution, the evolution of one species influences the evolution of other species to which it is intimately linked. This dynamic process has continuing mutual effects on each of the component entities; it can progressively augment the evolution and maturation of them all. For discussion see Chapter 2.

Coherence. An essential property of the laser beam. When the system is connected to a power source under appropriate conditions, a property referred to as 'coherence' can be induced in ordinary light; that is, the out-of-phase photons which by themselves were without much power, are rendered *in phase* (of the same wave length), i.e. in step with one another and thus can be launched in unison. For discussion see Chapter 2.

Cohort effect. Term used in a number of disciplines to describe the effect on an area of study of populations defined by some shared temporal or common life experience. In the context of the growth of the Bahá'í Faith, it is the effect of all those – whether registered Bahá'ís or not – who have the common experience of participating in and supporting the community-building efforts of the Bahá'í community. See discussion in Chapter 3.

Columbian Exchange. The exchange which took place with the New World in a process set in motion by Christopher Columbus in 1492. Some consider it as 'the most important event since the death of dinosaurs' (see Mann, *1493: Uncovering the New World Columbus Created*). As a result of the Columbian Exchange biological globalization had its start, as countless species of animals and plants as well as viruses and bacteria were introduced to the newly discovered lands and continents.

Constantine (the Great). 272–337 AD. Constantine I, Roman Emperor from 336–337. He was baptized as a Christian on his deathbed, and his role was pivotal in bringing about a turning point in the growth and expansion of Christianity in its 4th century.

Copernican Revolution. A tumultuous process which precipitated the overthrow of the geocentric model of the universe, with planet Earth at its centre, and its replacement with the heliocentric model, with the Sun at its centre. For discussion see Chapter 8.

Coup d'état. French, lit. 'strike against the state', resulting in an overthrow of the regime. In this writing, the term is used to signify the overthrow of an established way of thinking (i.e. a well-established paradigm is replaced with a more expansive paradigm) such as took place through the Copernican Revolution. For discussion regarding paradigm shift see Chapter 8.

Counsellors. The institution of the Boards of Counsellors was brought into being by the Universal House of Justice in 1968 to extend into the future the specific functions of protection and propagation conferred upon the Hands of the Cause of God. The members of these boards are appointed by the Universal House of Justice.

Covenant. In the religious context, a binding agreement between God and man whereby God requires of man certain behaviour in return for which He guarantees certain bounties and blessings. The **Greater Covenant** is what every **Manifestation of God** (q.v.) makes with His followers, promising that in the fullness of time a new Manifestation will be sent, and that they have the obligation to accept Him. As explained by 'Abdu'l-Bahá (*Bahá'í World Faith*, p. 358), Abraham made a covenant concerning Moses and gave the glad-tidings of His coming, Moses made a covenant concerning the advent of Christ, Christ gave the tidings of the coming of Muhammad, Muhammad made a covenant concerning the Báb, the Báb made a covenant concerning the coming of Bahá'u'lláh. Bahá'u'lláh refers to one who will become manifest no sooner than a thousand years hence. There is also a **Lesser Covenant**: the covenant that a Manifestation of God makes with His followers that they accept His appointed successor after Him. Bahá'u'lláh entered into a Covenant and Testament with all the Bahá'ís whereby they were all commanded to follow 'Abdu'l-Bahá, His appointed Centre of the Covenant, after His own passing. 'Abdu'l-Bahá continued the Covenant through Shoghi Effendi, the Guardian of the Bahá'í Faith. 'Abdu'l-Bahá's *Will and Testament* provides for the extension of the Covenant through the Guardianship and the Universal House of Justice.

Critical point. Term introduced by Erwin Laszlo as the 'chaos window' or 'decision window'. At this point, the system is exquisitely sensitive to a number of alternative small forces; the butterfly effect can take hold and any input, however small, 'can blow-up to change existing trends, bringing new trends and processes into existence'. The concept of critical point has been evoked by numerous other scholars and theorists and is used in other systems as the 'threshold', or the 'tipping point'. For discussion see Chapter 5.

Crusades. Between 1095 and 1291 AD, a series of wars called first by Pope Urban II and after him by succeeding Popes against the Muslims. The main goal was restoring to the Christians the control of the Holy Land.

Custodians. A group of nine **Hands of the Cause** (q.v.) designated after the passing of Shoghi Effendi in 1957 to live and serve at the Bahá'í World Centre as legal custodians of the Bahá'í Faith (see *The Ministry of the Custodians*, pp. 10-11). Together with the other Hands of the Cause, their mission was to direct the affairs of the Faith, to enable the Bahá'ís worldwide to complete the Ten Year Plan and to call for the election of the **Universal House of the Justice** (q.v.) in 1963.

Cyclic view of history. According to Toynbee, the cyclic view represents the Indo-Hellenic (Greco-Hindu) view of history. The pattern may be represented by recurrent cycles which repeat themselves over time. This view has the disadvantage of not accounting for progress in the course of history, but it has the advantage of lack of self-centredness. See discussion in Chapter 7.

Dante. Durante degli Alighieri, 1265–1321 AD, major Italian poet of the Middle Ages. His 'Comedia', *La Grande Comedia*, later called *Divina* by Boccaccio, is considered a literary masterpiece.

Diaspora. The term has varying definitions; some consider diasporas as the outcome of trade, war and persecution. Others consider them as also arising from going out to the world to spread respective teachings; it is in this light that the term may be applied to the Bahá'í Faith. Arnold J. Toynbee refines the definition to mean a world community of minorities which is not limited to one patch of earth but permeates the entire globe and has a global conscience. He believes that such communities of minorities with distinct identity hold the promise for the reunification of the world. It is in this sense that his reference to the Bahá'í diaspora finds its justification and acquires its fuller meaning. Diaspora is discussed in Chapter 10.

Directionality. In reference to the laser beam, this term means that the beam is organized, strong and concentrated, rather than weak and diffuse. See discussion in Chapter 2.

Dispensation. The period of time during which the authority of a Manifestation of God's social or temporal teachings endure. The eternal, spiritual truths taught by each Manifestation are not abrogated but affirmed by subsequent Manifestations. The Dispensation of the Báb lasted nine years (from 1844 with His declaration to 1850 with His martyrdom). The Dispensation of Bahá'u'lláh commenced in 1853 with the initiation of His Prophetic mission and will extend over a period of no less than one thousand years. It will constitute the first stage in a series of Dispensations to be established by future Manifestations of God. The Dispensation of Bahá'u'lláh includes the Heroic, the Formative and the Golden Ages.

Divine Elixir (see also **Elixir**). Bahá'u'lláh defines the Divine Elixir as the Word of God, the agent which can induce spiritual transformation in the human soul. Here an analogy is used from alchemy – the belief that base metal can be changed into gold through the use of an elixir.

DNA. Deoxyribonucleic acid. The arrangement of base sequences in the DNA carries the essential genetic code for every living organism. James Watson, Francis Crick and Maurice Wilkins are credited with discovering the double helix structure of DNA in 1953; this credit must also be extended to Rosalind Franklin whose research was significant in leading to this discovery.

Eccles, John Carew. 1903-1997. Born in Melbourne, Australia, Eccles received the Nobel Prize in Physiology and Medicine in 1963 for his work in neurophysiology. He followed Sherrington in developing a philosophy of the human person which is consonant with brain science. He addressed this in many of his lectures.

Elixir. Viewed by some as the 'elixir of life', a legendary drink that imparts love, eternal youth and eternal life. The term has been associated with the philosopher's stone and similar images. Among practitioners of alchemy the elixir is that agent which can transform base metal into precious gold.

Entry by troops. Frequently used Bahá'í terminology, from Shoghi Effendi: '[T]he advent of the day which, as prophesied by 'Abdu'l-Bahá (see **Central Figures**) will witness the **entry by troops** of peoples of divers nations and races into the Bahá'í world' (Shoghi Effendi, *Citadel of Faith*, p. 117).

Epicircles. Circles introduced within circles, an accommodation in the Aristotelian-Ptolemic model of universe. As Plato's view was that the perfect form of motion is a circular one, efforts were made to retain the circular orbits. The accommodation attempted to show that each planet travels along a small circle (epi-circle) that rolls along that planet's big orbital circle around the earth. Century after century, as the errors in this model grew increasingly evident, more epicircles were added to the model so that planets moved along epicircles within epicircles. Copernicus hoped to use 'modern' (16th-century) technology to improve on Ptolemy's measurements and hopefully eliminate some of the epicircles.

Equilibrium. Here used in reference to the science of Chaos. Systems that are *far from equilibrium* are significantly out of balance; that is, they are significantly unstable. In such systems a very small amount of additional energy can cause a very large change and even a complete reorganization of the system. Systems that are *in equilibrium* are stable and balanced. Systems which are *near equilibrium* are slightly out of balance – small changes in energy produces small changes in the system

Eschatology. From Greek *eschatos*: farthest, last. Eschatology is concerned with final events in history, such as the Kingdom of God, Advent of the Promised One, the Resurrection, the Day of Judgement. These metaphorical terms imply an end point, a culmination to the course of human history at which time an anticipated event will come to pass.

Eusebius of Caesarea. 263–339 AD. Court prelate during the reign of Constantine I, he played a significant role in formulating what is known as the **image doctrine** (q.v.), that Christianity and the Roman Empire were complementary.

Exclusivity of salvation. Belief that the only route to salvation is provided through one Manifestation (one Prophet-Founder of a religion). According to the doctrine instituted in Christianity, this means that the only path to salvation is through Jesus Christ.

First man. Term used by the author of this writing, based on the understanding of the station of the individual in the Bahá'í Faith, to refer to a spiritually evolved woman or man who manifests her/his inherent nobility – the purpose for which she/he was created. This marks the commencement of 'humanhood' – the outcome of fulfilment of the nobility inherent within each human being. Such transformation and transcendence bring forth a new race of women and men. The term 'first man' is offered in this writing as a counterpoint to the 'last man' discussed by Francis Fukuyama in *The End of History and the Last Man*. See Chapter 10.

Formative Age. Following the 'Heroic Age' of Bahá'u'lláh's Dispensation which ended with the passing of 'Abdu'l-Bahá in 1921, the Formative Age began; it is the age we are now in. It precedes the **Golden Age** (q.v.) of the Cause of Bahá'u'lláh.

Fractal. Coined by Benoit Mandelbrot in 1975, the term 'fractal' comes from the word 'fractional'; it signifies any image, feature, or process that displays the attribute of self-similarity at all levels of magnification. Thus the same pattern or feature is repeated at each level, across all scales. Examples are abundant in nature. Fractals are present in biological systems such as the branching of blood vessels, the airway passageways in the lung, and the folding of chromosomes. Fractals are seen in plants; the pattern of fronds of the fern plant is repeated at higher scales in the whole plant. Fractal dimensions can be derived from fractal equations (see Mandelbrot, *The Fractal Geometry of Nature*). See discussion of fractal in Chapter 5, and its implication in history in Chapter 7.

Fuentes, Carlos Macías. 1928–2012. Mexican writer; a well-known novelist and essayist in the Spanish-speaking world.

Galileo Galilei. 1564–1642. Italian physicist, mathematician, astronomer and philosopher. His public support of the heliocentric view of the cosmos was met with much opposition. The Catholic Church condemned the heliocentric view as 'false and contrary to Scripture'. Galileo later defended his views in *Dialogue Concerning the Two Chief World Systems*, published in 1632. He was tried by the Inquisition, found 'vehemently suspect of heresy', forced to recant, and spent the rest of his life under house arrest. See Chapter 8.

Generation of the laser beam. Light, in general, consists of many different, tiny packets of waves (quanta) of differing wave lengths. In ordinary light, these quanta are out of step (*out of phase*) with one another. When connected to a power source, however, under appropriate conditions, a property referred to as 'coherence' can be induced – that is, the out-of-phase quanta, which by themselves were without much power, are rendered *in phase* (of the same wave length) and coherent. Consequently, a laser beam can be generated with a power and intensity capable of performing a wide variety of tasks. Chapter 2 discusses the implications of the laser beam on growth.

Genghis Khan. c. 1162–1227. Founder and ruler of the Mongol Empire who reigned 1206–1227. Genghis Khan united many nomadic tribes of north-east Asia; by the end of his life the Empire included substantial parts of Central Asia and China. His invasions were accompanied by acts of violence, barbarism and brutality.

Geocentric model of the planetary system. The geocentric model places the Earth at the centre with the Sun and known planets revolving around it. See also **Heliocentric**.

Gestalt switch. Has to do with sudden change (switch) in perception. The work of the Hanover Institute provides this interesting metaphor. In an experiment, a subject who wore goggles with inverting lenses initially became disoriented, for the world was seen upside down; some time after, however, the visual field inverted over and the world was seen right side up (see Kühn, *The Structure of Scientific Revolution*).

Gibbon, Edward. 1737-1794. Author of the monumental six-volume *History of the Decline and Fall of the Roman Empire*. Against this background Gibbon discusses the rise and progress of Christianity.

Globalization. A term used in reference to the trend toward global consciousness that has been set in operation since the discovery of the new world, the Americas (See Mann, *1493: Uncovering the New World Columbus Created*). Globalization has implications which can have positive outcomes such as access to natural resources and financial liberalization of markets. On the other hand, globalization when miscarried can have negative implications.

Golden Age. According to the writings of Shoghi Effendi, the Golden Age of the Dispensation of Bahá'u'lláh lies far ahead in the future. Its advent must witness the proclamation of the Most Great Peace and the unfoldment of that world civilization which is the offspring and the primary purpose of that Peace (see Shoghi Effendi, *Citadel of Faith*, p. 7; 'The Unfoldment of World Civilization', in *The World Order of Bahá'u'lláh*, pp. 202-6).

Collingwood, Robin George. 1889-1943. English philosopher, historian and archeologist, known for his book *The Idea of History*, published posthumously in 1945. Though Collingwood was neglected in his time, he has become known for providing major inspiration to the philosophy of history.

Gravitational forces. In Newtonian physics gravitational forces are the forces of attraction between two masses. According to Newton's law of gravity, the gravitational force between two bodies is proportional to the product of their masses and inversely proportional to the square of the distance between them.

Growth-inducing milieu. An environment which has the necessary conditions for growth. The term is used in the plans of the Baháʼí Faith concerning the growth of the Baháʼí community.

Guardian. In the Baháʼí Faith, the title used for **Shoghi Effendi**, appointed by ʻAbduʼl-Bahá as Guardian of the Baháʼí Faith and Interpreter of its sacred texts. Shoghi Effendi was quite young when appointed by ʻAbduʼl-Bahá as his successor; he assumed the station of Guardianship after the passing of Abduʼl-Bahá in 1921 after the Will and Testament of Abduʼl-Bahá was read.

Gutenberg, Johannes. c. 1398–1468. German printer and publisher whose introduction of movable type to Europe in 1439 had an enormous impact on the Renaissance, the Scientific Revolution and a multitude of other areas. Leading to the widespread use of the printing press, Gutenberg's invention is considered among the most significant innovations, spurring a major turning point in the history of humankind.

Gyre. A circular or spiral motion. Sometimes used as a view of the historical process, e.g. by William Butler Yeats in his poem 'The Second Coming'. The gyre (**ascending spiral view**, q.v.) represents the Baháʼí view of history. For discussion see Chapter 7.

Habits of the mind. The American social scientist Howard Margolis (1932–2009) considered well-entrenched 'habits of the mind' to be barriers to a new paradigm (see Margolis, *Paradigms and Barriers: How Habits of Mind Govern Scientific Belief*).

Haldane, John. 1892–1964. British geneticist and evolutionary biologist who worked on 'prebiotic' conditions of life on Earth. The work of **Oparin** (q.v.) and Haldane – The Oparin-Haldane Hypothesis – calls attention to the fact that oxygen was rare or absent in the early atmosphere of Earth.

Hand of the Cause. Rank conferred on certain individuals by Baháʼuʼlláh, ʻAbduʼl-Bahá and Shoghi Effendi. The responsibility of the Hands of the Cause, as described by ʻAbduʼl-Bahá, is 'to diffuse the

Divine Fragrances, to edify the souls of men, to promote learning, to improve the character of all men . . .' ('Abdu'l-Bahá, *Will and Testament*, para. 21, p. 13).

Heliocentric model of the planetary system. The heliocentric model places the Sun at the centre with the Earth, the moon and the then known planets revolving around it. See also **Geocentric**. For discussion see Chapter 8.

House of Justice. 'The institution of the House of Justice consists of elected councils which operate at the local, national and international levels of society' (Note 49, in Bahá'u'lláh, *The Kitáb-i-Aqdas*, p. 188). See also **Universal House of Justice**.

Human genome project. An international project, involving many scientists, to determine the sequence of human genes on the 24 chromosomes. Information in the **DNA** (q.v.) is stored as a code made up of these four nucleotides: A, T, C and G (respectively: Adenine, Thymine, Cytosine and Guanine) each associated with a sugar, deoxyribose, and a phosphate group which make up the human DNA. The project was formally launched in 1990 and completed in 2003, showing that there are 3.1 billion letters of DNA arranged on 24 chromosomes.

Image doctrine. The idea that Christianity and the Roman Empire were complementary, indeed made for each other. This doctrine dominated the mindset of the 4th century AD; identifying Christianity with the political and social order of the Roman Empire was a powerful image and important to the growth of Christianity. Eusebius of Caesarea (q.v.), court prelate during the reign of Constantine I, played a significant role in formulating this doctrine.

Inquisition. Begun in the 12th century under the Roman Catholic Church with the intent of defending and maintaining the integrity of the Faith. Those judged as heretics were punished by torture and often by death. The Roman Inquisition tried Galileo in 1633 for his views on the cosmos.

Institute process. Term used in the plans of the Bahá'í Faith since 1994 to describe 'the two essential movements which continue to propel the process of growth, the steady flow of participants through the sequence of training institute courses and the movement of clusters along a continuum of development' (The Universal House of Justice, Riḍván Message, 2014, to the Bahá'ís of the World). Integral to the current plans of the Bahá'í world, the institute process is centred on participation in the 'core activities' – study circles, devotional meetings, children's classes and junior youth spiritual empowerment programmes. Ongoing learning is acquired through a pattern of study, service, consultation, action and reflection with others.

Interphase. The stage in the cell cycle which precedes mitosis, when the cell visibly divides into two. During the interphase the cell appears quiescent, offering no visible sign of doubling. See **Cell cycle** and the discussion in Chapter 1.

Israfil. According to Islamic tradition, Israfil is the beautiful angel of music. Israfil sings praises to God in a thousand different languages, injecting life into hosts of angels. Israfil is the angel responsible for signalling the coming of the Judgement Day by blowing a trumpet and sending out a blast of Truth.

Kepler, Johannes. 1571–1630. German mathematician and astronomer and a key figure in the 17th-century Copernican Revolution, best known for his laws of planetary movements.

Last man. Term used by Francis Fukuyama, author of *The End of History and the Last Man,* to mean the last generation of women and men before they achieve fulfilment in a liberal democracy. See also **First man** and the discussion in Chapter 10.

Linear view of history. According to Arnold J. Toynbee, the linear view represents the Judeo-Zoroastrian and the Christian-Muslim view of history. It marks the advent of their respective Prophet-Founders as the starting point of progress in the course of history. Their respective followers see this event as unique, not to be repeated again. Thereafter the trajectory of history takes an upward course, indicating progress. Toynbee finds advantage with this view as it accounts for progress in history, but disadvantage as it is self-centred. For a discussion on this theme see Chapter 7.

Local Spiritual Assembly. Local governing council in the Bahá'í community, instituted in every city, town, and village where nine or more adult believers are resident. The Local Spiritual Assembly is responsible for supervising all Bahá'í matters in its area. See also **National Spiritual Assembly** and **Universal House of Justice**. For discussion see Chapter 3.

Logos. Term used in various disciplines including philosophy, psychology, rhetoric and religion, and with various meanings. Heraclitus (535–475 BC) defined it as a principle of order and knowledge. In Christianity (John 1:1) it is identified with that through which all things are made divine. Christ was identified as the incarnation of the Logos, the 'Word'.

Lorenz, Edward Norton. 1917–2008. American mathematician and meteorologist and a pioneer in the science of Chaos. Lorenz is credited as the first to identify the process of Chaos in the field of meteorology.

Major Plan of God. Term used in Bahá'í thought to describe the purpose of God for humanity, its transformation. Its first goal is the Lesser Peace – the political unification of the world. Its ultimate object is the realization of the kingdom of God on earth. See also **Minor Plan**. See Chapter 2.

Manifestation of God. Designation used in the Bahá'í Faith to refer to the Founders of the great world religions such as Zoroaster, Krishna, Buddha, Moses, Jesus, Muhammad, the Báb and Bahá'u'lláh. It is not possible to explain this station adequately in few words. According to the Bahá'í sacred texts, the Manifestations of God are 'the representative and mouthpiece of God' (Bahá'u'lláh, *Gleanings from the Writings of Bahá'u'lláh*, XVIII, p. 70). Their works and acts are 'ordained by God, and are a reflection of His Will and Purpose' (ibid. XXIV, p. 59). They are the 'Vehicle for the transmission of the grace of the Divinity Itself, the Sovereign Lord of all' (ibid. XXVII, pp. 67–8).

Maxwell, James Clerk. 1831–1979. Scottish scientist. A Nobel laureate, Maxwell is considered by some as the father of modern mathematical physics. He developed the theory of electromagnetism and also made contributions to the fields of astronomy, mathematics and engineering. Einstein attributed the origin of the theory of relativity to Maxwell. Maxwell's work introduced significant changes to the Newtonian conception of reality.

Metaphor. Makes implicit or implied comparison between two things that are unrelated but have common characteristics. Bahá'u'lláh makes extensive use of metaphors to illuminate the mystical dimension of life, that invisible realm of the spirit that surrounds us. For example, He employs the metaphor of the sun to represent the centrality and incandescent power of truth – as in 'the Sun of Truth' – or the image of the ocean to represent the vastness and depth of divine revelation. Metaphors are used throughout this writing.

Minor Plan. The Minor Plan is the task of the Bahá'ís, to breathe life into the unified body of mankind toward creating a global civilization culminating in the Most Great Peace. The execution of the Minor Plan is through clearly delineated plans of the Bahá'í world, now aimed at the penetration of the message of Bahá'u'lláh throughout the world and its suffusion, leading to conversion and 'spiritualization' of the masses of humankind. See also **Major Plan of God**. See Chapter 2.

Mithraism. Religion centred around Mithras, with roots in pre-Zoroastrian Iran. Once it was introduced into Europe through Alexander's conquest, it spread rapidly and was the dominant religion of the Roman Empire from the 1st to the 4th centuries; it reached its zenith in the 3rd century and disappeared at the end of the 4th century when it lost competition to Christianity.

Mitosis. Period in the cell cycle whereby one cell becomes visibly two. Mitosis is a small fraction of the entire cell cycle. For example, while the cycle of a human cell may take as much as 24 hours, mitosis takes no more than one hour. The remaining 23 hours are taken up by the interphase period. See also **Cell cycle**, and discussion in Chapter 1.

Monochromaticity. A property of the laser beam. The generated beam is monochromatic in that it is of one specific wavelength. See discussion in Chapter 2.

Morse, Samuel Finley. 1791-1872. American inventor of Morse Code. The first telegraphic message was sent on 24 May 1844, from Washington to Baltimore, comprising words selected from the Bible: '*What Hath God Wrought*', with the word 'God' capitalized and underlined twice. Morse Code was initially used over land lines.

Moth and the flame. Metaphor used by mystics to represent sacrificial love. The moth symbolizes the lover and the flame the beloved. The light excites the moth, which circumambulates the flame closer and closer until it is consumed by the flame.

National Spiritual Assembly. Elected national governing council in the Bahá'í community. National Spiritual Assemblies (together with Regional Assemblies) are secondary **Houses of Justice** (q.v). Shoghi Effendi (*Bahá'í Administration*, p. 40) states that 'the friends in every country must elect a certain number of delegates, who in their turn will elect from among all the friends in that country the members of the National Spiritual Assembly'.

Nebuchadnezzar II. King of the Neo-Babylonian Empire, 605-562 BC.

Newly emergent entities. Phenomena that arise entirely new, not existing before. An example is gaseous oxygen in the Earth's atmosphere, which did not exist before animal life came into existence. Photosynthetic molecules in cyanobacteria, algae and plants produced oxygen from carbon dioxide and water. This made respiration possible; hence animal life was made possible and thrived thereafter.

Non-linear. In non-linear systems the outcome is not directly proportional to the input. A non-linear relationship follows mathematical principles of polynomial equations. Non-linear systems are unpredictable and appear random though they are not. A small change in one part of the system can produce complex effects throughout. A Chaotic process is non-linear. An example is the butterfly effect of the science of Chaos. See Chapter 5.

Oparin, Alexander. 1894–1980. Russian biochemist who worked independently from **John Haldane** (q.v.) on 'prebiotic' conditions of life on Earth. He is noted for his contributions to the theory of the origin of life.

Open networks. Networks that are open to all, whether affiliated or not. The concept was employed by Rodney Starke in his book *The Rise of Christianity*, where he provides a compelling discussion on the pivotal role which open networks played in the growth and development of Christianity during its earliest centuries. See Chapter 2.

Open portals. Paths to a Faith community that are open to and inviting to all. The core activities of Bahá'í communities are open portals; they welcome all, whether affiliated or not. A continually wider outreach to populations in the larger community is encouraged, with no distinctions made between believers and nonbelievers. Barriers to effective interaction are removed. See Chapter 2.

Organic growth. Term applied in this writing to describe the growth of the Bahá'í Faith. This characterization conveys that the Bahá'í Faith develops and grows as a living organism or as a viable organ in a biological system. This understanding implies that the ultimate structure of that viable organ, elegantly suited to its purpose, is inherent within it from its very beginning; that is, at the level of those first potent cells. Such an organ develops gradually and systematically until its purpose – its destiny – becomes ultimately manifest and its function becomes operational. See Chapter 1.

Origen Adamantius. 184/185–254/254 AD. Born in Alexandria, where he spent half his life, Origen was a noted Christian Greek scholar and theologian, considered one of the greatest Christian scholars. Many of his writings were later rejected by Christian orthodoxy.

Ozymandias. Greek name for the powerful Egyptian Pharoah Ramses II (1303–1213 BC). The collapse of powerful ancient empires made an indelible impression on the poet Shelley and inspired him to compose his celebrated poem of that name in 1817. See Chapter 10.

Pangaea. A single land mass on planet Earth up to 250 million years ago, before it split into Eurasia and the Americas.

Paradigm. From Greek *paradigmia*: a pattern or model, an exemplar. Paradigm signifies our worldview; how we believe knowledge or systems work. Paradigms, as the framework based on the knowledge of their time in a particular field of learning, have been invaluable to the advance of science. They serve to stimulate further thinking and research which in turn lead to new data and hence the need for expansion of the paradigm. For discussion see Chapter 8.

Paradigm expansion. A process analysed and discussed by Thomas Kühn, who is thought to have coined the term. A paradigm expansion expands a prevailing paradigm to one that is more in line with new data. Paradigm expansion bears somewhat similar meaning to **Paradigm shift**, explained below. See Chapter 8.

Paradigm shift. A process defined and explored by Thomas Kühn, who is thought to have coined the term. A paradigm shift changes an outworn paradigm (worldview, pattern of thinking) to one that is more relevant to the new findings and observations. In the context of the theme discussed in Chapters 8 and 9 it refers to the need to expand the pattern of one's thinking from a paradigm of truth exclusive to one religion, to a paradigm of truth encompassed by all religions. In the Bahá'í paradigm of the oneness of religions this paradigm shift is in reality a paradigm expansion. See the discussion in Chapter 8.

Parliament of World Religions. At this event convened in Chicago in 1893, reference was made to the Faith of Bahá'u'lláh for the first time in the North American continent. A Second Parliament of World Religions was convened in Chicago in 1993. The Parliament of World Religions has since continued to meet over the years; the latest occasion was in 2015 in Salt Lake City, Utah.

Phase transition. A change in phase such as the change of water from aqueous to steam form or from solid (ice) to aqueous form. At the boiling point of water, transition in phase from the liquid state to the vapour state begins to take place. See Chapter 2.

Philo of Alexandria. 20 BC–50 AD. Jewish Biblical philosopher, born in Alexandria. According to some scholars, his concept of Logos as God's creative principle or governing plan for the world influenced early Christology.

Philosophy of history. Study of discipline concerned with the purpose and outcome of the course of human history. For discussion see Chapter 7.

Photosynthesis. A process by which energy from the sun is absorbed by photosynthetic molecules such as chlorophyll in plants. These molecules capture the energy of sunlight and synthesize organic compounds, carbohydrates, from carbon dioxide and water with the release of oxygen essential to animal life. See Chapter 6.

Plato. c. 424/3–348/7 BC. Greek philosopher and mathematician, a student of Socrates and teacher of Aristotle. Plato was the founder of the Academy in Athens, the first institution of higher learning in the Western world. Together with Socrates and Aristotle, Plato helped to lay the foundations of western philosophy and science.

Population inversion. Term used in the context of the generation of the laser beam (q.v.). The population of in-phase quanta lock into each other and form the laser beam. This happens when over half of the population are in phase with one another. However, the quanta which are out of phase are of no consequence, as they cancel each other out; that is, the crest (the summit of the waves) and the trough (depressions between two waves) cancel each other. See Chapter 2.

Portals of entry. Routes for entry or affiliation with a faith community. The core activities comprising study circles, devotional meetings, neighbourhood children's classes and a programme for junior youth provide portals of entry to the Bahá'í Faith. See also **Open portals**. See Chapter 2.

Potential to the kinetic. Potential energy is the energy stored in a body and kinetic energy is the energy resulting from motion. Thus potential refers to that which is latent, kinetic that which becomes manifest and results in action. Conversion of the potential to the kinetic signifies conversion of the latent to the manifest.

Prebiotic. Prebiotic conditions of life on Earth refer to the origin of life: the spontaneous generation of life in a 'primordial soup' containing small organic molecules in salt water.

Prigogine, Ilya. 1917–2003. Belgian physical chemist, born in Russia. He received a Nobel Prize in 1977 for his work on the thermodynamics of non-equilibrium systems. His work contributes to the understanding of the science of Chaos in the natural sciences. Furthermore, its implications relate to social sciences and in particular to history. See Chapters 5 and 7.

Ptolemy, Claudius. 90–168 AD. Greco-Egyptian mathematician, geographer and astronomer. Ptolemy's model of the universe was **geocentric** (q.v.), with the earth at the centre. He was the author of several scientific treatises, including his treatise on astronomy, now known as the *Almagest*. See Chapter 8.

Qayyúmu'l-Asmá'. Commentary on the Surih of Joseph revealed by the Báb.

Reflex. A reflex works by means of an *arc*, i.e. through an incoming sensory input and an outgoing motor output. It is automatic: no further processing is required, no integration at a higher level of the nervous system is necessary. Reasoning and decision-making are not required. There are numerous examples of reflex from neuroscience, such as the knee-jerk reflex.

Renaissance. Cultural movement that spanned approximately the 14th to the 17th centuries. Beginning in Italy, it later spread to the rest of Europe, encompassing numerous fields including literature, science, art, politics and religion. The transformation which took place in many of these areas has contributed to the view that the Renaissance served as a bridge between the Middle Ages and the modern era.

Rúmí, Mawláná Jalálu'd-Dín. 1207–1273. Muslim poet, jurist, theologian and mystic.

Sa'di. 1210–1291. Celebrated Persian poet, lyricist and mystic from Shiraz, Iran. His best known books are *Bustan* (the Orchard) and *Gulistan* (the Rose Garden) as well as numerous other well-known poems.

Second law of thermodynamics. Entropy, a measure of disorganization, increases with time. See Chapter 7.

Self-transcendence. Transcending or going beyond one's self, one's ego. Spiritual self-transcendence is an objective of all the great religions of the world: for individuals to manifest the engraven image of God. In the Bahá'í Faith this is stated by Bahá'u'lláh in the *Hidden Words*: 'O Son of Spirit! Noble have I created thee, yet thou hast abased thyself. Rise then unto that for which thou wast created' (Arabic, no. 22). Arising to fulfil that innate nobility is transcending one's self.

Seneca, Lucius Annaeus. 4 BC–65 AD. Roman stoic statesman, philosopher and dramatist. Among the many works attributed to Seneca are philosophical essays and tragedies such as *Medea*.

Sensitive dependence on initial conditions. Term applied to the butterfly effect of the Chaos theory. A very small change under appropriate conditions (in non-linear systems) can have a very large outcome. See Chapter 5.

Sentient. Possessing powers of sense or sense perception; having or actually experiencing sensation or feeling: opposed to *inanimate* and *vegetal*. Sentient beings have the ability to feel and sense; they have a level of consciousness to be distinguished from the higher level of consciousness of humans.

Shelley, Percy Bysshe. 1792–1822. Major English poet and lyricist, considered among the finest.

Simile. Figure of speech that makes a direct comparison between two different things to show their similarities. Unlike metaphor, simile uses the words 'like' or 'as' to draw resemblance; for example, she 'talks like an angel', 'cries like a baby' or 'is lovely as a rose'.

Sin of hybris. Term used by Arnold J. Toynbee, but more commonly spelled 'hubris'. The sin of self-centredness.

Singular point. Term introduced by James Clerk Maxwell (q.v.), who draws this concept from his work on the simplest physical systems; he then extends this perception to the course of history. Maxwell proposes that at rare intervals in history there are moments which can be viewed as singular points. At these points a very small force, by its character and position in the whole constellation of events, can bring about a change of astonishing magnitude, as with a pebble starting an avalanche.

Síyáh-Chál. Farsi, lit. 'Black Pit'. The dark, foul-smelling, subterranean dungeon in Tehran, Iran where Bahá'u'lláh was imprisoned for four months. Here, in October 1852, He received the intimation of His Revelation; this marks the birth of His Prophetic Mission.

Social surface. As used in this book, this term refers to the ratio of the number of believers to the number of non-believers. It is the interface available for contact and interaction between the two. See Chapter 2.

Spengler, Oswald Arnold Gottfried. 1880–1936. German historian and philosopher of history, best known for his two-volume work entitled *The Decline of the West* (or *The Downfall of the Occident*) published in 1918 and 1922. This book met with resounding success and bore its influence on the thinking of the time and on a number of philosophers. In Spengler's view, civilizations have a life span; their development can be compared to that of an organism that goes through phases (seasons) of life.

Sustainability. Sustainable growth, characterized by endurance, perseverance and self-maintenance.

Synthesis phase. In this phase of mitosis (cell cycle division) synthesis (i.e. replication) of the genetic material, DNA, takes place. See **Cell cycle**, and also discussion in Chapter 1.

Tablets of the Divine Plan. Fourteen letters addressed by 'Abdu'l-Bahá to the Bahá'í communities in North America between 1916 and 1917. The formal presentation ('unveiling') of these Tablets took place at the end of the First World War in 1919 in New York City. They comprise the charter for the teaching and spread of the Bahá'í Faith throughout the world, toward the 'spiritual conquest' of the planet. See Chapter 3.

Theodosius the Great. 347–395 AD. Theodosius I, Roman Emperor who in 380 declared 'Catholic Christianity' the only legitimate religion of the Roman Empire.

Threshold level. In the context of the generation of a laser beam, the level where the number of quanta in an excited state exceeds the number of quanta in a lower energy state. The outcome is that the quanta that are in phase and have locked into each other form a laser beam. The quanta that remain out of phase cancel each other out; the laser beam predominates. This is known as 'population inversion'. See Chapter 2.

Tipping point. A term of recent usage referring to that certain point when the system changes, e.g. when trends catch on and become enormously popular.

Tissue culture. Living cells are isolated from organs and tissues and grown outside the organism in a medium supplied with all essential nutrients and under conditions optimal to their growth. Some cell lines have been continuously grown in such manner; these are of significant value to researchers. Examining the growth of a population of cells in a tissue-culture medium can provide a host of valuable information. For discussion see Chapter 1.

Tolstoy, Count Lev Nikolayevich. 1828–1910. Russian writer and philosopher, believed by many to be one of the greatest novelists of all time. More usually known in English as Leo Tolstoy.

Toynbee, Arnold Joseph. 1889–1975. British historian. With a broad perspective, he had an optimistic view of the course and outcome of history. He believed that religions play a significant role in the advance of civilizations. His 12-volume masterpiece, *A Study of History*, resonates the Bahá'í view on religions and their role in history.

Transmutation. A preferred choice of word to describe the level of transformation which takes place through the impetus of the Word of God, the Divine Elixir – divine revelation – whereby one becomes a new being, a new entity. This has its analogue in alchemy, i.e. the transmutation of a base metal into precious gold. The transmutation which takes place in the human soul is tantamount to a trans-substantiation.

Trans-substantiation. A change in substance. The change of a base metal into gold is more than transformation; it is trans-substantiation.

Triumphalism. An attitude of superiority, that one's beliefs are superior to others.

Turbulence. Turbulence has a number of implications in the field of physics. However, as a definition relevant to the discussion on Chaos in this writing, turbulence entails the introduction of disturbance or disorder into a system and the upsetting of its equilibrium. Turbulent flow is Chaotic. See Chapter 5.

Universal House of Justice. Supreme governing body of the Bahá'í Faith, instituted by Bahá'u'lláh in the *Kitáb-i-Aqdas* (Most Holy Book). 'Abdu'l-Bahá in His *Will and Testament* (para. 25) refers to the Universal House of Justice being indirectly elected. On the election of the first Universal House of Justice in 1963, see Chapter 3.

Virgin territories. In Bahá'í terminology, used to describe places – countries, islands and regions – to which the message of the Bahá'í Faith has not yet been taken. See Chapter 3.

Vital growth. Growth displayed by a living organism which has the capability of imparting continuation to its own life.

Yeats, William Butler. 1865–1939. Irish poet and playwright, and

Nobel laureate for literature in 1923. He was one of the foremost figures in 20th-century literature. His work has been described as 'inspired poetry'.

Worldview. From German: *Weltanschauung*, one's outlook on the world. The body of beliefs on life, the universe, and history held by individuals or groups. It is the perspective with which one views, understands and interprets the world. The term has wide philosophical and religious implications.

BIBLIOGRAPHY

Works by Bahá'u'lláh

— *Epistle to the Son of the Wolf.* Trans. Shoghi Effendi. Wilmette, IL: Bahá'í Publishing Trust, rev. ed. 1976.

— *Gems of Divine Mysteries: Javáhiru'l-Asrár.* Haifa: Bahá'í World Centre, 2002.

— *Gleanings from the Writings of Bahá'u'lláh.* Trans. Shoghi Effendi. Wilmette, IL: Bahá'í Publishing Trust, 2nd ed. 1976.

— *The Hidden Words of Bahá'u'lláh.* Trans. Shoghi Effendi. Wilmette, IL: Bahá'í Publishing Trust, 1970; New Delhi: Bahá'í Publishing Trust, 1987.

— *The Kitáb-i-Aqdas: The Most Holy Book.* Haifa: Bahá'í World Centre, 1992.

— *Kitáb-i-Íqán: The Book of Certitude.* Trans. Shoghi Effendi. Wilmette, IL: Bahá'í Publishing Trust, 2nd ed. 1950, 1981.

— *Prayers and Meditations by Bahá'u'lláh.* Trans. Shoghi Effendi. Wilmette,IL: Bahá'í Publishing Trust, 1938, 1987.

— *The Proclamation of Bahá'u'lláh to the Kings and Leaders of the World.* Haifa: Bahá'í World Centre, 1967.

— *The Seven Valleys and the Four Valleys.* Trans. M. Gail with A-K. Khan. Wilmette, IL: Bahá'í Publishing Trust, rev. ed. 1975.

— *The Summons of the Lord of Hosts: Tablets of Bahá'u'lláh.* Haifa: Bahá'í World Centre, 2002.

— *Tablets of Bahá'u'lláh Revealed after the Kitáb-i-Aqdas.* Comp. Research Department of the Universal House of Justice. Haifa: Bahá'í World Centre, 1978.

Works by the Báb

Selections from the Writings of the Báb. Comp. Research Department of the Universal House of Justice. Haifa: Bahá'í World Centre, 1976.

Other Sacred Scriptures

Bible. *Holy Bible.* King James version. London: Eyre and Spottiswoode, various dates.

Qur'án. *The Holy Qur'an.* Trans. Abdullah Yusuf Ali. 1934. Rev. ed. 2009/10, available at sacred-texts.com.

Works by 'Abdu'l-Bahá

— *'Abdu'l-Bahá in London* (1912, 1921). London: Bahá'í Publishing Trust, 1982.

— *Paris Talks: Addresses given by 'Abdu'l-Bahá in 1911* (1912). London: Bahá'í Publishing Trust, 12th ed. 1995.

— *The Promulgation of Universal Peace: Talks Delivered by 'Abdu'l-Bahá During His Visit to the United States and Canada in 1912* (1922, 1925). Comp. H. MacNutt. Wilmette, IL: Bahá'í Publishing Trust, 2nd ed. 1982.

— *The Secret of Divine Civilization.* Trans. M. Gail. Wilmette, IL: Bahá'í Publishing Trust, 1957.

— *Selections from the Writings of 'Abdu'l-Bahá.* Comp. Research Department of the Universal House of Justice. Haifa: Bahá'í World Centre, 1978.

— *Some Answered Questions* (1908). Comp. and trans. Laura Clifford Barney. Haifa: Bahá'í World Centre, rev. ed. 2014.

— *Tablets of Abdu'l-Bahá* (etext in the Ocean search engine; originally published as *Tablets of Abdul-Baha Abbas*. 3 vols. Chicago: Bahá'í Publishing Society, 1909–1916). Wilmette, IL: National Spiritual Assembly of the Bahá'ís of the United States, 1980.

— *Tablets of the Divine Plan.* Wilmette, IL: Bahá'í Publishing Trust, rev. ed. 1977.

— *Tablet to the Hague,* A letter written by 'Abdu'l-Bahá to the Central Organization for a Durable Peace, The Hague, 17 December 1919. London: Bahá'í Publishing Trust, n.d.

— *Will and Testament of 'Abdu'l-Bahá.* Wilmette, IL: National Spiritual Assembly of the Bahá'ís of the United States, 1944.

Works by Shoghi Effendi

— *The Advent of Divine Justice* (1939). Wilmette, IL: Bahá'í Publishing Trust, 1984.

— *Bahá'í Administration: Selected Messages 1922–1932.* Wilmette, IL: Bahá'í Publishing Trust, 1980.

— *The Bahá'í Faith 1844–1952: Information Statistical and Comparative.* Wilmette, IL: Bahá'í Publishing Trust, 1953.

— *The Bahá'í Faith – The World Religion: A Summary of Its Aims, Teachings and History.* Available at: http://bahairesearch.com/english/Baha'i/Authoritative_Baha'i/Shoghi_Effendi/Summary_Statement_-The_World_Religion.aspx.

— *Citadel of Faith: Messages to America, 1947–1957.* Wilmette, IL: Bahá'í Publishing Trust, 1965.

— *Dawn of a New Day: Messages to India 1923–1957.* New Delhi: Bahá'í Publishing Trust, n.d.

— *God Passes By* (1944). Wilmette, IL: Bahá'í Publishing Trust, rev. ed. 1974.

— *Messages to America 1932–1946*. Wilmette, IL: Bahá'í Publishing Trust, 1947. Published online by the Project Gutenberg.

— *Messages to the Bahá'í World, 1950–1957*. Wilmette, IL: Bahá'í Publishing Trust, 2nd ed. 1971.

— *The Promised Day Is Come* (1941). Wilmette, IL: Bahá'í Publishing Trust, rev. ed. 1980.

— *Unfolding Destiny: The Messages from the Guardian of the Bahá'í Faith to the Bahá'í Community of the British Isles*. London: Bahá'í Publishing Trust, 1981.

— *The World Order of Bahá'u'lláh: Selected Letters by Shoghi Effendi* (1938). Wilmette, IL: Bahá'í Publishing Trust, 2nd rev. ed. 1974.

Works by the Universal House of Justice

— *Century of Light*. Haifa: Bahá'í World Centre, 2001

— *The Constitution of the Universal House of Justice*. Haifa: Bahá'í World Centre, 1972.

— *The Five Year Plan, 2006–2011*. West Palm Beach, FL: Palabra Publications, 2006.

— *Institution of the Counsellors*. Haifa: Bahá'í World Centre, 2001.

— *Messages from the Universal House of Justice 1963–1986: The Third Epoch of the Formative Age*. Comp. Geoffry W. Marks. Wilmette, IL: Bahá'í Publishing Trust, 1996.

— Message to the Conference of the Continental Boards of Counsellors, 28 December 2010. Available at: http://www.bahai.org/library/authoritative texts/the-universal-house-of-justice/messages/.

— *The Ministry of the Custodians 1957–1963: An Account of the Stewardship of the Hands of the Cause*. Haifa: Bahá'í World Centre, 1992.

— *One Common Faith*. Haifa: Bahá'í World Centre, 2005; Wilmette, IL: Bahá'í Publishing Trust, 2005.

— Riḍván Messages to the Bahá'ís of the World: 2008, 2009, 2010, 2011, 2012, 2014, 2015, 2016. Available at: http://www.bahai.org/library/authoritative texts/the-universal-house-of-justice/messages/.

— *A Synopsis and Codification of the Kitáb-i-Aqdas*. Haifa: Bahá'í World Centre, 1973.

— *Turning Point: Selected Messages of the Universal House of Justice and Supplementary Materials, 1996–2006*. West Palm Beach, FL: Palabra Publications, 2006.

— *Wellspring of Guidance: Messages from the Universal House of Justice 1963–1968*. Wilmette, IL: Bahá'í Publishing Trust, 1976.

— *A Wider Horizon: Selected Messages of the Universal House of Justice, 1983–1992*. Riviera Beach, FL: Palabra Publications, 1992.

Other sources

Albers, Bruce; Johnson, Alexander; Lewis, Julian; Roberts, Keith; Walters, Peter. *Molecular Biology of the Cell*. New York: Garland Science, 5th ed. 2007.

Afroukhteh, Youness. *Memories of Nine Years in 'Akká*. Trans. Riaz Masrour. Oxford: George Ronald, 2003.

Atkins, Peter; de Paula, Julio. *Physical Chemistry*. Oxford: Oxford University Press/ W. H. Freeman, 9th ed. 2009.

Bahá'í Prayers: A Selection of Prayers Revealed by Bahá'u'lláh, The Báb, and 'Abdu'l-Bahá. Wilmette, IL: Bahá'í Publishing Trust, rev. ed. 1991.

The Bahá'í World: An International Record. Vol. III (1928-1930); vol. V (1932-1934); vol. X (1944-1946). Wilmette, IL: Bahá'í Publishing Trust. New series: *The Bahá'í World 2004-2005*. Haifa: Bahá'í World Centre, 2006.

Bahá'í World Faith: Selected Writings of Bahá'u'lláh and 'Abdu'l-Bahá. Wilmette, IL: Bahá'í Publishing Trust, rev. ed. 1956.

Bahíyyih Khánum, The Greatest Holy Leaf. Haifa: Bahá'í World Centre, 1982.

Barks, Coleman (trans.). *The Essential Rumi*. San Francisco: HarperCollins, 1995.

Barrett, David (ed.). *World Christian Encyclopedia*. Oxford: Oxford University Press, 1982.

Bausani, Alessandro. *Religions in Iran*. New York: Bibliotheca Persica, 2000.

Bergreen, Laurence. *Columbus: The Four Voyages, 1492-1504*. New York: Viking Penguin, 2011.

Boorstin, Daniel J. *The Discoverers: A History of Man's Search to Know His World and Himself.* New York: Vintage, 1985.

Britannica Book of the Year 1992. Ed. Daphne Daume. London: Encyclopaedia Britannica, 1992.

Butterfield, Herbert. *The Englishman and His History*. Cambridge: Cambridge University Press, 1944.

Campbell, Lewis; Garnett, William. *The Life of James Clerk Maxwell, with selections from his correspondence and occasional writings*. London, MacMillan and Co., 1884.

Carr, Edward Hallet. *What is History?* New York: Vintage, 1961.

Chadwick, Henry. 'The early Christian community', in J. McManners (ed.): *The Oxford Illustrated History of Christianity.* Oxford/New York: Oxford University Press, 1995.

Collingwood, R. G. *The Idea of History* (1945). Oxford: Oxford University Press, rev. ed. 1974.

The Compilation of Compilations. Prepared by the Universal House of Justice, 1963-1990. 2 vols. Sydney: Bahá'í Publications Australia, 1991.

Collins, Francis S. *The Language of God*. New York: Free Press, 2006.

Csikszentmihalyi, Mihalyi. *Flow: The Psychology of Optimal Experience*. New York: Harper Perennial, 1990.

Dahl, Gregory C. *One World One People: How Globalization is Facing Our Future*. Wilmette, IL: Bahá'í Publishing Trust, 2007.

Dante Alighieri (Durante degli Alighieri). *The Divine Comedy*. Trans. Allen Mandelbaum. New York: Everyman's Library, 1995.

Darwin, Charles. *On the Origin of Species By Means of Natural Selection* (1859). New York: Oxford University Press, 2009.

Developing Distinctive Bahá'í Communities. Evanston, IL: National Spiritual Assembly of the Bahá'ís of the United States, 1998.

Diamond, Jared. *Collapse: How Societies Choose to Fail or Succeed*. New York: Penguin, 2011.

Dover, Gabriel. 'Molecular drive: A cohesive mode of species evolution', in *Nature*, 299:111–7, 1982.

Dray, William H. *Philosophy of History*. Englewood Cliffs, NJ: Prentice Hall, 1964.

Dunbar, Hooper C. *Forces of Our Time: The Dynamics of Light and Darkness*. Oxford: George Ronald, 2010.

Edmonds, L. N. Jr. *Cellular and Molecular Basis of Biological Clocks*, Sixth Edition, New York: Springer, 6th ed., 2008.

Ehrlich, P. R.; Raven, P. H. 'Butterflies and plants: A study in coevolution', in *Evolution*, 18:586–608, 1964.

England, A. Marjorie; Wakely, Jennifer. *Color Atlas of the Brain & Spinal Cord: An Introduction to Normal Neuroanatomy*. St. Louis: Mosby Year Book, 1991.

Fananapazir, Lameh. *Islam at the Crossroads*. Oxford: George Ronald, 2015.

Fraser, Gordon. *The New Physics for the Twenty First Century*. Cambridge/New York: Cambridge University Press, 2nd rev. ed., 2006.

Frontiers of Learning, video, available at http://www.bahai.org/frontiers.

Fukuyama, Francis. *The End of History and the Last Man*. New York: The Free Press, 1992.

— *The Great Disruption: Human Nature and the Reconstruction of Social Order*. New York: The Free Press, 1999.

— *Trust: The Social Virtues and the Creation of Prosperity*. New York: The Free Press, 1996.

Funk & Wagnalls New International Dictionary of the English Language. Chicago, IL: World Book, 1996.

Gebser, Jean. *The Ever Present Origin*. Trans. Noel Barstad with Algis Mickunas. Athens, OH: Ohio University Press, 1991.

Gibbon, Edward. *The History of the Decline and Fall of the Roman Empire*. Abridged, ed. Dero A. Saunders. New York: Penguin, 1985.

Gladwell, Malcolm. *The Tipping Point*. New York: Little Brown, 2000.

Gleick, James. *Chaos: Making a New Science*. New York: Penguin, 1987.

Hegel, George W. F. *The Philosophy of History*. Trans. J. Sibree. New York: Dover, 2004.

Heimer, Lennart. *The Human Brain and Spinal Cord*. New York: Springer, 1983.

Holley, Horace. 'Survey of current Bahá'í activities 1928-1930', in *The Bahá'í World*, vol. III (1928-1930).

Hunt, Brian R.; Yorke, James A. 'Maxwell on Chaos', in *Nonlinear Science Today*, 3:1, 1993.

Huntington, Samuel P. *The Clash of Civilizations and the Remaking of World Order*. New York: Simon & Schuster, 1996.

Hoyningen-Huene, Paul. *Reconstructing Scientific Revolutions*. Trans. Alexander T. Levine. Chicago: University of Chicago Press, 1993.

Jantsch, Erich. *The Self-Organizing Universe: Scientific and Human Implications of the Emerging Paradigm of Evolution*. Oxford: Pergamon Press, 1980.

Johns, Jeremy. 'Christianity and Islam', in J. McManners (ed.): *The Oxford Illustrated History of Christianity*. Oxford/New York: Oxford University Press, 1995.

Khodadad, Jena Khadem. 'The Bahá'í worldview on unity of religions, "progressive revelation": The application of principles and insights from the history of science', in: *Lights of Irfán*, vol. 10. Darmstadt: Asr-i-Jadid, 2009, pp. 43-70.

— 'The course of human history is directed toward unified history of humankind and a global civilization', in *Proceedings of the Eighth International Conference on Globalization for the Common Good*. Chicago, Layola University, 2009.

— 'The religious and spiritual philosophy of the Bahá'í Faith on globalization', in *Proceedings of the Ninth International Conference on Globalization for the Common Good*. Thousand Oaks, CA: California Lutheran University, 2010.

— ; Loew, Jerome M.; Weinstein, Ronald S. 'Freeze-fracture and freeze-etch electron microscopy of membrane proteins', in C. Ian Ragan and Richard J. Cherry (eds.): *Techniques for Analysis of Membrane Proteins*. London: Chapman and Hall, 1986, pp. 275-314.

Kühn, Thomas. *The Structure of Scientific Revolution*. Chicago: University of Chicago Press, 2nd ed. 1970.

Lample, Paul. *Revelation and Social Reality: Learning to Translate What is Written into Reality*. West Palm Beach, FL: Palabra Publications, 2009.

Langer, William (ed.) *An Encyclopedia of World History* (1940). Updated and ed. Peter N. Stearns. New York: Houghton Mifflin, 6th ed. 2001.

Laszlo, Erwin. *The Chaos Point*. Newburyport, MA: Hampton Roads, 2006.

Lewis, David Levering. *God's Crucible: Islam and the Making of Europe, 570–1215*. New York/London: W. W. Norton, 2008.

Lights of Guidance: A Bahá'í Reference File. Comp. H. Hornby. New Delhi: Bahá'í Publishing Trust, 5th ed. 1997.

Loehle, Craig, *Blueprint for a New World*. Oxford: George Ronald, 2007.

Ma'ani Ewing, Soveida. *Collective Security Within Reach*. Oxford: George Ronald, 2007.

Mandelbrot, Benoit. *The Fractal Geometry of Nature*. New York: W. H. Freeman and Co., 1982.

Mann, Charles C. *1493: Uncovering the New World Columbus Created*. New York: Alfred A. Knopf, 2011.

Marcus, Robert. 'From Rome to the barbarian kingdoms', in J. McManners (ed.): *The Oxford Illustrated History of Christianity*. Oxford/New York: Oxford University Press, 1995.

Margolis, Howard. *Paradigms and Barriers: How Habits of Mind Govern Scientific Belief*. Chicago: University of Chicago Press, 1993.

McLean, J. A. *A Celestial Burning: A Selective Study of the Writings of Shoghi Effendi*. New Delhi: Bahá'í Publishing Trust, 2012.

McManners, John. 'Introduction', in J. McManners (ed.): *The Oxford Illustrated History of Christianity*. Oxford/New York: Oxford University Press, 1995.

— 'The expansion of Christianity', in J. McManners (ed.): *The Oxford Illustrated History of Christianity*. Oxford/New York: Oxford University Press, 1995.

Melzer, A. M; Weinberger, J.; Zinman, M. R. *History and the Idea of Progress*. Ithaca, NY: Cornell University Press, 1995.

Miller, Donald L. *Lewis Mumford: A Life*. New York: Grove Press, 1989.

Mumford, Lewis. *The Transformations of Man*. New York: Harper and Rowe, 1956.

Nakhjavání, 'Alí. *Shoghi Effendi: Author of Teaching Plans*. Rome: Casa Editrice Bahá'í, 2nd ed. 2007.

Nicholson, Reynard. *The Mathnawi of Jalalu'ddin Rumi*. 6 vols. Cambridge: E.J.W. Gibb Memorial Trust, 1926.

Nolte, John. *The Human Brain, An Introduction to Its Functional Anatomy*. Philadelphia, PA: Elsevier, 6th ed. 2009.

Oparin, Alexander. *The Origin of Life*. New York: Dover, 1952, 1973.

Pinker, Steven. *The Better Angels of Our Nature: Why Violence has Declined*. New York: Penguin, 2011.

Prigogine, Ilya; Stengers, Isabelle. *Order Out of Chaos*. New York: Bantam, 1984.

Promoting Entry by Troops. Comp. Research Department of the Universal House of Justice. Wilmette, IL: Bahá'í Publishing Trust, 1993. Available on the Ocean search engine.

Rabbání, Rúḥíyyih. *The Priceless Pearl*. London: Bahá'í Publishing Trust, 1969.

Rifkin, Jeremy. *The Empathic Civilization: The Race to World Consciousness in a World in Crisis*. Boston/Cambridge/Oxford: Polity Press, 2009.

Russell, Peter. *The Global Brain: The Awakening Earth in a New Century*. Edinburgh: Floris Books, 3rd ed. 2008.

Saiedi, Nader. *Logos and Civilization: Spirit, History and Order in the Writings of Bahá'u'lláh*. Bethesda, Maryland: University Press, 2000.

Schaefer, Udo. *The Imperishable Dominion: The Bahá'í Faith and the Future of Mankind*. Trans. J. Rawling-Keitel, D. Hopper and P. Crampton from the German. Oxford: George Ronald, 1983.

— *The Light Shineth in Darkness*. Oxford: George Ronald, 1980.

Shelley, Percy Bysshe. *Miscellaneous and Posthumous Poems of Percy Bysshe Shelley*. London: W. Benbow, 1826.

Smith, Wilfred Cantwell. *Toward a World Theology: Faith and the Comparative History of Religion*. Philadelphia: Westminster Press, 1981.

Spengler, Oswald. *The Decline of the West*. Trans. C. F. Atkinson from the German: *Der Untergang des Abendlandes* (2 vols, 1918, 1922). Vol 1: *Form and Actuality*; vol. 2: *Perspectives of World History*. New York: Alfred A. Knopf, 1926, 1928, 1932.

Starke, Rodney. *The Rise of Christianity*. New York: Harper Collins, 1997.

Star of the West: The Bahai Magazine. Periodical, 25 vols. 1910–1935. Vols. 1–14 RP Oxford: George Ronald, 1978. Complete CD-ROM version: Talisman Educational Software/Special Ideas, 2001.

Stendardo, Luigi. *Leo Tolstoy and the Bahá'í Faith*. Trans. Jeremy Fox from the French. Oxford: George Ronald, 1985.

Stockman, Robert H. *The Bahá'í Faith in America*. Vol. 1: *Origins 1892-1900*. Wilmette, IL: Bahá'í Publishing Trust, 1985. Vol. 2: *Early Expansion, 1900-1912*. Oxford: George Ronald, 1995.

Strauss, William; Howe, Neil. *An American Prophecy: The Fourth Turning*. New York: Broadway Books, 1997.

Taherzadeh, Adib. *The Child of the Covenant: A Study Guide to the Will and Testament of 'Abdu'l-Bahá*. Oxford: George Ronald, 2000.

— *The Covenant of Bahá'u'lláh*. Oxford: George Ronald, 1992.

— *The Revelation of Bahá'u'lláh*. 4 vols. Oxford: George Ronald, 1974–1987.

Taleb, Nassim Nicholas. *The Black Swan: The Impact of the Highly Improbable*. New York: Random House, 2007.

Teilhard de Chardin, Pierre. *The Future of Man.* Trans. Norman Denny from the French. New York: Doubleday, 1964.

Thomas, June Manning. *Planning Progress: Lessons from Shoghi Effendi.* Ottawa: Bahá'í Studies, 1999.

Toffler, Alvin. *The Third Wave.* New York: William Morrow and Company, 1980.

Toynbee, Arnold J. *Change and Habit.* Oxford: OneWorld, 1992.

— *Civilization on Trial.* Oxford: Oxford University Press, 1948.

— *An Historian's Approach to Religion.* Oxford: Oxford University Press, 1956.

— *A Study of History.* 12 vols. Oxford: Oxford University Press, 1934–1961.

Unlocking the Power of Action. Comp. Research Department of the Universal House of Justice. Wilmette, IL: Bahá'í Publishing Trust, 1994. Available on the Ocean search engine.

Whinfield, E. H. (tr.). *Masnavi I Masnavi: The Spiritual Couplets of Maulana Jalalu-d'in Muhamad I Rumi.* London: Trubner & Co., 1887.

Wright, Robert. *Non-Zero: The Logic of Human Destiny.* New York: Pantheon, 2000.

Yeats, William Butler. *The Collected Works of W. B. Yeats.* Ed. Richard J. Finneran. New York: Simon and Schuster, 1996.

NOTES AND REFERENCES

Preface
1. 'Abdu'l-Bahá, *Some Answered Questions*, Chapter 16, pp. 93-6.
2. Shoghi Effendi was appointed by 'Abdu'l-Bahá as his successor when quite young; he assumed the station of Guardianship after the passing of 'Abdu'l-Bahá in 1921 when the Will and Testament of 'Abdu'l-Bahá was read.
3. Served on the National Teaching Committee from 1996 to 2000, focused on an extensive media campaign.
4. Served on the Regional Council of the Central States from 1997 to 2010.
5. The Universal House of Justice, Riḍván Message, 1990, to the Bahá'ís of the World, in *Entry by Troops*, p. 17.
6. The Green Lake Conference takes place annually in Green Lake, Wisconsin. It is the longest running Bahá'í Conference in the United States.
7. See the 2004 *New Zealand Bahá'í Newsletter*.
8. Bahá'u'lláh, quoted in Shoghi Effendi, *God Passes By*, p. 184.
9. 'Abdu'l-Bahá, *Some Answered Questions*, Chapter 16, pp. 93-6.
10. The Universal House of Justice, Riḍván Message, 2015, to the Bahá'ís of the World.
11. ibid.
12. See Rabbání, *The Priceless Pearl*, p. 2.
13. The Sixth Script, in *The Principles of Chinese Writing*, quoted in Edmonds, *Cellular and Molecular Basis of Biological Clocks*, and in Nolte, *The Human Brain*, prefatory page.
14. Rumi, 'The Granary Floor', trans. Coleman Barks, *The Essential Rumi*, p. 249, based on Nicolson, II: 156-93.

Acknowledgements
1. Bahá'u'lláh, *The Seven Valleys and the Four Valleys*, p. 34.

Introduction
1. The intimation to Bahá'u'lláh of His mission was in 1853 in the Síyáh-Chál (see the Glossary); the disclosure (declaration) of His Prophetic mission was on 21 April 1863 in Baghdad.
2. 1893 was a landmark date, when the Bahá'í Faith was mentioned for the first time on the continent of North America, at the First Parliament of World Religions in Chicago.
3. Shoghi Effendi makes this statement in 'America and The Most Great Peace', dated 21 April 1933; in Shoghi Effendi, *The World Order of Bahá'u'lláh*, p. 88.

4   Through a series of national plans and the Ten Year Global Crusade (1953-1963).
5   The Universal House of Justice, Message to the Conference of the Continental Boards of Counsellors, 28 December 2010, para. 12.
6   2005 figures, from statisticians at the Bahá'í World Centre.
7   The Universal House of Justice, Riḍván Message, 2010, to the Bahá'ís of the World.
8   The size of the worldwide Bahá'í community is reported variously by some sources at approximately 5.0 to 5.5 million, by others at 5.5 to 6 million and by still others at close to 7 million.
9   Shoghi Effendi, *Messages to the Bahá'í World, 1950-1957*, p. 154. The Adamic cycle includes the revelations starting from Adam and ending with the Báb. It has within its compass the Hindu, Zoroastrian, Buddhist, Jewish, Christian and Muslim religions, with Muḥammad the seal – the end of that cycle – linked to the Manifestation of the Báb. Shoghi Effendi (*God Passes By*, p. 57) explains that the advent of the Báb in the Adamic Cycle 'at once signalized the termination of the "Prophetic Cycle" and the inception of the "Cycle of Fulfilment"'.

Regarding the Adamic cycle, see Taherzadeh, *The Covenant of Bahá'u'lláh*, pp. 32-3. Taherzadeh describes the unique placement of the advent of the Báb in the course of religious history: 'He stood between two religious cycles. With his advent He closed, on the one hand, the "Prophetic Cycle", which began with Adam as the first Manifestation of God in recorded history and ended with the Dispensation of Islám and, on the other, He opened the "Cycle of Fulfilment" whose duration, according to the Writings of Bahá'u'lláh and 'Abdu'l-Bahá, will be at least five thousand centuries.'
10 These national plans were initiated by eleven National Spiritual Assemblies throughout the world.
11 This was the Ten Year Global Crusade launched in 1953 by Shoghi Effendi to culminate in 1963.
12 The 'Formative Age' followed the 'Heroic Age' of Bahá'u'lláh's Dispensation which ended with the passing of 'Abdu'l-Bahá. The Formative Age is the age we are currently in, and is aimed at the erection of the Administrative Order throughout the planet, the establishment of its institutions and the effects of its 'society building' powers.
13 Far ahead lies what Shoghi Effendi called the 'Golden Age' of the Dispensation of Bahá'u'lláh. Its advent 'must witness the proclamation of the Most Great Peace and the unfoldment of that world civilization which is the offspring and the primary purpose of that Peace' (Shoghi Effendi, *Citadel of Faith*, p. 7). See also the Universal House of Justice, *Century of Light*, pp. 55, 56.
14 Shoghi Effendi, *Messages to the Bahá'í World, 1950-1957*, p. 154.
15 The Universal House of Justice, Riḍván Message, 1964, to the Bahá'ís of the World, p. 1.
16 The Universal House of Justice, Riḍván Message, 2011, to the Bahá'ís of the World.
17 See the Universal House of Justice, *Century of Light*, p. 69.
18 'Abdu'l-Bahá's Tablets of the Divine Plan are the fountainhead of all subsequent plans of the Bahá'í Faith.
19 The Universal House of Justice, Message to the Conference of the Continental Boards of Counsellors, 28 December 2010, para. 3.

20 'Entry by troops' is a phrase frequently used in Bahá'í terminology, from Shoghi Effendi: '{T}he advent of the day which, as prophesied by 'Abdu'l-Bahá, will witness the entry by troops of peoples of divers nations and races into the Bahá'í world' (*Citadel of Faith*, p. 117).
21 Institute process: 'the two essential movements which continue to propel the process of growth' are 'the steady flow of participants through the sequence of training institute courses and the movement of clusters along a continuum of development' (The Universal House of Justice, Riḍván Message, 2014, to the Bahá'ís of the World). The institute process is integral to the current plans of the Bahá'í world. It is centred on participation in the core activities: study circles, devotional meetings, children's classes and spiritual empowerment programmes for junior youth.
22 See the Universal House of Justice, Riḍván Message, 2010, to the Bahá'ís of the World.
23 The Universal House of Justice, Message to the Conference of the Continental Boards of Counsellors, 28 December 2010, para. 12.
24 The Universal House of Justice, Message to the Conference of the Continental Boards of Counsellors, 29 December 2015, and other recent messages.
25 ibid.
26 The Five Year Plan (2011–2016) was part of a series of plans launched in 2001 following the termination of the Four Year Plan. The Five Year Plans include four global enterprises, each of a five year time span, up to the year 2021. That year 2021 marks the centenary of the passing of 'Abdu'l-Bahá and the conclusion of the first century of the Formative Age of the Bahá'í Faith.
27 Specified in the Five Year Plan (2011–2016) as five thousand 'clusters', a term used to define geographical areas in the Bahá'í community for the purpose of a focus on growth. Clusters were introduced by the Universal House of Justice and became fundamental units of growth in the Five Year Plans.
28 The Universal House of Justice, Riḍván Message, 2015, to the Bahá'ís of the World.
29 The Universal House of Justice, Message to the Conference of the Continental Boards of Counsellors, 28 December 2010.
30 An autocatalytic process implies that the catalysis of the process is powered from within the system. In an autocatalytic process the reaction product serves also as a reactant. An autocatalytic process is a self-catalyzing process whereby catalysis progresses continuously, gathering speed over time. As an analogy in the context of this writing, when an autocatalytic process sets in, the wave of transformation propagates and escalates.
31 The Universal House of Justice, Riḍván Message, 2010, to the Bahá'ís of the World.
32 'Abdu'l-Bahá, *'Abdu'l-Bahá in London*, p. 80.
33 The words 'infuse', 'diffuse', 'penetrate' and 'suffuse' were used by Shoghi Effendi to describe sequential phases in the dissemination of the Divine Word through Bahá'u'lláh's Revelation (Shoghi Effendi, *Messages to the Bahá'í World, 1950–1957*, p. 154).
34 See Bahá'u'lláh, *The Proclamation of Bahá'u'lláh to the Kings and Rulers; The Summons of the Lord of Hosts: Tablets of Bahá'u'lláh*.

35 These principles and others have been expounded by Bahá'í scholars; see for example Dahl, *One World One People: How Globalization is Facing Our Future*; Ma'ani Ewing, *Collective Security Within Reach*; Schaefer, *The Imperishable Dominion* and *The Light Shineth in Darkness*.
36 'Wherefore fear ye, O My well-beloved ones? Who is it that can dismay you? A touch of moisture sufficeth to dissolve the hardened clay out of which this perverse generation is moulded' (Bahá'u'lláh, *Tablets of Bahá'u'lláh Revealed after the Kitáb-i-Aqdas*), pp. 84–5.

1. Nature of Growth

1 Letter from the Universal House of Justice to a National Spiritual Assembly, 27 July 1980, in *Promoting Entry by Troops*, p. 11.
2 The term 'adherent' is used throughout this book to signify avowed believers. Other terms, which may be perceived as synonyms, are: followers, affiliated, believers, and registered Bahá'ís. However, the term 'avowed believers' carries a greater depth of meaning; from the perspective of this author it implies confirmed believers.
3 Edward Gibbon, the great historian of the Roman Empire (1737–1794) wrote the monumental six-volume *History of the Decline and Fall of the Roman Empire* which discusses and explores the factors underlying the decline and fall that great Empire. Against this background, Gibbon discusses the rise and progress of Christianity. Shoghi Effendi was a great admirer of this work.
4 Gibbon, *The Decline and Fall of the Roman Empire*, p. 317.
5 *The Bahá'í World*, 2004–2005; see also earlier estimates in *Encyclopedia Britannica, 1992 Book of the Year* and *The World Christian Encyclopedia* (1982).
6 *The Bahá'í World*, 2004–2005.
7 As provided by the US Census Bureau Estimates.
8 See the video *Frontiers of Learning* (2013), on progress in advanced clusters, available at: http://www.bahai.org/frontiers; for more recent videos see http://www.bahai.org/action.
9 The Universal House of Justice, Riḍván Message, 2015, to the Bahá'ís of the World.
10 The Universal House of Justice, Message to the Conference of the Continental Boards of Counsellors, 29 December 2015.
11 'Abdu'l-Bahá, *Some Answered Questions*, Chapter 37, p. 170.
12 ibid. Chapter 29, pp. 135–6.
13 ibid. Chapter 37, p. 170.
14 ibid. Chapter 16, pp. 93–6.
15 Letter written on behalf of Shoghi Effendi to an individual believer, 18 February 1932, in *Promoting Entry by Troops*, p. 3.
16 The Universal House of Justice, Riḍván Message, 1989, to the Bahá'ís of the World.
17 Shoghi Effendi, *Bahá'í Administration*, p. 66.
18 'Abdu'l-Bahá, *Tablets of the Divine Plan*, p. 49.
19 Bahá'u'lláh, Kalimát-i-Firdawsíyyih, in *Tablets of Bahá'u'lláh Revealed after the Kitáb-i-Aqdas*, p. 71.
20 Bahá'u'lláh, Bishárát, ibid. p. 24; see also Bahá'u'lláh, *The Kitab-i-Aqdas*, Note 61, p. 195.

REFERENCES

21 See 'Abdu'l-Bahá, *The Promulgation of Universal Peace*, p. 187.
22 See discussion in Chapter 3, *The Flow of Plans and Growth*.
23 Covenant: see the Glossary; also Taherzadeh, *The Covenant of Bahá'u'lláh*.
24 'Abdu'l-Bahá, *The Promulgation of Universal Peace*, p. 420.
25 See Albers et al., *Molecular Biology of the Cell*.
26 The Universal House of Justice, Message to the Conference of the Continental Boards of Counsellors, 28 December 2010, para. 2.
27 Letter from the Universal House of Justice to a National Spiritual Assembly, 27 July 1980, in *Promoting Entry by Troops*, p. 11.
28 'Abdu'l-Bahá, *The Promulgation of Universal Peace*, pp. 43-4; cited in the Universal House of Justice, *Century of Light*, p. 111.
29 Bahá'u'lláh, Tablet of Aḥmad, in *Bahá'í Prayers*, p. 209.
30 Bahá'u'lláh, *Gems of Divine Mysteries*, p. 26.
31 Bahá'u'lláh, *Epistle to the Son of the Wolf*, p. 95.
32 Shoghi Effendi, *The Advent of Divine Justice*, p. 7.
33 Shoghi Effendi, *Citadel of Faith*, p. 43.
34 The Universal House of Justice, Riḍván Message, 2010, to the Bahá'ís of the World.
35 The Universal House of Justice, Message to the Conference of the Continental Boards of Counsellors, 29 December 2015.
36 ibid.
37 ibid.; see also The Universal House of Justice, Riḍván Message, 2010, to the Bahá'ís of the World.
38 The Universal House of Justice, Message to the Conference of the Continental Boards of Counsellors, 28 December 2010, para. 3.

2. Enhancing Growth from Within

1 Abdu'l-Bahá, *Selections from the Writings of Abdu'l-Bahá*, no. 207, p. 260.
2 For examples, see *Frontiers of Learning*, video, available at: http://www.bahai.org/frontiers.
3 The Universal House of Justice, Message to the Bahá'ís of the World, 5 December 2013.
4 Gen. 1:26-7.
5 Bahá'u'lláh, *Gleanings from the Writings of Bahá'u'lláh*, CXXII, pp. 259-60.
6 Bahá'u'lláh, *Hidden Words*, Arabic no. 22.
7 *Converting potential to the kinetic*: **Potential** energy is the energy stored in a body and kinetic energy is the energy resulting from motion. Thus potential refers to that which is latent; **kinetic** that which becomes manifest as a result of action. It produces motion. Conversion of the potential to the kinetic signifies conversion of the latent to the manifest.
8 Thomas, *Planning Progress: Lessons from Shoghi Effendi*.
9 In the nervous system a reflex is an involuntary, stereotyped response to a sensory input (see Nolte, *The Human Brain*, p. 238; Heimer, *The Human Brain and Spinal Cord*, p. 158; England and Wakely, *Color Atlas of the Brain & Spinal Cord*, p. 171).
10 Bahíyyih K͟hánum, *The Greatest Holy Leaf*, p. 142.
11 ibid. p. 10.

12 Mawláná Jalálu'd-Dín Rúmí (1207–73), born in Persia, a Muslim poet, jurist, theologian, and mystic.
13 *Mathnavi of Rumi* (trans. E. H. Whinfield), *The Masnavi*, vol. 3.
14 Afroukhteh, *Memories of Nine Years in 'Akká*, p. 51.
15 'Abdu'l-Bahá, *Tablets of Abdul-Baha Abbas*, vol. 3, p. 530.
16 ibid. p. 502.
17 Letter on behalf of Shoghi Effendi to the Manchester Spiritual Assembly, 28 July 1950, in *Unfolding Destiny*, p. 406.
18 Bahá'u'lláh, *Prayers and Meditations*, XXXVIII, p. 54.
19 Bahá'u'lláh, *Gleanings from the Writings of Bahá'u'lláh*, XCII, p. 183.
20 ibid. XCIX, p. 200.
21 Letter from the Universal House of Justice to a National Spiritual Assembly, 19 May 1994, in *Unlocking the Power of Action* (comp.), p. 2.
22 The Universal House of Justice, Riḍván Message, 1988, to the Bahá'ís of the World, in *A Wider Horizon*, p. 58.
23 Letter from Shoghi Effendi to the American Bahá'í community, 28 July 1954, in *Citadel of Faith*, p. 130.
24 The Universal House of Justice, Riḍván Message, 2010, to the Bahá'ís of the World.
25 The active medium is a medium which is capable of becoming activated; it can be energized for the generation of the laser beam. See Fraser, *The New Physics for the Twenty First Century*; and *How Stuff Works, Hungry Minds*.
26 The source of external energy energizes the active medium, pumping atoms in the medium from an inactive state to a higher energy state; that is, to an excited state. The excited electrons fall back to a lower orbit, emitting photons of a specific wavelength. Ultimately, a laser beam is generated with the specific properties of monochromaticity, coherence, and directionality.
27 The property of monochromacity (of one specific wavelength) as applied to the Bahá'í population does not imply uniformity. Rather, it implies oneness of purpose in dedication to the mission of Bahá'u'lláh for humanity.
28 'Abdu'l-Bahá, *Selections from the Writings of 'Abdu'l-Bahá*, no. 207, p. 260.
29 This is known as 'population inversion'. The quanta that are in phase and have locked into each other form the laser beam. However, the quanta which are out of phase are of no consequence as they cancel each other out; that is, the crest (the summit of the waves) and the trough (depressions between two waves) cancel each other.
30 See *Frontiers of Learning*, video, available at: http://www.bahai.org/frontiers.
31 In the natural sciences it is often exemplified by the boiling point, that point in transition in the phase of water from the liquid state to the vapour state; in some other systems it is the 'critical mass'. In yet other systems it is referred to as the 'threshold': this term is used by several authors in relationship to events in recent history.
32 Gladwell, *The Tipping Point*.
33 Letter from the Universal House of Justice to a National Spiritual Assembly, 19 May 1994, in *Unlocking the Power of Action* (comp.), p. 2.
34 The Universal House of Justice, *Century of Light*, p. 69. The 'Greater Plan of God' can be understood as the Major Plan of God.
35 'The institution of the Boards of Counsellors was brought into being by the

Universal House of Justice in 1968 to extend into the future the specific functions of protection and propagation conferred upon the Hands of the Cause of God. The members of these boards are appointed by the Universal House of Justice' (The Universal House of Justice, *Constitution*, By-Laws no. IX). For further information see the Universal House of Justice, *Institution of the Counsellors*.

36 Letter from the Universal House of Justice to a National Spiritual Assembly, 19 May 1994, in *Unlocking the Power of Action* (comp.), p. 3.
37 ibid.
38 'Abdu'l-Bahá, *Selections from the Writings of 'Abdu'l-Bahá*, no. 73, p. 111.
39 ibid. no. 207, p. 260.
40 See Fukuyama, *Trust: The Social Virtues and the Creation of Prosperity*.
41 See Shoghi Effendi, *Bahá'í Administration*, p. 28.
42 'Abdu'l-Bahá, *Selections from the Writings of 'Abdu'l-Bahá*, no. 45, pp. 87-8.
43 See 'Abdu'l-Bahá, *Tablets of the Divine Plan*, 1977
44 'Abdu'l-Bahá, *Selections from the Writings of 'Abdu'l-Bahá*, no. 35, p. 75.
45 Shoghi Effendi, *The World Order of Bahá'u'lláh*, p. 144.
46 See Darwin, *On the Origin of Species by Means of Natural Selection* (1859).
47 Ehrlich and Raven, 'Butterflies and plants: A study in coevolution', in *Evolution*, 18:586-608 (1964).
48 Dover, 'Molecular drive: A cohesive mode of species evolution', in *Nature*, 299:111-117 (1982).
49 Jantsch, *The Self-Organizing Universe: Scientific and Human Implications of the Emerging Paradigm of Evolution*.
50 The Universal House of Justice, Riḍván Message, 2008, to the Bahá'ís of the World.
51 Csikszentmihalyi, *Flow: The Psychology of Optimal Experience*.
52 These plans were preceded by a number of plans devised by the Guardian of the Faith, Shoghi Effendi, and by the Universal House of Justice in the first three decades of its existence. See Chapter 3, *The Flow of Plans and Growth*.
53 The Universal House of Justice, Message to the Conference of the Continental Boards of Counsellors, 26 December 1995, in *Turning Point*, pp. 3-14; Message to the Bahá'ís of the World, 31 December 1995, ibid. pp. 15-18; Riḍván Message, 1996, to the Bahá'ís of the World, ibid. pp. 21-37; to the Bahá'ís in various continents and countries, ibid. pp. 39-85; and Riḍván Message, 2000, to the Bahá'ís of the World, ibid. pp. 125-39.
54 The Universal House of Justice, Message to the Bahá'ís of the World, 26 November 1999, ibid. pp. 119-21; Riḍván Message, 2000, to the Bahá'ís of the World, ibid. pp. 125-39.
55 The Universal House of Justice, Message to the Conference of the Continental Boards of Counsellors, 9 January 2001, ibid. pp. 141-8; Message to the Bahá'ís of the World, 16 January 2001, ibid. pp. 153-5; Riḍván Message, 2001, to the Bahá'ís of the World, ibid. pp. 157-62.
56 See the Universal House of Justice, *The Five Year Plan, 2006 2011*.
57 The Universal House of Justice, Message to the Conference of the Continental Boards of Counsellors, 28 December 2010; Message to the Bahá'ís of the World, 1 January 2011; Riḍván Message, 2011, to the Bahá'ís of the World; Message to

all National Spiritual Assemblies, 12 December 2011.Available at: http://www.bahai.org/library/authoritative-texts/the-universal-house-of-justice/messages/.
58 The Universal House of Justice, Message to the Conference of the Continental Boards of Counsellors, 29 December 2015. Available at: http://www.bahai.org/library/authoritative-texts/the-universal-house-of-justice/messages/.
59 The Universal House of Justice, Riḍván message, 2000, to the Bahá'ís of the World, in *Turning Point*, p. 125; Message to the Bahá'ís of the World, 16 January 2001, ibid. p. 154; Riḍván Message, 2010, to the Bahá'ís of the world.
60 The Universal House of Justice, Riḍván Message, 2009, to the Bahá'ís of the World.
61 See Starke, *The Rise of Christianity*.
62 The Universal House of Justice, Riḍván Message, 1996, to the Bahá'ís of the World, in *Turning Point*, p. 29.
63 The Universal House of Justice, Riḍván Message, 1998, to the Bahá'ís of the World, ibid. pp. 104–5.
64 Shoghi Effendi, *The Advent of Divine Justice*, p. 61.
65 The Universal House of Justice, *Century of Light*, p. 138.
66 See the Universal House of Justice, *A Wider Horizon*, p. 70.
67 Letter from Shoghi Effendi to the Bahá'ís of the United States, 20 August 1954, in *Citadel of Faith*, p. 140.

3. The Flow of Plans and Growth

1 'The Call', by Joseph H. Hannen was composed for the unveiling of the Tablets of the Divine Plan at the Eleventh Annual Convention and Bahá'í Congress held in New York City, 26–30 April, 1919 (see *Star of the West*, vol. X, no. 4 (May 1919), pp. 50, 53).
2 The duration of the Báb's ministry was from 23 May 1844 (the declaration of His mission) to 9 July 1850 (His martyrdom). The duration of Bahá'u'lláh's ministry was from 1853 – the secret intimation to Him of His mission – to 1992 when He passed away in Akka.
3 In this chapter, certain comparisons are made between the growth of the Bahá'í Faith and Christianity, currently the predominant religion in the Western hemisphere. It must be borne in mind, however, that the Zoroastrian, Jewish, Hindu, Buddhist and Muslim revelations are all revered by the Bahá'í Faith and viewed as emanating from the same divine source. The intent of this chapter is not a comprehensive comparison between the growth of the Bahá'í Faith and all of the other great religions of the world; nor does it aim to provide an exhaustive comparison between the growth of the close to 160-year-old Bahá'í Faith with 2,000-year old-Christianity. Certain comparisons, however, are deemed of value, as they shed light on the question of the growth of the Bahá'í Faith.
4 See Chadwick, 'The early Christian community', in McManners (ed.): *The Oxford Illustrated History of Christianity*.
5 See 'The rise and expansion of Islam', in Langer (ed.) (updated Stearns, ed.), *Encyclopedia of World History*, 6th ed. pp. 610–945; Johns, 'Christianity and Islam', p. 169; Lewis, *God's Crucible: Islam and the Making of Europe, 570–1215*.
6 The Bahá'í Era commenced in 1844 AD with the declaration of the Báb.
7 See Shoghi Effendi, *The World Order of Bahá'u'lláh*, p. 88.
8 Shoghi Effendi, *Citadel of Faith*, p. 105.

9   See Gibbon, *History of the Decline and Fall of the Roman Empire*, p. 29.
10 See Starke, *The Rise of Christianity*, pp. 6-8.
11 Barrett (ed.), in *The World Christian Encyclopedia*, published in 1982, reported the decade-long work of Christian demographers on the number of Christians worldwide as well as the followers of other religions. According to this source, although during that period some sects or sub-groups of Christianity and Islam grew at a faster rate than the Bahá'í Faith, none had followers in more than a hundred countries. Thus for that particular point in time, the Bahá'í Faith was viewed as the most widely spread religion. The *Britannica Book of the Year 1992* provides statistics confirming that the Bahá'í Faith had communities in 205 countries and territories.
12 See *The Bahá'í World, 2004-2005*.
13 See Shoghi Effendi, *The Bahá'í Faith 1844-1952: Information Statistical and Comparative*; Rabbaní, *The Priceless Pearl*, p. 390.
14 See *The Bahá'í World, 2004-2005*. The Bahá'í Faith has been embraced by some 2,112 indigenous tribes, races and ethnic groups.
15 See Gibbon, *History of the Decline and Fall of the Roman Empire*, p. 317.
16 Origen Adamantius (184/185-254/254 AD), a noted Christian Greek scholar and theologian.
17 See Gibbon, *History of the Decline and Fall of the Roman Empire*, p. 317.
18 See Starke, *The Rise of Christianity*, pp. 6-8.
19 This number was reported at approximately five and a half million by the *Britannica Book of the Year 1992*, and more recently (2005) by the statisticians at the Bahá'í World Centre. A higher number – over 6.5 million – has been reported by other sources.
20 7.4 billion according to estimates by the United Nations Department of Economics and Social Affairs (UNDESA), Population Division, July 2015.
21 Constantine the Great (272-337 AD), Emperor from 336-337. He was pivotal in bringing about a turning point in the growth and expansion of Christianity.
22 Eusebius of Caesarea (260/265-339/340), Roman historian and scholar.
23 See Marcus, 'From Rome to the Barbarian kingdoms', in McManners (ed.): *The Oxford Illustrated History of Christianity*, pp. 70-72.
24 Theodosius the Great, Roman Emperor 379-395 AD.
25 Augustine of Hippo (354–430 AD), an important figure in the development of Western Christianity.
26 See McManners, 'The expansion of Christianity', Ch. 9 in McManners (ed.): *The Oxford Illustrated History of Christianity*, p. 301.
27 ibid. pp. 306-8.
28 Matt. 5:39.
29 Matt. 26:52
30 Luke 22:36.
31 Matt. 10:34.
32 Pope Urban II (1035-1099) called the First Crusade on 27 November 1095. He proclaimed that God had willed it, thus justifying the use of sword against infidels.
33 There were nine Crusades launched by the Christians against the Muslims in the Holy Land in order to regain Jerusalem.

34 Bahá'u'lláh, *Tablets of Bahá'u'lláh Revealed after the Kitáb-i-Aqdas*, p. 21.
35 Bahá'u'lláh, *Epistle to the Son of the Wolf*, p. 25.
36 See Bahá'u'lláh, *Gleanings from the Writings of Bahá'u'lláh*, CXXXIX, p. 303.
37 ibid. XLIII, p. 92.
38 See Shoghi Effendi, *God Passes By*; Bahá'u'lláh, *The Proclamation of Bahá'u'lláh to the Kings and Rulers*; Bahá'u'lláh, *The Summons of the Lord of Hosts*; Ma'ani Ewing, *Collective Security Within Reach*.
39 The first mention of the Bahá'í Faith on the North American continent seems to have taken place at the first Parliament of World Religions in Chicago in 1893; see 'Abdu'l-Bahá, *Tablets of the Divine Plan*, p. 67.
40 The Universal House of Justice, *Century of Light*, p. 35.
41 Shoghi Effendi, *Citadel of Faith*, p. 62.
42 The earlier Tablets had been sent to the North American Bahá'í communities. However, due to the disruption of the First World War, the later Tablets had not been communicated. On 26 April the two Tablets revealed for the Northeastern States were unveiled to the music of a harp as Margaret Randall and Bertha Holley drew aside the curtains revealing the beautifully framed embossed Tablets. On Sunday 27 April the two Tablets revealed for the Southern States were unveiled. On 28 April the Tablets to the Central States were unveiled; that same evening the Tablets to the Western States were unveiled. See *Star of the West*, vol. X, no. 4 (May 1919).
43 ibid. p. 52.
44 The Paris Peace Conference opened on 18 January 1919 and came to a close on 21 January 1920. There is general agreement that its terms, in the Treaty of Versailles, set the stage for other conflicts, notably the Second World War.
45 The Universal House of Justice, *Century of Light*, p. 33: 'The vindictive peace treaty, imposed by the Allied powers on their defeated enemies, succeeded only, as both 'Abdu'l-Bahá and Shoghi Effendi have pointed out, in planting the seeds of another, far more terrible conflict. The ruinous reparations demanded of the vanquished – and the injustice that required them to accept the full guilt for a war for which all parties had been, to one degree or another, responsible – were among the factors that would prepare demoralized peoples in Europe to embrace totalitarian promises of relief which they might not otherwise have contemplated.'
46 *Star of the West*, vol. X, no. 4 (May 1919), pp. 50, 53. Joseph H. Hannen of Washington DC was a devoted and active teacher of the Bahá'í Faith. In 1916 'Abdu'l-Bahá sent the first Tablet of the Divine Plan to the Southern states in care of Hannen, who was later named a Disciple of 'Abdu'l-Bahá by Shoghi Effendi (see Stockman, *The Bahá'í Faith in America*, vol. 2, pp. 137, 224–6).
47 'Abdu'l-Bahá, *Tablets of the Divine Plan*, p. 47.
48 ibid. p. 34. According to Islamic Traditions, Israfil is the beautiful angel of music, singing praises to God in a thousand different languages and injecting life into hosts of angels. Israfil is the angel responsible for signalling the coming of the Judgement Day by blowing a trumpet and sending out a blast of Truth.
49 ibid.
50 ibid. pp. 37–8.
51 ibid. p. 38.

52 ibid. p. 6.
53 The process associated with the revelation of the Tablets constituting the Charter of 'Abdu'l-Bahá's Divine Plan was 'held in abeyance for well-nigh twenty years while the fabric of an indispensable Administrative Order, designed as a divinely appointed agency for the operation of that Plan, was being constructed' (Shoghi Effendi, *Citadel of Faith*, p. 32). See also the Universal House of Justice, *Century of Light*, p. 39; Shoghi Effendi, *Messages to the Bahá'í World, 1950-1957*, p. 18.
54 In one of his messages to the Bahá'í World, Shoghi Effendi described a vast ten-part majestic process which was set in motion at the dawn of the Adamic cycle. The **eighth part** of that process he described as the **diffusion** of that light to over 94 sovereign states, dependencies and islands of the planet as a result of the prosecution of a series of national plans. The **ninth part** of the process he described as the **further diffusion** of that same light over 131 additional territories and islands in both the Eastern and Western hemispheres, through the operation of a decade-long world spiritual crusade. For further information, see the Introduction.
55 Bahá'u'lláh quoted in Shoghi Effendi, *Messages to the Bahá'í World, 1950-1957*, p. 117.
56 'Abdu'l-Bahá, *Tablets of the Divine Plan*, p. 71.
57 ibid. p. 34.
58 See, for example, National Spiritual Assembly of the Bahá'ís of the United States, *Developing Distinctive Bahá'í Communities*.
59 'Abdu'l-Bahá, *Tablets of the Divine Plan*, p. 34.
60 Shoghi Effendi, 'America and The Most Great Peace', 21 April 1933, in Shoghi Effendi, *The World Order of Bahá'u'lláh*, pp. 87-8.
61 ibid.
62 The Universal House of Justice, *Century of Light*, pp. 67, 75.
63 Shoghi Effendi, *Messages to the Bahá'í World, 1950-1957*, p. 152.
64 Cablegram from Shoghi Effendi to the 1936 American Convention, 1 May 1936, in Shoghi Effendi, *Messages to America*, p. 6; see also *The Bahá'í World*, vol. 14, p. 294.
65 See Shoghi Effendi, *Citadel of Faith*.
66 'Issue forth from your cities, O peoples of the West, and aid God ere the Day when the Lord of mercy shall come down unto you . . .' (Chapter XLVI, in *Selections from the Writings of the Báb*, p. 56). The Qayyúmu'l-Asmá', Commentary on the Surih of Joseph (in the Qur'án), was revealed by the Báb on 22 May 1844, the night of the declaration of His mission to Mullá Ḥusayn.
67 Shoghi Effendi, *Citadel of Faith*, p. 1.
68 The Universal House of Justice, *Century of Light*, p. 76.
69 Shoghi Effendi, *Citadel of Faith*, pp. 87-8.
70 Cable from Shoghi Effendi to the National Spiritual Assembly of the Bahá'ís of the United States and the National Spiritual Assembly of the Bahá'ís of the British Isles, 16 January 1951, in Shoghi Effendi, *Unfolding Destiny*, p. 256.
71 Letter from Shoghi Effendi, 15 June 1950, ibid. p. 251.
72 See Shoghi Effendi, *The Bahá'í Faith 1844-1952: Information Statistical and Comparative*.
73 See Shoghi Effendi, *Dawn of a New Day: Messages to India 1923-1957*, p. 225.

74 Shoghi Effendi, *Citadel of Faith*, p. 120.
75 ibid. pp. 154, 155.
76 Shoghi Effendi, *Messages to the Bahá'í World, 1950-1957*, p. 152.
77 The Universal House of Justice, *Century of Light*, p. 77.
78 *The Ministry of the Custodians*, p. 92.
79 Shoghi Effendi, *Messages to the Bahá'í World, 1950-1957*, p. 69.
80 *The Ministry of the Custodians*, p. 13.
81 ibid. p. 93.
82 ibid. p. 13.
83 Shoghi Effendi, *The World Order of Bahá'u'lláh*, p. 78.
84 Message from the Universal House of Justice to the Bahá'ís of the World, Naw-Rúz 1974, in *Messages from the Universal House of Justice, 1963-1986*, no. 141, p. 261.
85 See Thomas, *Planning Progress: Lessons from Shoghi Effendi*.
86 Shoghi Effendi, *Messages to America*, pp. 65, 67 and 70; as quoted in *The Ministry of the Custodians*, p. 260. These letters were written on eve of the first All-America Convention in 1944 on the centenary of the Declaration of the Báb.
87 Shoghi Effendi, *Citadel of Faith*, p. 114.
88 Letter from Shoghi Effendi to the National Spiritual Assembly of the United States, 28 June 1954, in *Citadel of Faith*, p. 132.
89 Letter from Shoghi Effendi to all National Spiritual Assemblies, April 1956, in Shoghi Effendi, *Messages to the Bahá'í World, 1950-1957*, p. 101.
90 Shoghi Effendi, *God Passes By*, p. 253.
91 Shoghi Effendi, *Citadel of Faith*, p. 120.
92 Shoghi Effendi, *The World Order of Bahá'u'lláh*, p. 145.
93 See Bahá'u'lláh, *The Kitáb-i-Aqdas*, Notes, no. 49, p. 188; see also the Universal House of Justice, *A Synopsis and Codification of the Laws and Ordinances of the Kitáb-i-Aqdas*: 'In the Kitáb-i-Aqdas Bahá'u'lláh ordains both the Universal House of Justice and the Local Houses of Justice. In many of His laws He refers simply to "the House of Justice" leaving open for later decision which level or levels of the whole institution each law would apply to' (note 1, p. 55).
94 Shoghi Effendi, *The World Order of Bahá'u'lláh*, p. 5.
95 Shoghi Effendi, *Bahá'í Administration*, p. 63.
96 Quoted in *The Ministry of the Custodians*, p. 13.
97 See Shoghi Effendi, *God Passes By*, p. 331. For further information on Local Spiritual Assemblies see 'The Local Spiritual Assembly', in *The Compilation of Compilations*, vol. 2, pp. 39 et seq.
98 See Shoghi Effendi, *Bahá'í Administration*.
99 'It is expressly recorded in 'Abdu'l-Bahá's Writings that these National Assemblies must be indirectly elected by the Friends; that is, the Friends in every country must elect a certain number of delegates, who in their turn will elect from among all the Friends in that country the members of the National Spiritual Assembly' (Shoghi Effendi, *Bahá'í Administration*, pp. 39-40). For further information on National Spiritual Assemblies see 'The National Spiritual Assembly' in *The Compilation of Compilations*, vol. 2, p. 82 et seq.
100 '. . . two of which already existed but would change names and areas of jurisdiction, thus adding eleven in number; these eleven, plus three more which had been elected in Africa in 1956, brought the total number formed by the

Guardian during his thirty-six-year ministry to twenty-six' (*The Ministry of the Custodians*, p. 13).

101 The Universal House of Justice, *Century of Light*, p. 83. On the Hands of the Cause: 'Alongside the decision-making authority devolved on the elective institutions of the Faith, a parallel function of the Administrative Order is to exert a spiritual, moral and intellectual influence on both these institutions and the lives of the individual members of the community. Conceived by Bahá'u'lláh Himself, this responsibility "to diffuse the Divine Fragrances, to edify the souls of men, to promote learning, to improve the character of all men . . ." is vested by the Master's Will and Testament particularly in the Hands of the Cause of God' (The Universal House of Justice, *Century of Light*, p. 79). Shoghi Effendi appointed Hands of the Cause, in accordance with the provisions of the Will and Testament of 'Abdu'l-Bahá (see *The Ministry of the Custodians*, p. 49). Between 1952 and 1957, he appointed a total of 27 individuals to this rank (ibid. p. 21). In his message of October 1957 to the Bahá'ís of the World, he entrusted the Hands of the Cause with the all-important duty of protecting and propagating the Cause and of guarding the Bahá'í communities throughout the world. The Guardian called the Hands of the Cause in this message 'the Chief Stewards of Bahá'u'lláh's embryonic World Commonwealth' (Shoghi Effendi, *Messages to the Bahá'í World, 1950-1957*, p. 127; see also *The Ministry of the Custodians*, p. 45).

102 See *The Ministry of the Custodians*, p. 340.
103 ibid.
104 Bahíyyih Khánum was the distinguished daughter of Bahá'u'lláh and to whom He gave the title Greatest Holy Leaf. The monument marking her resting place was erected on Mt. Carmel by Shoghi Effendi. See *Bahíyyih Khánum, The Greatest Holy Leaf*, pp. 92-4 (including photographs of the monument).
105 The Universal House of Justice, *Century of Light*, p. 139.
106 The Universal House of Justice, *Wellspring of Guidance*, p. 1.
107 Shoghi Effendi, *The World Order of Bahá'u'lláh* p. 196.
108 Among the steps taken by the Universal House of Justice was to bring into being the institution of the Boards of Counsellors 'to extend into the future the specific functions of protection and propagation conferred upon the Hands of the Cause of God. The members of these boards are appointed by the Universal House of Justice' (The Universal House of Justice, *Constitution*, By-Laws no. IX).
109 The Universal House of Justice, *Century of Light*, p. 98.
110 The Universal House of Justice, *Messages from the Universal House of Justice, 1963-1986*, p. xxxiii.
111 The Universal House of Justice, Riḍván Message, 1993, to the Bahá'ís of the world, in *Promoting Entry by Troops*, p. 19.
112 ibid.
113 The Universal House of Justice, Message to the Bahá'ís of the World, 31 December 1995, in *Turning Point*, pp. 3-14; and Riḍván Message, 1996, to the Bahá'ís of the World, ibid. pp. 21-37.
114 The Universal House of Justice, Message to the Bahá'ís of the World, 26 November 1999, ibid. pp. 119-21.
115 The Universal House of Justice, Riḍván Message, 1996, to the Bahá'ís of the World, ibid. p. 31.

116 The Universal House of Justice, *Century of Light*, pp. 99-108; 108-111.
117 ibid.
118 ibid.
119 ibid. pp. 101-2.
120 The Universal House of Justice, Riḍván Message, 1996, to the Baháʼís of the World, in *Turning Point*, p. 27.
121 ibid.
122 Core activities include study circles, devotional meetings, children's classes and junior youth empowerment programmes.
123 The Universal House of Justice, *Century of Light*, p. 108.
124 The Universal House of Justice, Riḍván Message, 2010, to the Baháʼís of the World.
125 ibid.
126 The Universal House of Justice, Riḍván Message, 2014, to the Baháʼís of the World.
127 The Universal House of Justice, Riḍván Message, 2008, to the Baháʼís of the World.
128 ibid.
129 The Universal House of Justice, Riḍván Message, 2010, to the Baháʼís of the World.
130 ibid.
131 ibid.
132 ibid.
133 The stage of penetration is the tenth part of the vast majestic process Shoghi Effendi described, see note 54 above, and the explanations in the Introduction and Glossary.
134 The Universal House of Justice, Riḍván Message, 2009, to the Baháʼís of the World.
135 The Universal House of Justice, Riḍván Message, 2010, to the Baháʼís of the World.
136 ibid.
137 The Universal House of Justice, Message to the Baháʼís of the World, 26 November 1999, in *Turning Point*, p. 120.
138 See discussion by Paul Lample, *Revelation and Social Reality: Learning to Translate What is Written into Reality*.
139 The Universal House of Justice, Riḍván Message, 2008, to the Baháʼís of the World.
140 The Universal House of Justice, Riḍván Message, 2009, to the Baháʼís of the World.
141 The Universal House of Justice, Message to the Conference of the Continental Boards of Counsellors, 28 December 2010, para. 2.
142 ibid. para. 2.
143 During the period of the ministry of the Báb these countries were Iraq and Persia (Iran). Added to these during the period of ministry of Baháʼuʼlláh were Azerbaijan, Armenia, Burma, Egypt, Georgia, India, Israel, Lebanon, Pakistan, Sudan, Syria, Turkey and Turkmenistan (Shoghi Effendi, *The Baháʼí Faith 1844-1952: Information Statistical and Comparative*, 1953, p. 9).

144 The Bahá'í Faith was mentioned in 1893 at the First Parliament of World Religions which ran from 11 to 27 September in Chicago. It was by far the largest of several congresses held in conjunction with the Columbian Exposition. Shoghi Effendi writes in *God Passes By*: 'It was on September 23, 1893, that a paper written by Rev. Henry H. Jessup, D.D., Director of Presbyterian Missionary Operations in North Syria, was read by Rev. George A. Ford of Syria, at the World Parliament of Religions, held in Chicago, in connection with the Columbian Exposition, commemorating the four-hundredth anniversary of the discovery of America, it was announced that "a famous Persian Sage," "the Bábí Saint," had died recently in 'Akká, and that two years previous to His ascension "a Cambridge scholar" had visited Him, to whom He had expressed "sentiments so noble, so Christ-like" that the author of the paper, in his "closing words," wished to share them with his audience' (p. 256).
145 See Thomas, *Planning Progress: Lessons from Shoghi Effendi*.
146 For progress in advanced clusters see *Frontiers of Learning*, video, available at http://www.bahai.org/frontiers; see also http://www.bahai.org/action.
147 The Universal House of Justice, Riḍván Message, 2015, to the Bahá'ís of the World.
148 ibid.
149 ibid.
150 The Universal House of Justice, Message to the Conference of the Continental Boards of Counsellors, 28 December 2010, para. 12.
151 The Universal House of Justice, Riḍván Message, 2010, to the Bahá'ís of the World.
152 In 2016, the UN estimates world population to grow to eight billion by 2024 and nine billion by 2037.
153 See also discussion in Chapter 6, *The Twofold Process and Growth*.
154 Shoghi Effendi, *The World Order of Bahá'u'lláh*, p. 203.
155 See Taherzadeh, *The Revelation of Bahá'u'lláh*, vol. 1, p. 217.
156 Shoghi Effendi, *The World Order of Bahá'u'lláh*, p. 195.

4. Crystallization and Growth

1 Shoghi Effendi, *The World Order of Bahá'u'lláh*, p. 168.
2 The author presented certain concepts of crystallization covered in this chapter to audiences in several forums (conferences in the United States of America as well as in Auckland, New Zealand) between the years 1994 and 2011.
3 Shoghi Effendi, *Messages to the Bahá'í World, 1950-1957*, p. 106.
4 In 1928 the Soviet Government nationalized all places of worship, including the Bahá'í House of Worship in Ishqabad, Turkmenistan.
5 See *The Bahá'í World, 2004-2005*. The figure of 120,000 is by two orders of magnitude greater than the number estimated for localities in 1919.
6 See Holley, 'Survey of current Bahá'í activities 1928-1930', in *The Bahá'í World*, vol. III (1928-1930), pp. 34-43.
7 Shoghi Effendi, *The World Order of Bahá'u'lláh*, pp. 195-6.
8 *Funk and Wagnalls New International, Dictionary of the English Language*.
9 Shoghi Effendi, *The World Order of Bahá'u'lláh*, p. 98.
10 Shoghi Effendi, *Messages to America 1932-1946*, p. 52.

11 The Universal House of Justice, Message to the Conference of the Continental Board of Counsellors, 27 December 2005, in *Turning Point*, p. 195.
12 See Dunbar, *Forces of Our Time: The Dynamics of Light and Darkness*; Loehle, *Blueprint for a New World*.
13 For further reading on crystallization see Atkins and de Paula, *Physical Chemistry*.
14 The Universal House of Justice, Message to the Conference of the Continental Boards of Counsellors, 28 December 2010, para. 3.
15 See the Universal House of Justice, Riḍván Message, 2009, to the Bahá'ís of the World.
16 The Universal House of Justice, Message to the Conference of the Continental Boards of Counsellors, 28 December 2010, para. 15.
17 In an autocatalytic process the reaction product serves also as a reactant. An autocatalytic process is self-catalyzing; it speeds up with time as the process catalyzes itself. In the context of this writing, when the autocatalytic process sets in, it spreads and escalates.
18 The Universal House of Justice, Message to the Conference of the Continental Boards of Counsellors, 28 December 2010, paras. 2 and 3.

5. The Science of Chaos and Thousandfold Growth

1 Letter from Shoghi Effendi, 18 July 1953, in Shoghi Effendi, *Citadel of Faith*, p. 117.
2 See for example Teilhard de Chardin, *The Future of Man*; Mumford, *The Transformations of Man*; Toffler, *The Third Wave*; Wright, *Non-Zero: Logic of Human Destiny*.
3 Letter on behalf of Shoghi Effendi to an individual believer, 18 February 1932, in *Promoting Entry by Troops*, p. 1.
4 The Universal House of Justice, Riḍván Message, 1990, to the Bahá'ís of the World, ibid. p. 17.
5 Letter on behalf of Shoghi Effendi to an individual believer, 18 February 1932, in *Promoting Entry by Troops*, p. 1
6 The term 'growth inducing milieu' is used in the plans of the Universal House of Justice.
7 Letter from Shoghi Effendi, 18 July 1953, in Shoghi Effendi, *Citadel of Faith*, p. 117.
8 See the Universal House of Justice, Riḍván Message, 2010, to the Bahá'ís of the World.
9 Letter from Shoghi Effendi, 18 July 1953, in Shoghi Effendi, *Citadel of Faith*, p. 117.
10 Bahá'u'lláh, *Gleanings from the Writings of Bahá'u'lláh*, LXX, p. 136.
11 ibid. IV, p. 7.
12 Fractal: a mathematical feature of chaos. Fractal is derived from the word 'fractional'; it signifies any image or process that displays the attribute of self-similarity at all scales. Simply put, fractal is repetition of a pattern or a property at all levels of magnification and enlargement. Thus the same pattern or feature is repeated at each level.
13 See Gleick, *Chaos: Making a New Science*.
14 See Hunt and Yorke, 'Maxwell on Chaos'. James Clerk Maxwell (1831–79) is

considered by some as the father of modern physics. He developed the theory of electromagnetism and also made contributions in astronomy, mathematics and engineering. Albert Einstein attributed the origin of the theory of relativity to Maxwell, saying that his work introduced significant change in conception of reality since the time of Newton.
15 Edward Norton Lorenz (1917–2008), American mathematician and meteorologist.
16 See Gleick, *Chaos: Making a New Science;* Prigogine and Stengers, *Order Out of Chaos.*
17 ibid.
18 Provisional translation, in Saiedi, *Logos and Civilization: Spirit, History and Order in the Writings of Bahá'u'lláh*, p. 29.
19 Edward Lorenz, at the 139th meeting of the American Association for the Advancement of Science in 1972.
20 Bahá'u'lláh, *Prayers and Meditations*, CLXXVIII, p. 296.
21 From Haggai 2:6.
22 Prigogine and Stengers, *Order Out of Chaos*, p. 14. Ilya Prigogine received the Nobel Prize for chemistry in 1977 for his work on the thermodynamics of non-equilibrium systems.
23 See Laszlo, *The Chaos Point.*
24 Shoghi Effendi, *The World Order of Bahá'u'lláh*, p. 170.
25 See McManners, 'Introduction', in McManners (ed.): *The Oxford Illustrated History of Christianity*, p. 7. Although scholars debate the exact origin of Mithraism, many agree that it has Iranian roots in pre-Zoroastrian Iran. Once it was introduced into Europe through conquest by Alexander, it spread rapidly over the whole Roman Empire. It was the dominant religion of the Empire from the first to the fourth century CE; it reached its zenith in the third and disappeared at the end of fourth century. Mithraism posed competition to Christianity; see also Bausani, *Religions in Iran*, p. 29.
26 See Prigogine and Stengers, *Order Out of Chaos*, pp. 163–4.
27 See Mumford, *The Transformations of Man*, p. 140.
28 Cited in Campbell and Garnett, *The Life of James Clerk Maxwell*, p. 443.
29 Shakespeare, *Julius Caesar*, 4:3.
30 Miller, *Lewis Mumford: A Life*, p. 448.
31 See Taleb, *The Black Swan: The Impact of the Highly Improbable.*
32 Shoghi Effendi, *Citadel of Faith*, p. 117.
33 Quoted by Shoghi Effendi, *The World Order of Bahá'u'lláh*, p. 169.
34 Shoghi Effendi, *Citadel of Faith*, p. 117.
35 Cited by Russell, *The Global Brain: The Awakening Earth in a New Century*, p. 180.

6. The Twofold Process of Growth
1 Shoghi Effendi, *The World Order of Bahá'u'lláh*, p. 169.
2 The Universal House of Justice, Riḍván Message, 2010, to the Bahá'ís of the World.
3 Letter from Shoghi Effendi, 18 July 1953, in Shoghi Effendi, *Citadel of Faith*, p. 117.

4   *de novo:* Latin, lit. 'from new'.
5   Aleksandr Oparin, a Russian biochemist notable for his contributions to the theory of the origin of life, and John Haldane, a British geneticist and evolutionary biologist, are credited with the Oparin-Haldane hypothesis, Oparin in 1924 and Haldane in 1929.
6   John Carew Eccles (1903–97) was born in Melbourne, Australia. He received the Nobel Prize in physiology and medicine in 1963 for his work in neurophysiology. Eccles followed Sherrington in developing a philosophy of the human person which is consonant with brain science.
7   Prebiotic evolution or the origin of life refers to the spontaneous generation of life in a 'primordial soup' containing small organic molecules in salt water.
8   Photosynthetic molecules such as chlorophyll in plants, most algae and cyanobacteria, capture the energy of light (sunlight) and synthesize carbohydrates from carbon dioxide and water, releasing oxygen. Oxygen is essential to animal life. Cyanobacteria are thought to have converted the reducing atmosphere to an oxidizing atmosphere.
9   Oxygen was present on earth in combination with other elements such as carbon; however, as O_2 it was absent in the early atmosphere of the earth. O_2 is essential to respiration of animals including humans.
10 Sentient: 'possessing powers of sense or sense perception; having or actually experiencing sensation or feeling, opposed to *inanimate* and *vegetal*' (*Funk and Wagnalls New International Dictionary of the English Language*).
11 Shoghi Effendi, *The World Order of Bahá'u'lláh*, p. 98.
12 Bahá'u'lláh, *Prayers and Meditations*, CLXXVIII, p. 295.
13 Bahá'u'lláh, *The Summons of the Lord of Hosts*, p. 25.
14 ibid.
15 Shoghi Effendi, *The World Order of Bahá'u'lláh*, p. 169.
16 Bahá'u'lláh, *Prayers and Meditations*, CLXXVIII, p. 296.
17 Shoghi Effendi, *The World Order of Bahá'u'lláh*, p. 170.
18 ibid.
19 ibid.
20 ibid.
21 Shoghi Effendi, *The Promised Day Is Come*, p. 118.
22 Shoghi Effendi, *The World Order of Bahá'u'lláh*, p. 170.
23 ibid.
24 ibid.
25 ibid.
26 See for example Gen.1:27: 'So God created man in his own image, in the image of God created he him; male and female created he them.'
27 Bahá'u'lláh, *Hidden Words*, Arabic no. 22.
28 Shoghi Effendi, *The World Order of Bahá'u'lláh*, p. 168.
29 Bahá'u'lláh, *Gleanings from the Writings of Bahá'u'lláh*, IV, p. 7.
30 ibid. LXX, p. 136.
31 Bahá'u'lláh, *Tablets of Bahá'u'lláh Revealed after the Kitab-i-Aqdas*, p. 171; *Gleanings from the Writings of Bahá'u'lláh*, CX, pp. 215–16.
32 See Chapter 5 for the discussion of Chaos, using the analogy of the flow of water in a riverbed.

33 Shoghi Effendi, *The World Order of Bahá'u'lláh*, p. 36.
34 ibid.
35 ibid. p. 170.
36 ibid. p. 169.
37 ibid.
38 See for example his book *The Third Wave*. Born in 1928, Alvin Toffler is an American writer and futurist, known for his works discussing the digital revolution, communication revolution and technological singularity.
39 Carlos Fuentes Macías (b. 1928), Mexican writer and a well-known novelist and essayist in the Spanish-speaking world
40 'Abdu'l-Bahá, *Selections from the Writings of 'Abdu'l-Bahá*, no. 40, p. 82.
41 Steven Pinker (b. 1954), cognitive scientist, psychologist, linguist, and author of books on mind, language and human nature, for example *The Better Angels of Our Nature: Why Violence Has Declined*.
42 See the Universal House of Justice, *Century of Light*.
43 Lucius Annaeus Seneca (4 BC-65 AD), statesman, Stoic philosopher and dramatist. Among the many works attributed to him are philosophical essays and tragedies. This quotation is from *Medea*, one of his tragedies, as quoted in Boorstin, *The Discoverers*, p. 255.
44 See Bergreen, *Columbus: The Four Voyages 1492-1504*. These dates were significant markers in the process of globalization; see Boorstin, *The Discoverers*.
45 Pedro Nunes (1502-78), Portuguese mathematician and cosmographer, who made significant contributions to navigation; see Boorstin, op. cit., p. 626.
46 Columbian Exchange: the term used for the exchange which took place with the new world in the process set in motion by Columbus in 1492. Some consider this to be 'the most important event since the death of dinosaurs'; see Mann, *1493: Uncovering the New World Columbus Created*.
47 Num.23:23. Morse Code was invented by the American Samuel Finley Morse (1791-1872). In this first message it was used over land lines.
48 Such as Goethe, or Tennyson in *Locksley Hall*.
49 For instance, Isa. 2:4, 11:6, and many others; see Shoghi Effendi, *God Passes By*, pp. 94-6 for anticipation of such an age in all great religions of the world.
50 Genghis Khan (1162-1227 AD), founder and ruler of the Mongol Empire, united many nomadic tribes of northeast Asia; by the end of his life the Empire included substantial parts of Central Asia and China but his invasions were accompanied by acts of violence, barbarism and brutality. Alexander III (356-23 BC), King of Macedonia and conqueror of the Persian Empire, is considered one of the greatest military geniuses of all times, but he died without designating a successor to the Macedonian Empire and his reign and conquests were also bloody and brutal. Napoleon Bonaparte (1769-1821), Emperor of the French 1804-14, made several of his relatives crowned heads of European countries and introduced Napoleonic law – still in operation today – but was at last defeated and died in exile on the island of St Helena.
51 Shoghi Effendi, *The World Order of Bahá'u'lláh*, p. 44.
52 ibid. p. 46.
53 'Abdu'l-Bahá, *Selections from the Writings of 'Abdu'l-Bahá*, no. 15, p. 32; for an extensive discussion see the Universal House of Justice, *Century of Light*.

54 Shoghi Effendi, *The Advent of Divine Justice*, p. 6.
55 The Universal House of Justice, Riḍván Message, 2010, to the Baháʼís of the world.
56 See Baháʼu'lláh, *The Summons of the Lord of Hosts*; also *The Proclamation of Baháʼu'lláh to the Kings and Rulers*.
57 See Khodadad, 'The religious and spiritual philosophy of the Baháʼí Faith on globalization', in *Proceedings of the Ninth International Conference on Globalization for the Common Good*.
58 See Chapter 5, *The Science of Chaos and Thousandfold Growth*.
59 The invention of movable type introduced by Johannes Gutenberg (1398-1468) started the printing revolution and thus the spread of learning. The invention of the printing press is considered the most important event of modern times. It played a key role in development of the Renaissance, the Reformation, and the Scientific Revolution in the Age of Enlightenment.
60 See Collins, *The Language of God: A Scientist Presents Evidence for Belief*.
61 Shoghi Effendi, *The World Order of Baháʼu'lláh*, pp. 42-3.
62 ibid.
63 ibid. p. 203.
64 ibid.
65 Baháʼu'lláh, quoted in Shoghi Effendi, *God Passes By*, p. 184.

7. The Flow of History and Growth

1 Strauss and Howe, *An American Prophecy: The Fourth Turning*, p. 257.
2 For the relevant discussions by these writers, see Teilhard de Chardin, *The Future of Man*; Mumford, *The Transformations of Man*; Toffler, *The Third Wave*; Wright, *Non-Zero: Logic of Human Destiny*; Campbell and Garnett, *The Life of James Clerk Maxwell*, p. 443.
3 Teilhard de Chardin, *The Future of Man*, p. 74.
4 Mumford, *The Transformations of Man*, p. 138.
5 Wright, *Non-Zero: Logic of Human Destiny*, p. 3.
6 Melzer, Weinberger and Zinman, *History and the Idea of Progress*, p. 147.
7 ʻAbduʼl-Bahá, Tablet to the Hague, letter to the Central Organization for a Durable Peace, 17 December 1919, in *Selections from the Writings of ʻAbduʼl-Bahá*, no. 227, p. 303.
8 ʻAbduʼl-Bahá, *ʻAbduʼl-Bahá in London*, p. 30.
9 ʻAbduʼl-Bahá, *The Secret of Divine Civilization*, p. 60.
10 ʻAbduʼl-Bahá, *Selections from the Writings of ʻAbduʼl-Bahá*, no. 227, p. 303.
11 ibid. no. 225, p. 283. See also the Universal House of Justice, Riḍván message, 2008, to the Baháʼís of the World.
12 ʻAbduʼl-Bahá, *The Secret of Divine Civilization*, pp. 60-61; quoting Qurʼán 12:44; 21:5; 24:39.
13 Shoghi Effendi, *The Baháʼí Faith – The World Religion: A Summary of Its Aims, Teachings and History*.
14 George Wilhelm Friedrich Hegel (1770-1831), in *The Philosophy of History*; Oswald Arnold Gottfried Spengler (1880-1936) in his two-volume work *The Decline of the West*; Robin George Collingwood (1889-1943) best known for his book *The Idea of History*, published posthumously in 1945, and Arnold J.

Toynbee (1889-1975) in his 12-volume *Study of History*.
15 Carr, *What is History?* p. 63.
16 For further discussion of this point see Dray, *Philosophy of History*; McLean, *A Celestial Burning*, Ch. 6.
17 In *Civilization on Trial* (1948) Toynbee identifies these two alternative views of history as Greco-Hindu and Judeo-Christian. In a later work, *An Historian's Approach to Religion* (1956), he renames these fundamental views respectively as Indo-Hellenic and Judeo-Zoroastrian.
18 Toynbee, *An Historian's Approach to Religion*, pp. 4-5.
19 John 16:12-13.
20 Toynbee, *An Historian's Approach to Religion*, p. 13.
21 Strauss and Howe, *An American Prophecy: The Fourth Turning*, pp. 8-11.
22 See Shoghi Effendi, *God Passes By*, pp. 94-6.
23 ibid. p. 100.
24 ibid.
25 See discussion on progressive revelation in Chapter 8, *Oneness of Religion and Growth*.
26 Yeats, 'The Second Coming', in Finneran, *The Collected Works of W. B. Yeats*. William Butler Yeats (1865–1939), Irish poet and playwright, Nobel laureate (1923), was one of the foremost figures in 20th-century literature. His work has been described as 'inspired poetry'.
27 Butterfield, *The Englishman and His History*, p. 103, quoted in Carr, *What is History?*, p. 63. Sir Herbert Butterfield (1900–79) was a British historian and philosopher of history.
28 John 1:1-4.
29 'Logos' is an important term in various disciplines, including philosophy, psychology, rhetoric and religion. In Christianity, Logos is identified with that through which all things are made divine (John 1:1).
30 Philo of Alexandria (20 BC–50 AD), born in Alexandria, was a Jewish Biblical philosopher. He viewed Logos as God's governing plan for the world, God's creative principle. According to some scholars his concept influenced early Christology.
31 See Wright, *Non-Zero: Logic of Human Destiny*, p. 333.
32 The term 'higher religions' was used by Toynbee.
33 Eschatology: derived from the Greek 'eschatos', it means farthest, last. Eschatology is concerned with the ultimate destiny of humankind. Eschatology is concerned with final events in history, such as the Kingdom of God, the Advent of the Promised One, the Resurrection, the Day of Judgement.
34 Isa. 2:4.
35 ibid. 11:6.
36 The second law of thermodynamics states that entropy – disorganization – always increases with time.
37 See Mandelbrot, *The Fractal Geometry of Nature*. He coined the term 'fractal' in 1975.
38 Shoghi Effendi, *The Promised Day Is Come*, p. 117.
39 ibid.
40 ibid.

41 See Prigogine and Stengers, *Order Out of Chaos*.
42 See Ma'ani Ewing, *Collective Security Within Reach*.
43 Shoghi Effendi, *The World Order of Bahá'u'lláh*, p. 45.
44 Prigogine and Stengers, *Order Out of Chaos*, p. xxiii.
45 Shoghi Effendi, *The World Order of Bahá'u'lláh*, pp. 12, 194; *The Advent of Divine Justice*, p. 73.
46 The Universal House of Justice, Message to the Conference of the Continental Boards of Counsellors, Riḍván 158, in *Turning Point*, p. 148.
47 Lord Acton, letter to the contributors to the *Cambridge Modern History*, 12 March 1898, cited in Arnold Toynbee, *A Study of History*, vol. I.
48 Wright, *Non-Zero: Logic of Human Destiny*, p. 7.
49 Rifkin, *The Empathic Civilization: The Race to World Consciousness in a World in Crisis*.
50 Shoghi Effendi, *The Promised Day Is Come*, p. 117.
51 The Universal House of Justice, *One Common Faith*, p. 14.
52 'Abdu'l-Bahá, *The Secret of Divine Civilization*, p. 95.
53 See Toynbee, *An Historian's Approach to Religion*.
54 See Toynbee, *Civilization on Trial*.
55 Chrysalis: a protective covering within which the butterfly undergoes its development and its metamorphosis.
56 Shoghi Effendi, *The Advent of Divine Justice*, p. 6.
57 Beginning in Italy, the cultural movement known as the Renaissance later spread to the rest of Europe, encompassing numerous fields including literature, science, art, politics and religion. The transformation that took place has contributed to the view that the Renaissance served as a bridge between the Middle Ages and the modern era.
58 The Universal House of Justice, Message announcing the Four Year Plan, 31 December 1995, in *Turning Point*, p. 15.
59 The Universal House of Justice, Riḍván Message, 1996, to the Bahá'ís of the World, in *Turning Point*, p. 21.
60 Mumford, *The Transformations of Man*, p. 139.
61 'Abdu'l-Bahá, *Tablets of 'Abdu'l-Bahá*, vol. 3, p. 690.
62 Bahá'u'lláh, *Kitáb-i-Íqán: The Book of Certitude*, p. 240.
63 The Universal House of Justice, Riḍván Message, 2010, to the Bahá'ís of the World.
64 ibid.
65 Lample, *Revelation and Social Reality*, p. 109.
66 The Universal House of Justice, Riḍván Message, 2010, to the Bahá'ís of the World.
67 Wright, *Non-Zero: Logic of Human Destiny*, pp. 7–9.
68 See Teilhard de Chardin, *The Future of Man*.
69 Toynbee, *An Historian's Approach to Religion*, p. 298.
70 Elixir: a legendary drink that imparts love, eternal youth and eternal life. Among the practitioners of alchemy, an elixir is that agent that can transmute base metal into precious gold. The use of the term 'Elixir' in the Writings of Bahá'u'lláh refers to that agent which can transform – or rather transmute and transubstantiate – the character of the individual and society. The Word of God is that divine

Elixir (Bahá'u'lláh, *Gleanings from the Writings of Bahá'u'lláh*, XCIX, p. 199).
71 Wright, *Non-Zero: Logic of Human Destiny*, p. 332.
72 Strauss and Howe. *An American Prophecy: The Fourth Turning*, p. 257.

8. The Paradigm of Oneness of Religion and Growth

1 I wish to express my appreciation to Dr Feridun Khodadadeh for his encouragement and interest in the ideas and diagrams in Chapters 8 and 9 and the diagrams in Chapter 9. Some of the salient points of this concept were first presented by the author at the 2008 Irfán Colloquium and later published as 'The Bahá'í worldview on unity of religions, "progressive revelation": The application of principles and insights from the history of science', in *Lights of Irfán*, vol. 10, pp. 43–70.
2 Mumford, *The Transformations of Man*, p. 157.
3 ibid.
4 ibid.
5 The term 'spark of history' is used by Strauss and Howe, *An American Prophecy: The Fourth Turning*.
6 The Universal House of Justice, *One Common Faith*, p. 41.
7 This belief has been expressed variously in the great religions of the world. It is fundamental to the theology of all religions: man is a spiritual being capable of transcendence.
8 See Huntington, *The Clash of Civilizations and the Remaking of World Order*; and Chapter 7 of the present book, *The Flow of History and Growth*.
9 Bahá'u'lláh, *Tablets of Bahá'u'lláh Revealed after the Kitáb-i-Aqdas*, p. 129.
10 'Abdu'l-Bahá, *The Promulgation of Universal Peace*, p. 298.
11 ibid. p. 175.
12 'Abdu'l-Bahá, *The Secret of Divine Civilization*, p. 80.
13 'Abdu'l-Bahá, *The Promulgation of Universal Peace*, p. 179.
14 ibid.
15 Toynbee, *An Historian's Approach to Religion*, p. 274.
16 'Abdu'l-Bahá, *Paris Talks*, no. 41, p. 139.
17 See the Universal House of Justice, *One Common Faith*.
18 Toynbee, *An Historian's Approach to Religion*, p. 265.
19 ibid. p. 298.
20 'Abdu'l-Bahá, *The Promulgation of Universal Peace*, p. 140.
21 See Kühn, *The Structure of Scientific Revolution*.
22 See the *Oxford English Dictionary*. There are numerous examples of paradigm and paradigm expansion in science; of particular interest to the author of this writing is the expansion of paradigm of the structure and function of biological membranes. The expansion of this paradigm has progressed through several models to the present fluid mosaic model of membrane; this has spurred further research on the structure and function of biological membranes and their constituent membrane proteins (see Khodadad, Loew and Weinstein, 'Freeze-fracture and freeze-etch electron microscopy of membrane proteins', in Ragan and Cherry (eds): *Techniques for Analysis of Membrane Proteins*, pp. 275-314).
23 Augustine of Hippo (354–430 AD), Bishop of Hippo in the Roman Africa Province, philosopher and theologian. In his early years he was heavily influenced

by Manichaeism but later converted to Christianity and was baptized in 387 AD. Augustine developed his own approach to and perspective on philosophy and theology; his writings were influential in the development of Western Christianity.
24 Aristotle (384-322 BC), Greek philosopher and one of Plato's greatest students. He produced important works on logic.
25 Claudius Ptolemy (90 –168 AD), Greek mathematician, geographer and astronomer and author of several scientific treatises, including the astronomical treatise now known as the *Almagest*.
26 Plato (c.424/423-348/347 BC), Greek philosopher and mathematician. He was a student of Socrates and founded the Academy in Athens, the first institution of higher learning in the Western world. Together with Socrates and Aristotle, Plato helped to lay the foundations of Western philosophy and science.
27 Two points to be noted here for further clarification: first, even the learned of Islam seemed to believe in the Ptolemaic theory of the universe; second, certain verses in the Qur'án pointed to the contrary. One of these verses states, 'The sun moves in a fixed place' (36:37), clearly indicating that the sun is fixed and moves around an axis. Another Quranic verse states, 'And each star moves in its own heaven' (36:38).
28 Dante degli Alighieri (c. 1265–1321), author of one of the first major literary masterpieces to be written in Italian rather than Latin. His *Comedia*, later given the name 'Divina' by the poet Boccaccio, with its descriptions of Hell, Purgatory and Heaven, has influenced centuries of Western art and literature.
29 Bahá'u'lláh, *Gleanings from the Writings of Bahá'u'lláh*, LXXXII, pp. 162-3.
30 Letter written on behalf of Shoghi Effendi to an individual, 9 February 1937, in *Lights of Guidance*, no. 1581, p. 478.
31 'Abdu'l-Bahá, *Selections from the Writings of 'Abdu'l-Bahá*, no. 19, p. 41.
32 The Second Parliament of World Religions convened in Chicago in 1993, on the centenary of the First Parliament of World Religions held in 1893. The particular session referred to in the text centred on 'The Christ of the Twentieth Century'.
33 Epicircles: circles introduced within circles. This was an accommodation in the model of the universe whereby each planet travels along a small circle (epicircle) that rolls along that planet's big orbital circle around the earth. Century after century, the errors in this model grew more and more evident. More epicircles were added to the model so that planets moved along epicircles within epicircles. Copernicus hoped to use 'modern' (16th-century) technology to improve on Ptolemy's measurements in an attempt to eliminate some of the epicircles.
34 Giordano Bruno (1548–1600), Italian philosopher, mathematician and astronomer.
35 Tycho Brahe (1546-1601), Danish astronomer. He designed and built instruments, calibrated them and checked their accuracy periodically. He thus revolutionized astronomical instrumentation.
36 Johannes Kepler (1571–1630), German mathematician and astronomer. He was a key figure in the 17th-century Copernican Revolution, best known for his laws of planetary movements.
37 Galileo Galilei (1564-1642), Italian physicist, mathematician, astronomer and

philosopher. His data and public support of the heliocentric view was met with opposition. The Catholic Church condemned heliocentrism as 'false and contrary to Scripture'. Galileo defended his views in *Dialogue Concerning the Two Chief World Systems*, published in 1632. He was tried by the Inquisition, found 'vehemently suspect of heresy', forced to recant, and spent the rest of his life under house arrest.

38 See Margolis, *Paradigms and Barriers: How Habits of Mind Govern Scientific Belief*.
39 Bahá'u'lláh, quoted in *The Bahá'í World*, vol. 5, p. 608.
40 The work of the Hanover Institute on visual gestalt provides an interesting metaphor. In experiments where the subject wears a goggle with inverting lenses, initially he becomes disoriented, for the world is seen upside down; some time after, however, the visual field inverts and the world is seen right side up (see Kühn, *The Structure of Scientific Revolution*).

9. Progressive Revelation and Growth

1 'Abdu'l-Bahá, *The Promulgation of Universal Peace*, p. 344.
2 See Fananapazir, *Islam at the Crossroads*, pp. 389-99.
3 See the Universal House of Justice, *One Common Faith*.
4 'Abdu'l-Bahá, *The Promulgation of Universal Peace*, p. 140.
5 Shoghi Effendi, *The Promised Day Is Come*, Preface to 3rd ed., p. v.
6 Shoghi Effendi, *God Passes By*, p. 100.
7 'Abdu'l-Bahá, *The Promulgation of Universal Peace*, p. 97.
8 ibid. pp. 404-5.
9 ibid. p. 393.
10 Shoghi Effendi, *The World Order of Bahá'u'lláh*, p. 60.
11 ibid. p. 115
12 ibid.
13 Shoghi Effendi, *The Promised Day Is Come*, Preface to 3rd ed., p. v.
14 Bahá'u'lláh, *Gleanings from the Writings of Bahá'u'lláh*, XXXI, p. 74.
15 Shoghi Effendi, *The World Order of Bahá'u'lláh*, p. 103.
16 Letter on behalf of Shoghi Effenidi to an individual, 4 October 1950, in *The Compilation of Compilations*, vol. I, p. 22.
17 Shoghi Effendi, *God Passes By*, p. 57.
18 Taherzadeh, *The Covenant of Bahá'u'lláh*, pp. 32-3.
19 See Kühn, *The Structure of Scientific Revolution*.
20 Tolstoy was informed about the Bahá'í Faith; see Stendardo, *Leo Tolstoy and the Bahá'í Faith*.
21 Shoghi Effendi, *The Promised Day Is Come*. p. 119.
22 ibid.
23 See Boorstin, *The Discoverers, A History of Man's Search to Know His World and Himself*; Mann, *Uncovering the New World Columbus Created*.
24 DNA: deoxynucleic acid. It carries the essential genetic code for every living organism. The discovery in 1953 of the double helix structure of DNA is credited to James Watson and Francis Crick as well as Rosalind Franklin. Franklin's X-ray diffraction studies on DNA were important to the discovery of the structure of DNA by Watson and Crick. The Nobel Prize was awarded to Watson,

Crick and Wilkins. Rosalind Franklin died before the prize was awarded. A case was made to also honour her posthumously.

10. The Worldwide Bahá'í Community and the Unification of World Society

1. Shoghi Effendi, *The Promised Day is Come*, p. 123.
2. See Introduction.
3. Shoghi Effendi, *The Advent of Divine Justice*, p. 72.
4. Shoghi Effendi, *The World Order of Bahá'u'lláh*, p. 169.
5. Bahá'u'lláh, quoted in Shoghi Effendi, ibid. pp. 161-2.
6. Bahá'u'lláh, *Tablets of Bahá'u'lláh Revealed after the Kitáb-i-Aqdas*, pp. 84-5.
7. Dan. 2:31-40. Nebuchadnezzar, king of the Neo-Babylonian Empire, ruled from 605 to 562 BC.
8. Shelley, 'Ozymandias', in *Miscellaneous and Posthumous Poems of Percy Bysshe Shelley*, p. 100.
9. See discussion in Chapter 6, *The Twofold Process and Growth*, and Chapter 7, *The Flow of History and Growth*.
10. Bahá'u'lláh, *Tablets of Bahá'u'lláh Revealed after the Kitáb-i-Aqdas*, pp. 84-5.
11. Shoghi Effendi, *The World Order of Bahá'u'lláh*, p. 171.
12. Shoghi Effendi, *God Passes By*, p. 305.
13. Shoghi Effendi, *Citadel of Faith*, p. 125.
14. Nakhjavání, *Shoghi Effendi: Author of Teaching Plans*, p. 64.
15. Shoghi Effendi, *The World Order of Bahá'u'lláh*, p. 171.
16. ibid. p. 202.
17. Shoghi Effendi, *Citadel of Faith*, p. 39.
18. Bahá'u'lláh, *Tablets of Bahá'u'lláh Revealed after the Kitáb-i-Aqdas*, pp. 84-5.
19. Shoghi Effendi, *The World Order of Bahá'u'lláh*, p. 24.
20. The Universal House of Justice, *The Promise of World Peace*, p. 7.
21. Bahá'u'lláh, *Gleanings from the Writings of Bahá'u'lláh*, CIX, p. 214.
22. Provisional translation, in Saiedi, *Logos and Civilization: Spirit, History and Order in the Writings of Bahá'u'lláh*, pp. 59-60.
23. Bahá'u'lláh, *Tablets of Bahá'u'lláh Revealed after the Kitáb-i-Aqdas*, p. 84.
24. Shoghi Effendi, *The World Order of Bahá'u'lláh*, p. 25.
25. See Bahá'u'lláh, *Hidden Words*.
26. Shoghi Effendi, *The World Order of Bahá'u'lláh*, p. 163.
27. ibid.
28. Shoghi Effendi, *The Advent of Divine Justice*, p. 14.
29. The Universal House of Justice, Riḍván Message, 2009, to the Bahá'ís of the World.
30. Bahá'u'lláh, *Gleanings from the Writings of Bahá'u'lláh*, CIX, p. 214.
31. Mumford, *The Transformations of Man*, p. 138.
32. Toynbee, *Change and Habit*. The term 'diaspora' has been defined variously. Some consider diasporas arising as the outcome of trade, war and persecution. Others consider them as also arising from going out to spread the teachings of a respective religion. It is through this latter definition that the term may be applied to the Bahá'í worldwide community. The worldwide spread of the Bahá'í Faith has been due to dedicated individuals who set out to settle in new localities – often under harsh, inhospitable and difficult conditions - for the sole reason

of spreading the transforming message of Bahá'u'lláh and making it accessible to humanity, as a prelude to the oneness of the human race and a planetary civilization.
33 Shoghi Effendi, *Citadel of Faith*, p. 119.
34 ibid. p. 120.
35 Shoghi Effendi, *The World Order of Bahá'u'lláh*, p. 195.
36 The Universal House of Justice, Message to the Bahá'ís of the world acting under the Mandate of 'Abdu'l-Bahá, 26 March 2016. The term 'Blessed Beauty' refers to Bahá'u'lláh.
37 See Toynbee, *Change and Habit*.
38 See Thomas, *Planning Progress: Lessons from Shoghi Effendi*.
39 Shoghi Effendi, *The Promised Day Is Come*, p. 123.
40 Shoghi Effendi, *The World Order of Bahá'u'lláh*, p. 41.
41 See for example Luke 22:47; Matt. 26:47–49.
42 McManners, 'Introduction', in *The Oxford Illustrated History of Christianity*.
43 Shoghi Effendi, *God Passes By*, p. 253.
44 The Universal House of Justice, Message to the Bahá'ís of the world acting under the Mandate of 'Abdu'l-Bahá, 26 March 2016.
45 ibid.
46 ibid.
47 ibid.

ABOUT THE AUTHOR

Jena Khadem Khodadad was born in Tehran, Iran. She holds a doctorate degree in Biological Sciences from Northwestern University and has pursued an academic career on the faculty of Rush Medical College as professor of Cell Biology and Anatomy. Her research was focused on the molecular organization of biological membranes and her teaching on cell and molecular biology and neuroscience. Jena's publications are in scientific journals and books. She has presented her research at national and international scientific forums in the United States, Spain, China and Japan. Jena is an advocate of human rights and has presented before a number of human rights organizations, including Amnesty International and the American Jewish Committee, on the denial of higher education to Bahá'ís in Iran. As an active member of an interfaith organization, she is dedicated to the enhancement of interfaith understanding and dialogue. Jena has served on the institutions of the Bahá'í Faith at national, regional and local levels. She and her husband, Manucher, live in the United States in the Chicago area.